FATHERING DAUGHTERS

FATHERING
DAUGHTERS

EDITED BY

REFLECTIONS BY MEN

DeWitt Henry and
James Alan McPherson

BEACON PRESS   BOSTON

Beacon Press
25 Beacon Street
Boston, Massachusetts 02108-2892
www.beacon.org

Beacon Press books
are published under the auspices of
the Unitarian Universalist Association of Congregations.

03 02 01 00 99 98   8 7 6 5 4 3 2 1

This book is printed on recycled acid-free paper that contains at
least 20 percent postconsumer waste and meets the uncoated paper
ANSI/NISO specifications for permanence as revised in 1992.

Book design by Boskydell Studio
Composition by Wilsted & Taylor Publishing Services

Library of Congress Cataloging-in-Publication Data
Fathering daughters : reflections by men / edited by DeWitt Henry
    and James Alan McPherson.
        p.   cm.
    ISBN 0-8070-6218-9 (cloth)
    1. Fathers and daughters.   2. Parenting.   I. Henry, DeWitt.
II. McPherson, James Alan, 1943–   .
HQ755.85.F386   1998
306.874′2—dc21   97-50222

for the daughters

CONTENTS

INTRODUCTION

THIS PROJECT BEGAN in conversations between the editors, James Alan McPherson and DeWitt Henry. We have been friends since meeting in Cambridge, Massachusetts, in the 1970s. Over the years we have visited together in Iowa City and in Boston, and now our daughters have become friends.

Our conversations tended to be philosophical, taking the measure of American culture, good and bad, on the pulses of our personal lives. We spoke of decadence in the culture, of racism, of feminism, of our writing students, and of our lives as men. Sometimes our daughters joined in, and sometimes DeWitt's wife, Connie, sometimes other friends, men and women from different callings and backgrounds. Our conversations continued the preoccupations of our writing (especially McPherson's stories in *Elbow Room* and in his more recent nonfiction) and in the 1980s led to our co-editing a special issue of *Ploughshares* magazine, entitled "Confronting Racial Difference."

But besides our common interests as writers and teachers, our central concern was our parenting, and especially our parenting of daughters. In these closing years of the century, as our daughters attain adulthood, we fear for the worst and hope for the best, both personally and culturally; fear the forces of social division and hate; hope for civility, imagination, and social justice. DeWitt brought William Butler Yeats into the conversation, turning to the poem "A Prayer for My Daughter," from 1919, and wondered how other writers who were fathers today might contemplate the future for their daughters.

"It never fails," Jim wrote later from Iowa City. "As soon as we start brooding together, something positive happens, and we make a book."

A number of fathers (and one father-to-be) from different backgrounds have now joined us by writing essays for this collection, and we hope that their words may encourage others to speak.

While the discussion of fathering daughters has been appropriated by daughters for the past twenty years, there has been too much silence on the part of fathers. There is a sense of release in these essays, of pent-up feelings and of honest, complex witness; sometimes confession, sometimes confusion, sometimes apology, sometimes protest or appeal, sometimes meditation and prayer. What are our responsibilities as fathers? What do we want, in personal and in social terms, for our daughters?

To prepare for our task as editors of this collection, we visited bookstores in Harvard Square to become acquainted with books on the shelves. We found vast women's studies sections in each bookstore and a conspicuous absence of men's studies, other than a small section of gay studies.

We felt self-conscious about drawing stares. Here we were, two grumpy old men, clearly middle aged, one African-American, one WASP, browsing the feminist shelves in evident astonishment. Studies by women touching on fathers ranged from psychology to sociology, to cultural criticism, to fiction and poetry. Women's studies questioned assumptions about everything from the female body to the psyche, from home to the workplace, all seeking to remedy a widespread discontent and pathology. Women exhorted women to childless careers, to recovered memories of abuse, to celibacy, to "wildzones" of creativity. A virtual industry of ideology was in place, and where were we, as fathers, in this call for change?

In volume after volume, fathers were identified as embodiments of "patriarchy," and were portrayed as abusive, tyrannical, overpowering, predatory, absent, distant, shadowy, irresponsible, and victims themselves of traditions that denied women full human potential. According to many daughters, fathers were at the heart of their unhappiness as women. Historically, of course, fathers favored sons. Adrienne Rich was frequently invoked as a woman who looked past the personal to the cultural figure of her father: "There was an ideology at last which let me dispose of you, identify the suffering you caused, hate you righteously as part of a system, the kingdom of the fathers" ("Sources" in *Your Native Land, Your Life: Poems*).

We were glad to find other books addressed at least in part to fathers, texts by women to help daughters and fathers talk and work together to "reframe the relationship." These writers, instead of taking a divisive stand, have adopted an earlier, Betty Friedan style of feminism that called for equality rather than blame between the sexes.

In the essays here, for what feels to us like the first time, fathers themselves are expressing the perplexities of parenting daughters during these decades of questioning, polarization, and social change. In our invitation for essays, we asked fathers to write about their love for and their responsibilities to their daughters, about their perspectives on culture, about the future, and about the impact of feminist criticisms on their hearts and minds. We asked for honest explorations of conscience.

To voice their relationships, as fathers, and to voice them honestly, presumes a dilemma of conscience. As one father put it:

> I think a published essay by me on "the perplexities of fathering a daughter" might well *add* to those perplexities. That is, I would have to write about strained times, blessedly past I hope, between my daughter and me that she would not want to read about. Joan Didion somewhere says that the first responsibility of the writer is to betray his/her subject in the service of the piece. . . . But I guess I'm not that confident in the redemptive powers of art or the cathartic effects of truth-telling.

Similarly, some ten years ago, in editing a collection of essays by women writers about their fathers, Ursula Owen commented: "Some women simply refused, finding it too painful, or fearing it would stir up old family dramas best left alone, or would hurt the people involved. And for many women who agreed to contribute, there turned out to be anxieties which took them by surprise" (*Fathers: Reflections by Daughters*).

The conversation is not an easy one, but one we feel is necessary. The risk is one of love. Clearly the father-daughter bond in our society has been under profound strain and is in need of nurturing. The highly personal accounts here are directed toward rediscovering each other, as fathers, daughters, husbands, and wives; toward confronting the future; and toward strengthening the bond.

Let the conversation continue.

DeWitt Henry and James Alan McPherson

1

Arrivals

Delivering Lily

Phillip Lopate

EVER SINCE expectant fathers were admitted into delivery rooms a few decades ago, they have come armed with video cameras and awe. Before I became a father, I often heard men describe seeing the birth of their baby as "transcendental": the greatest experience in their lives. They would recall how choked up they got, even boast about their tears. It sounded very kitschy, like the ultimate sunrise. Being a nontranscendentalist, with suspicions, moreover, about my affective capacities, I was unsure how I would react. I had seen birthing scenes often enough in movies: how much more surprising could the reality be? I wondered, as someone who used to pass out at the sight of my own blood filling syringes, would I prove useless and faint? Or would I rise to the occasion, and be so moved in the bargain that at last I could retire those definitions of myself as a detached skeptic and accept the sweet, decent guy allegedly underneath?

Whatever reactions would befall me, I prepared myself for a minor role. The star of any birth is the mother; her co-star, Baby; her supporting leads, the medics. At nativity, every father feels himself a Joseph.

September 16, 1994, around four in the afternoon, I came across my wife, Cheryl, lying on the couch. She said she had "spotted" earlier, and wondered if this teaspoon's worth of sanguineous discharge could be what the books referred to, more scarletly, as "the bloody show."

I had already made a date with a friend—poet and fellow Brooklynite Harvey Shapiro—to attend the end of Yom Kippur services at the local temple, after which I was to bring Harvey back to our house to break fast together. Harvey would supply the traditional challah bread and herring, and Cheryl the rest of the meal. I promised her I would return with Harvey no later than seven.

At the Kane Street Synagogue, the rabbi was taking her own sweet time, and I knew Cheryl would be annoyed if her dinner got cold, so I prevailed on Harvey to leave the service early. Just as well. We were sitting around the table, getting ready to enjoy Cheryl's lamb and baked potatoes, when she pointed mysteriously to her belly.

"What's up?" I asked.

"I think it's starting."

She smiled. If it was indeed starting, she could skip her appointment the following week for an artificial induction. The fetus was at a good weight, and the doctors hadn't wanted to take the chance of the placenta breaking down, as happened often with overdue deliveries. Cheryl had felt sad at the thought of being artificially induced—missing the suspense of those first contractions—but now the baby seemed to be arriving on her due date, which meant we were in for the whole "natural" experience after all.

First-time parents, we had wondered whether we would really be able to tell when it was time. Would we embarrass ourselves by rushing off to the hospital days early, at the first false quiver? How to be sure whether the sensations Cheryl reported were the contractions? As instructed, we began timing them. Meanwhile, our downstairs neighbor Beth popped in, and stayed to witness potential history.

Harvey, a man in his late sixties and a grizzled veteran of parenthood, distracted us with stories of his boys' infancies while I kept my eye on the second hand. The contractions seemed to be spaced between five and seven minutes apart. We phoned our obstetricians. The office was closed for the Jewish holiday, but the answering service relayed the message to Dr. Arita, who was on call that night. Dr. Arita told Cheryl not to come into the hospital until contractions began occurring regularly, at five minutes apart, and lasted a full minute.

As soon as we had clocked two one-minute contractions in a row, I was impatient to start for the hospital. I had no wish to deliver a baby on the kitchen floor. Cheryl seemed calmer as she described her condition to Dr. Arita. It was now ten P.M., and he told her she would probably be coming into the hospital "sometime that night." This phraseology sounded too vague to me. I marveled at my wife's self-possessed demeanor. Cheryl was manifesting her sweet, lovely, modest, cheerfully plucky side—the side she presented to my friends and to outsiders; it was not a lie, but it gave no hint of her other self, that anxious, morose perfectionist she often produced when we were alone.

At ten-thirty the contractions began to arrive five minutes apart, and with more sharpness. Arita, beeped, said to come in. I pulled together a few last items (rubber ball, ice pack) on the checklist of things to take to the delivery room, and, saying good-bye to our guests, had gotten halfway to the door when I noticed Cheryl was, as usual, not quite ready to leave the house. She decided she had to water the mums.

For months, we had debated which neighborhood car service to call for the hour-long trip from Carroll Gardens to Mount Sinai Hospital, on the Upper East Side of Manhattan. Cheryl, a superb driver with no faith in my own lesser automotive skills, had even considered taking the wheel herself when the time came. Now suddenly she turned to me and said, "You drive. Just don't speed."

I maneuvered the car with caution over the Brooklyn Bridge, then up the FDR Drive, while Cheryl spoke happily of feeling empowered and in control. The contractions, she said, were not that painful: "I like these intense experiences that put you in contact with life and death." Premature bravado, I thought, but kept this to myself, glad to have her confidently chatting away; it meant she wouldn't have as much chance to find fault with my driving.

We parked the car in the hospital's indoor lot. Cheryl began walking very slowly up the ramp, holding her back. "I can't walk any faster," she snapped (the first sign of a change in mood?), as if responding to an un-spoken criticism she sensed me making about her pace, when in fact I was stumbling all over myself to support her.

It was close to midnight as we entered the eerily quiet Klingenstein Pavilion. I approached the security guard, busy flirting with a nurse's aide, for directions. We had preregistered weeks before to avoid red tape at zero hour. After signing in, we were directed down a long, creepy corridor into Birthing Room C. Mount Sinai Hospital has one of the largest maternity wards in the country, which is one reason we chose it;

but suddenly its very magnitude made us uneasy. We felt no longer dramatic or special, but merely one more on the assembly line, popping babies up and down the hall.

The expectant couple was deposited in Room C, and left alone. It would be difficult to describe Room C except in regard to absences: it was not cozy, it was not charming, it was not tiny, it was not big, it was not even decrepit, it had nothing for the eye to fasten on. It was what you expected, more or less, of an anonymous hospital room with a quick turnover; but Cheryl, I sensed, had hoped for more—more ambiance, amenities, *something* for the money. A visual designer by trade, she could, I knew, be preternaturally sensitive to new environments. Like a bride who finds herself in a nondescript wedding chapel, Cheryl may have long nurtured a fantasy of the ideal first-time birthing chamber, and something told me this was not it.

Often I allow myself to be made captive to my wife's moods, registering in an instant her first signs of discontent, and trying (usually without success) to gentle her out of it. I suspect that this catering to her anxiety—if only by playing the optimist to her pessimist—is really laziness of my part: it saves me the trouble of having to initiate emotions on my own.

Cheryl was given a hospital gown to wear. The moment she put it on, her confidence evaporated. She became an object, a thing to cut open. I cast about for ways to regain the light mood we had had in the car, but it was no use. "Let's get out of this room. It gives me the willies," she said.

We went for a walk around the ward, opening doors and peering inside like naughty children. Our best discovery was a conference room, dark and coffee-machined and air-conditioned—freezing, in fact—which suited her just fine. We hid out for fifteen minutes in this nonmedical haven. But her contractions eventually drove us back to Room C.

Cheryl lay down. She took an instant dislike to her berth, saying, "I don't like this bed!" and fiddling with the dials to raise and lower it. (An aversion, I thought, to proneness itself, which brought with it the surrender of her last sense of control). I turned on the TV to distract her. The second half of *Working Girl*, with Melanie Griffith, was on; Cheryl said she didn't want to hear the dialogue, so I was to keep the sound just loud enough to provide a background of "white noise." This was certainly a temperamental difference between us: If I had been giving birth, whatever the ordeal, I think I would have wanted the dialogue as well as the visuals of the movie on television. But I obliged; besides, we had already seen it.

For some reason, I had imagined our being swamped by medical personnel the moment we entered the hospital. We had not anticipated these quarter-hours of waiting alone, without instructions. We sat about like useless tourists who arrive in an economy hotel after a long trip, too tired to attempt the streets of a foreign city, yet too hemmed in by the unlovely room to enjoy a siesta.

How glad we were to see Dr. Arita walk in! A silver-mustached, suavely Latin, aristocratic type, he was one of Cheryl's favorites on the team. (She had been instructed to "establish a rapport" with all four obstetricians, since you never knew who was going to be on call during the actual delivery.) Cheryl had once admitted to me she thought Arita handsome, which made me a little jealous of him. He wore the standard green cotton scrubs with "Property of Mt. Sinai Hospital" printed on the material (still wrinkled, pulled straight from the dryer, no doubt; in former times, they would have been crisply ironed, to maintain authority and morale) and, improbably, a shower cap, which suggested he had come straight from surgery. This fashion accessory, I was happy to see, reduced somewhat his matinee-idol appeal.

It was Dr. Arita who had, months before, performed the amniocentesis, which ascertained among other things that our baby was to be a girl. Dr. Arita had a clinical terseness, never taking five words to say what four could accomplish. He asked Cheryl if she wanted Demerol to cut the pain and help her sleep.

Cheryl had her speech all ready. "No, I don't want Demerol. Demerol will make me groggy. It'll turn my brain to mush, and I hate that sensation."

"All right. If you change your mind, let me know." With those succinct words, he exited.

*

From time to time a nurse would see how Cheryl was getting along. Or the resident on the floor would pop in and say, "You're doing great, you're doing great!" Increasingly, Cheryl wasn't. Her contractions had become much more intense, and she began making a gesture with her hands of climbing the wall of pain, reaching her arms toward the ceiling. Finally she cried out:

"Painkiller. Painkiller. DEMEROL."

I ran to fetch the resident.

"I'd give it to my wife," he said, which seemed to soothe Cheryl somewhat. Exhausted by her pain, she had entered a cone of self-absorption, and only a doctor's or nurse's words seemed able to reach her. She had tuned me out, I thought, except as a potential irritant—a lowly servant who was not doing his job. "More ice," she said, rattling the cup as though scornful of the lousy service in this joint.

During prenatal Lamaze pep talks, the husband was always being built up as an essential partner in the birthing process. This propaganda about the husband's importance, the misapplied fallout of equal sharing of domestic responsibilities in modern marriage, struck me as bunk, since the husband's parturient chores appeared menial at best. One of my spousal duties was to replenish the ice that Cheryl sucked on or rubbed across her forehead. Throughout the night I made a dozen of these ice runs, dashing into the kitchenette and filling the cup with chips. Back in the room, Cheryl would cry out "Ice," then "Ice, ice!" with mounting urgency, as though the seconds between her request and my compliance were an eternity marking my bottomless clumsiness. I was rushing as fast as I could (though I must confess that when someone yells at me to fetch something or perform any manual action, it releases a slight physical hesitation on my part, perhaps no longer than 1.5 seconds, but this 1.5-second delay was enough to drive Cheryl wild. It is, you might say, the 1.5-second factor that makes conjugal life so continuously absorbing). Also, if I gave her a piece she deemed too small or too large, she would berate me in tones of "How could you be so stupid?" This went on for hours.

Her underlying reproach seemed to be that I was not hooked into her brain—was not able to anticipate her needs through ESP or heightened sensitivity—and she would have to waste precious breath articulating them. I would occasionally try to ease the tension by giving her a neck rub or caressing her hand, all recommended consolations by the Lamaze instructor. She shook me off like a cockroach. We husbands had been instructed as well to make "eye contact" with our wives. But whenever I tried this, Cheryl acquired the look of a runaway horse made acutely distressed by an unwanted obstacle in her path.

Sadly, I was not sufficiently generous to rise above feelings of being unfairly attacked. Days later, it surprised me to hear Cheryl telling people I had been wonderful during labor: "like a rock." Why, if this was so, I asked her, had she been so mean to me at the time? She explained rather reasonably that she was just taking her pain and putting it on me as fast as possible.

Sometimes, during contractions, she would literally transfer her pain to me by gouging my leg. Mistakenly thinking she was attached to my foot, I offered it to her, only to have it pushed away. "No, not the foot, I don't want the foot, I want the hand!" she screamed. (Being abnormally sensitive to smells all during pregnancy, she had picked up an unpleasant odor from my socks.)

What she liked best, it turned out, was to grip my trousers belt and yank hard. Eventually we worked out a routine: As soon as she started climbing a contraction, I would jump out of my chair, which was on her left side, run over to her right side and stand beside her as she pulled and thrashed at my belt for the duration of the spasm. All the while I would be counting off every five seconds of the contraction. I was not entirely sure what purpose I served by counting aloud in this fashion; they had told us husbands to do so in Lamaze class, in connection with certain breathing exercises, but since we had thrown those exercises out the window soon after coming to the hospital, why, I wondered, was it necessary to keep up a count?

I should explain that we had never been ideal Lamaze students. We were too preoccupied with our lives to practice the breathing regularly at home, or perhaps unable to overcome the feeling that it was a bit silly. When the actual labor came, it was so unremitting that we could not be bothered trying to execute these elegant respiratory tempi. It would be like asking a drowning woman to waltz. Cheryl continued to breathe, willy-nilly; that seemed enough for both of us. (I can hear the Lamaze people saying: Yes, but if only you had followed our instructions, it would have gone so much easier . . .) In any event, I would call out bogus numbers to please Cheryl, sensing that the real point of this exercise was for her to have the reassurance of my voice, measuring points on the arc of her pain, as proof that I was equally focused with her on the same experience.

In spite of, or because of, this excruciating workout, we were both getting very sleepy. The wee hours of the morning, from two to six, saw the surreal mixture of agony merging with drowsiness. Cheryl would be contorted with pain, and I could barely stop from yawning in her face. She too would doze off, between contractions. Waking suddenly as though finding herself on a steeply ascending roller coaster, she would yowl "Ooowwwww!" I'd snap awake, stare at my watch, call out a number, rush to the other side of the bed and present my belt for yanking. When it was over I would go back to my chair and nod off again, to the sound of some ancient TV rerun. I recall Erik Estrada hopping on a motorcycle in *CHiPs*, and *Hawaii Five-O*'s lead-in music; and early morning catnap dreams punctuated by a long spate of CNN, discussing the imminent invasion of Haiti; then *CBS News*, Dan Rather's interview with the imperturbable dictator, Raoul Cedras; and "Ice, ice!"

During this long night, Cheryl put her head against my shoulder and I stroked her hair for a long while. This tenderness was as much a part of the experience as the irritation, though I seem to recall it less. It went without saying that we loved each other, were tied together; and perhaps the true meaning of intimacy was not to have to put on a mask of courtesy in situations like these.

Demerol had failed to kill the pain: Cheryl began screaming "PAIN-KILLER, PAINKILLER, HELP!" in that telegraphic style dictated by her contractions. I tracked down the resident, and got him to give her a second dose of Demerol. But less than an hour later, her pain had reached a knuckle-biting pitch beyond Demerol's ministrations. At six in the morning, I begged the doctors to administer an epidural, which would numb Cheryl from the waist down. "Epidural"—the "open sesame" we had committed to memory in the unlikely event of unbearable pain—was guaranteed to be effective, but the doctors tried to defer this as long as possible, because the numbness in her legs would make it harder to push the baby out during the active phase. (My mind was too fatigued to grasp ironies, but it perked up at this word *active,* which implied that all the harsh turmoil Cheryl and I had undergone for what seemed like forever was merely the latent, "passive" phase of labor.)

The problem, the reason the labor was taking so long, was that while Cheryl had entered the hospital with a membrane eighty percent "effaced," her cervix was still very tight, dilated only one centimeter. From midnight to about five in the morning, the area had expanded from one to only two centimeters; she needed to get to ten centimeters before delivery could occur. To speed the process, she was now given an inducement drug, Proactin—a very small amount, since this medication is powerful enough to cause seizures. The anesthesiologist also hooked Cheryl up to an IV for her epidural, which was to be administered by drops, not all at once, so that it would last longer.

Blessedly, it did its job.

Around seven in the morning Cheryl was much calmer, thanks to the epidural. She sent me out to get some breakfast. I never would have forgiven myself if I had missed the baby's birth while dallying over coffee, but Cheryl's small dilation encouraged me to take the chance. Around the corner from the hospital was a Greek coffee shop, Peter's, where I repaired and ate a cheese omelette and read the morning *Times.* I can't remember if I did the crossword puzzle: Knowing me, I probably did, relishing these quiet forty minutes away from the hospital, and counting on them to refresh me for whatever exertions lay ahead.

Back on the floor, I ran into Dr. Raymond Sandler, Cheryl's favorite obstetrician on the team. Youthfully gray-haired, with a melodious South African accent and kind brown eyes, he said the same things the other doctors did, but they came out sounding warmer. Now, munching on some food, he said, "She looks good!" Dr. Sandler thought the baby would come out by noon. If so, delivery would occur during his shift. I rushed off to tell Cheryl the good news.

Momentarily not in pain, she smiled weakly as I held her hand. Our attention drifted to the morning talk shows. (Cheryl had long ago permitted me to turn up the volume.) Redheaded Marilu Henner was asking three gorgeous soap opera actresses how they kept the zip in their marriage. What were their secret ways of turning on their husbands? One had the honesty to admit that, ever since the arrival of their baby, sex had taken a backseat to exhaustion and nursing. I liked her for saying that, wondering at the same time what sacrifices were in store for Cheryl and me. Marilu (I had never watched her show before, but now I felt like a regular) moved on to the question of what first attracted each woman to her husband. "His tight buns." The audience loved it. I glanced over at Cheryl, to see how she was taking this. She was leaning to one side with a concentrated expression of oncoming nausea, her normally beautiful face looking drawn, hatchet-thin. She seemed to defy the laws of perspective: a Giacometti face floating above a Botero stomach.

We were less like lovers at that moment than like two soldiers who had marched all night and fallen out, panting, by the side of the road. The titillations of the TV show could have come from another planet, so far removed did they feel from us; that Eros had gotten us here in the first place seemed a rumor at best.

Stubbornly, in this antiseptic, torture-witnessing cubicle, I tried to recover the memory of sexual feeling. I thought about how often we'd made love in order to conceive this baby—every other night, just to be on the safe side, during the key weeks of the month. At first we were frisky, reveling in it like newlyweds. Later, it became another chore to perform, like moving the car for alternate-side-of-the-street parking, but with the added fear that all our efforts might be in vain. Cheryl was thirty-eight, I was fifty. We knew many other couples around our age who were trying, often futilely, to conceive—a whole generation, it sometimes seemed, of careerists who had put off childbearing for years, and now wanted more than anything a child of their own, and were deep into sperm motility tests, in vitro fertilizations, and the lot. After seven months of using the traditional method, and suffering one miscarriage in the process, we were just about to turn ourselves over like lab rats to the fertility experts when Cheryl got pregnant. This time it took. Whatever torment labor brought, we could never forget for a moment how privileged we were to be here.

"You've got to decide about her middle name!" Cheryl said with groggy insistence, breaking the silence.

"OK. Just relax, we will."

"Elena? Francesca? Come on, Phillip, we've got to get this taken care of or we'll be screwed."

"We won't be 'screwed.' If worse comes to worse, I'll put both names down."

"But we have to make up our minds. We can't just—"

"Well, which name do you prefer?"

"I can't think straight now."

A new nurse came on the day shift: a strong, skillful West Indian woman named Jackie, who looked only about forty but who told us later that she was a grandmother. As it turned out, she would stay with us to the end, and we would become abjectly dependent on her—this stranger who had meant nothing to us a day before, and whom we would never see again.

At nine centimeters' dilation, and with Jackie's help, Cheryl started to push. "Pretend you are going to the toilet," Jackie told Cheryl, who obeyed, evacuating a foul-smelling liquid.

"She made a bowel movement, that's good," Dr. Sandler commented in his reassuring way. Jackie wiped it up with a towelette, and we waited for the next contraction. Jackie would say with her island accent, "Push, push in the bottom," calling to my mind that disco song, "Push, push in the bush." Cheryl would make a supreme effort. But now a new worry arose: The fetal monitor was reporting a slower heartbeat after each contraction, which suggested a decrease in the baby's oxygen. You could hear the baby's heartbeat amplified in the room, like rain on a tin roof, and every time the sound slowed down, you panicked.

Dr. Sandler ordered a blood sample taken from the infant's scalp, to see if she was properly aerated (that is, getting enough oxygen). In addition, a second fetal monitor was attached to the fetus's scalp (don't ask me how). My poor baby, for whom it was not enough to undergo the birth trauma, was having to endure the added insult of getting bled while still in the womb.

The results of the blood test were positive. "Not to worry," Dr. Sandler said. But just in case, he ordered Cheryl to wear an oxygen mask for the remainder of the labor. This oxygen mask frightened us, with its bomb shelter associations.

"How will the baby be delivered?" Cheryl asked, as the apparatus was placed over her face. "Will they have to use forceps?"

"That will depend on your pushing," answered Dr. Sandler, and then he left. I did not like the self-righteous sound of this answer, implying it was ours to screw up or get right. We had entrusted ourselves to the medical profession precisely so that they could take care of everything for us!

Often, after a push, the towelette underneath Cheryl was spattered with blood. Jackie would swoop it up, throw it on the floor, kick it out of the way, raise Cheryl's lower half from the bed and place a fresh towelette underneath. The floor began to smell like a battleground, with blood and shit underfoot.

"Push harder, push harder, harder, harder, harder," Jackie chanted in her Barbados accent. Then: "Keep going, keep going, keep going!" Cheryl's legs were floppy from the epidural; she reported a feeling of detachment from her body. In order for her to have a counterpressure to push against, I was instructed to lift her left leg and double it against the crook of my arm. This maneuver, more difficult than it sounds, had to be sustained for several hours; a few times I felt that my arm was going to snap and I might end up hospitalized as well. It was probably the hardest physical work I've ever done—though nothing compared, of course, to what Cheryl was going through. I feared she would burst a blood vessel.

Around eleven, Jackie went on her lunch break, replaced by a nurse who seemed much less willing to get involved. A tense conversation ensued between Dr. Sandler and the new nurse:

"This patient is fully effaced," he said.

"My other patient is fully, too."

He sighed, she shrugged, and the next minute, they were both out the door. Left alone with a wife buckling in pain, I felt terrified and enraged: How dare Jackie take a food break now? Couldn't we page her in the cafeteria and tell her to get her ass back? It was no use; I had to guide Cheryl through her contractions as if I knew what I was doing. This meant watching the fetal monitor printout for the start of each contraction (signaled by an elevating line), then lodging her leg against my arm, and chanting her through the three requisite pushes per contraction, without any firm idea exactly when each was supposed to occur. The first time I did this I got so engrossed pressing her leg hard against me that I forgot the cheerleading. I have a tendency to fall silent during crises, conserving energy for stock taking and observation. This time I was brought up short by Cheryl yelling at me: "How am I supposed to know how long to push?" I wanted to answer: I'm not a trained medic, I have no idea myself. The next time, however, I bluffed. "Push, push in the bottom!" doing my best Jackie imitation until Jackie herself came back.

Sometime near noon, Dr. Sandler made an appearance with his colleague, Dr. Schiller, and began explaining the case to her. Cheryl had never felt as confident about Laura Schiller as she had about Dr. Sandler and Dr. Arita, either because Dr. Schiller was the only woman on the team (not that Cheryl would have agreed with this explanation), or because Dr. Schiller had a skinny, birdlike, tightly wound manner that did not immediately inspire tranquillity, or because the two women had simply not had the opportunity to "develop a rapport." With a sinking sensation, we began to perceive that Dr. Sandler was abandoning us. Actually, he probably would have been happy to deliver Lily, if only she had arrived when he had predicted, before noon. Now he had to be somewhere else, so he turned the job over to his capable colleague.

Dr. Schiller brought in a younger woman—a resident or intern— and they discussed whether the baby was presenting OA or OR (whatever that meant). Now they turned to the expectant mother and got serious. Dr. Schiller proved to be a much tougher coach than Jackie. "Come on, Cheryl, you can try harder than that," she would say. Cheryl's face clouded over with intense effort, her veins stood out, and half the time her push was judged effective, the other half, not. I could never fathom the criteria used to separate the successes from the failures; all I knew was that my wife is no shirker, and I resented anyone implying she was. If some of Cheryl's pushes lacked vigor, it was because the epidural had robbed her of sensation below, and because the long night of pain, wasted on a scarcely increased dilation, had sapped her strength.

Over the next hour, doctor's and patient's rhythms synchronized, until something like complete trust developed between them. Dr. Schiller cajoled; Cheryl responded. We were down to basics; the procedure of birth had never seemed so primitive. I couldn't believe that here we were in the postindustrial era, and the mother still had to push the fetus by monstrously demanding effort, fractions of an inch down the vaginal canal. It was amazing that the human race survived, given such a ponderous childbearing method. With all of science's advances, delivering a baby still came down to three timeworn approaches: push, forceps, or Caesarean.

This particular baby, it seemed, did not want to cross the perineum. "If the baby's no closer after three more pushes," Dr. Schiller declared, "we're going to have to go to forceps."

Forceps would necessitate an episiotomy—a straight surgical cut of the pubic region to keep it from fraying and tearing further. An episiotomy also would leave Cheryl sore and unable to sit for weeks. Knowing that I would probably be accused of male insensitivity, and sensing my vote counted marginally at best, I nevertheless expressed a word in favor of forceps. Anything to shorten the ordeal and get the damn baby out. Cheryl had suffered painful contractions for eighteen hours; she was exhausted; I was spent—and I was dying with curiosity to see my little one! I couldn't take the suspense any longer, obviously not a legitimate reason. Cheryl worried that the forceps might dent or misshape the baby's skull. Dr. Schiller explained that the chances of that occurring were very slight, given the improved design of modern instruments.

Cheryl pushed as hard as she could, three times, with a most desperate look in her eyes. No use.

"I always try to give a woman two hours at best to push the baby out. But if it doesn't work—then I go to forceps," Dr. Schiller said authoritatively. Cheryl looked defeated. "Okay, we'll try one more time. But now you really have to push. Give me the push of the day."

The Push of the Day must have felt like a tsunami to Lily, but she clung to the side of her underwater cave.

They readied the scalpel for an episiotomy. I turned away. Some things you can't bear to watch done to a loved one. Dr. Schiller, kneeling, looked inside Cheryl and cried out, "She's got tons of black hair!" Standing over her, I could make out nothing inside; the fact that someone had already peeked into the entranceway and seen my baby's locks made me restless to glimpse this fabled, dark-haired creature.

The last stage was surprisingly brief and anticlimactic. The doctors manipulated the forceps inside Cheryl, who pushed with all her might. Then I saw the black head come out, followed by a ruddy, squirming body. Baby howled, angry and shocked to find herself airborne in such a place. It was such a relief I began to cry. Then I shook with laughter. All that anguish and grief and triumph just to extract a writhing jumbo shrimp—it was comic.

The doctor passed the newborn to her mother for inspection. She was (I may say objectively) very pretty: like a little Eskimo or Mexican babe, with her mop of black hair and squinting eyes. Something definitely Third World about her. An overgrown head on a scrawny trunk, she reversed her mother's disproportions. A kiss from Cheryl, then she was taken off to the side of the room and laid on a weighing table (seven pounds, four ounces) and given an Apgar inspection by Jackie, under a heat lamp. Lily Elena Francesca Lopate had all her fingers and toes, all her limbs, and obviously sound vocal chords. She sobbed like a whip-poorwill, then brayed in and out like an affronted donkey.

Abandoned. For, while Cheryl was being stitched up by Dr. Schiller (who suddenly seemed to us the best doctor in the world), Lily, the jewel, the prize, the cause of all this tumult, lay on the table, crying alone. I was too intimidated by hospital procedure to go over there and comfort her, and Cheryl obviously couldn't move, and Jackie had momentarily left the room. So Lily learned right away how fickle is the world's attention.

Dr. Schiller told Cheryl she would probably have hemorrhoids for a while, as a result of the episiotomy. Cheryl seemed glad enough that she had not died on the table. She had done her job, delivered up safely the nugget inside her. I admired her courage beyond anything I had ever seen.

Happy, relieved, physically wrung out: these were the initial reactions. For hours (I realized after the fact) I had been completely caught up in the struggle of labor, with no space left over for self-division. But that may have had more to do with the physically demanding nature of assisting a birth than with any transcendental wonderment about it. In fact, it was less spiritually uplifting and more like boot camp. I felt as if I had gone through combat.

That night, home from the hospital, I noted in my diary all I could recall. Consulting that entry for this account, I see how blurred my understanding was—remains—by the minutiae of medical narrative. What does it all mean, exactly? On the one hand, an experience so shocking and strange; on the other hand, so typical, so stupefyingly ordinary.

When people say that mothers don't remember the pain of labor, I think they mean that of course they remember, but that the fact of the pain recedes next to the blessing of the child's presence on earth.

Odd: What I remember most clearly from that long night and day is the agitated pas de deux between Cheryl and me, holding ourselves up like marathon dancers, she cross at me for not getting her ice fast enough, me vexed at her for not appreciating that I was doing my best. Do I hold on to that memory because I can't take in the enormity of seeing a newborn burst onto the plane of existence, and so cut it down to the more mundane pattern of a couple's argument? Or is it because the tension between Cheryl and me that night pointed to a larger truth: that a woman giving birth finds herself inconsolably isolated? Close as we normally were, she had entered an experience into which I could not follow her; the promise of marriage—that we would both remain psychically connected—was of necessity broken.

I remember Cheryl sitting up, half an hour after Lily was born, still trembling and shaking.

"That's natural, for the trembling to last a while," said Dr. Schiller.

Weeks afterward, smiling and accepting congratulations, I continue to tremble from the violence of the baby's birth. In a way, I am still trembling from it. The only comparison that comes to mind, strangely enough, is when I was mugged in the street, and I felt a tremor looking over my shoulder, for months afterward. That time my back was violated by a knife; this time I watched Cheryl's body ripped apart by natural forces, and it was almost as if it were happening to me. I am inclined to say I envied her and wanted it to be happening to me—to feel that intense an agony, for once—but that would be a lie, because at the time, not for one second did I wish I were in Cheryl's place. Orthodox Jews are taken to task for their daily prayer, "Thank God I am not a woman." And they should be criticized, since it is a crude, chauvinistic thought; but it is also an understandable one in certain situations, and I found myself viscerally "praying" something like that, while trying to assist Cheryl in her pushes.

Thank God I am not someone else. Thank God I am only who I am. These are the thoughts that simultaneously create and imprison the self. If ego is a poisonous disease (and it is), it is one I unfortunately trust more than its cure. I began as a detached skeptic and was shoved by the long night into an unwilling empathy, which saw Cheryl as a part of me, or me of her, for maybe a hundred seconds in all, before returning to a more self-protective distance. Detachment stands midway between two poles: at one end, solipsism; at the other end, wisdom. Those of us who are only halfway to wisdom know how far we still lean toward the chilliness of solipsism.

It is too early to speak of Lily. This charming young lady, willful, passionate, and insisting on engagement on her terms, who has already taught me more about unguarded love and the dread meaning of responsibility than I ever hoped to learn, may finally convince me there are other human beings as real as myself.

In praying for my daughter, I pray for myself.

A Story for Ancient Moon

Adam Schwartz

TODAY IS September 14, 1996: the first day of Rosh Hashanah, a time when we celebrate the New Year, a time when we think about new beginnings. Today's date is also an occasion for me to think about my daughter's beginnings. Almost a year ago today, on September 16, 1995, my daughter Annie was found on the steps of a middle school in Wuhan, China. She was five months old and had probably been left by her birth mother, and almost certainly because she was a girl. As many of you know, China has a one-child-per-family policy, with brutal economic penalties for couples who have more than one child. And because sons are more highly valued than daughters, many thousands of baby girls are abandoned in China every year.

I have other dates to celebrate my daughter's beginnings: her birthday, of course—April 26, 1995; and the date she was placed in our arms—April 15, 1996. So why would September 16, 1995, the day she was abandoned, also be sacred to me?

Baby girls adopted from China come to their adoptive parents with virtually no history. The orphanage provides a birth date, which may or may not be accurate, and a name, which may or may not be the one given by the birth parents. About the only real information you get is the certificate of abandonment, a document stating where and when the child was abandoned. I already knew many people who had adopted babies from China, and I was surprised to hear some of them tell me that they had very little curiosity about their daughters' lives before the adoption. One woman said to me that she felt her daughter's life began the moment she was placed in her arms. I was dumbfounded by this attitude. Perhaps I was projecting my concerns onto the daughter I had not even met yet, but it struck me as unbearably sad that she would never be able to contact her birth mother if she wanted to, that she would never be able ask questions of the woman who gave birth to her and then abandoned her. Would this missing knowledge, these unanswered questions, keep her from feeling whole?

Before we left for China, we knew our daughter's birthday, April 26, 1995, and her Chinese name, Wu Guyue, which means "ancient moon." We also had a black and white passport-size photo of her. She looked exactly like her name—a high moonscape of a forehead, and eyes like a pair of shiny black pearls. Her eyes stared calmly back at the camera, a look so clear and knowing that she truly did have an ancient countenance. Her eyes were exactly like the "ancient, glittering eyes" of the Chinamen in Yeats' poem "Lapis Lazuli." We showed her name to some Chinese friends, all of whom said it was unique, not like the generic names commonly used by the orphanage. Between this information and her photograph, I was sure my daughter had been named by someone who knew and loved her.

We arrived in Wuhan on Sunday night, April 14, and at ten-thirty the next morning, in a dim, dilapidated government office, our daughter was handed to us. She cried nonstop for an hour. Then she fell asleep, and when she woke up later that afternoon in our hotel room she smiled and laughed with my wife and I as if she had known us all twelve months of her life. In the hotel restaurant the next evening, she cried when I left the table to retrieve something from our room; I looked back, and my daughter was reaching out to me with her doll-sized hands.

After two days with Annie, I could better understand the woman who felt that her daughter's life began at the moment they met. The love I felt for Annie was so completely transforming, so shockingly powerful, and the bond between us so deep and immediate, that I believed, in every cell of my body, that we were meant to be father and daughter. I couldn't imagine another fate for either of us. Of course I knew that she existed because some time in July of 1994 a man and woman in China made love and conceived a child. But this fact was—and still is—as remote to me as the idea that God created the world in seven days, or any other creation myth.

On our third day in China, officials from the orphanage came by our hotel room with some documents, among them the certificate of abandonment. This is what it said:

> This is to certify that Wu Guyue, female, born on April 26, 1995, was found to be abandoned at the Xingou Middle School, Dongxihu District, Wuhan City, Hubei Province on September 16, 1996. Then she was sent to our court by the People's Government of Xingou Town, Dongxihu District, Wuhan City, Hubei Province on September 16, 1995. Her innate parents couldn't be found.

My blood pounded as I read this. Perhaps it was the official, unsentimental account of a heart-shattering act; perhaps it was a reminder that my daughter did indeed have a history, but a history she would never know. Then I noticed the date again. Her birth mother had kept her for nearly five months. I knew that most of the babies are abandoned after only a couple of days or weeks at the most. The more I looked at this date—April 16, 1995—the more it looked like a sliver of light, a small fragment of evidence that Annie's birth mother wanted desperately to keep her.

Very soon that sliver of light turned into a small window; only fifteen minutes after I had read the certificate of abandonment, my wife and I found another document, this one unofficial and completely unexpected. Two days earlier, when Annie was handed to us, she, like all the babies in our group, was swaddled in many layers of clothing, even though it was the middle of April and warm in Wuhan. After we brought her back to our hotel room, it took us about twenty minutes to peel off all the layers of clothing. We wanted to keep it of course, and sent it to the hotel laundry. The clothing was delivered to our room just before the orphanage officials came by. As my wife was putting it away, she noticed a red cloth stitched over the heart of the innermost garment. She looked closer and saw that this red cloth had writing on it. We called our translator. He examined the cloth, told us it was a letter from her foster mother, and then read it to us. This is what it said:

> To Guyue's parents: Greetings to you. I am Guyue's foster mother. Baby Guyue was brought from the orphanage to my house to be in my foster

care more than half a year ago, and now she is adopted by you two kind-hearted people. I feel happy for her, but at the same time it is hard to accept that she is leaving me to cross the ocean to the other shore. I would like to ask you to take good care of baby Guyue, and on her birthday every year, please send back some pictures to relieve my longing for her.

As the translator read this letter, I was holding Annie in my arms, my eyes damp with tears. I was crying, I think, because I realized we had come upon something very valuable for my daughter. She would have a personal and direct connection back to her homeland; she would have more than a certificate of abandonment to account her origins; she would know, without question, that she had been deeply loved before she was adopted.

When I heard this letter, I couldn't help but think of Annie's birth mother, who had cared for her for nearly the same amount of time as the foster mother. I couldn't begin to imagine the depths of her grief and longing. Or perhaps I could, and the mystery for me was not the abandonment itself but how she, or any parent, could bear such a terrible loss. I asked our translator why her birth mother would have waited five months before giving her up. He clearly wasn't comfortable with my curiosity and questions, but finally he said that the husband has all the power in a marriage and very possibly Annie's mother tried to keep her for as long as possible. I thanked him very much; that was exactly the answer I was hoping for.

Not long after we returned to the United States, I had a dream about Annie's birth mother. In my dream, I am crossing a wide, traffic-choked avenue in Wuhan. Coming toward me is a woman with the dazed, pallid look of someone recovering from a long illness. In the middle of the avenue our eyes meet; I think she senses something familiar about me, knows that we are connected in some way, but can only offer me a pained, perplexed gaze. I want to tell her who I am, want to let her know that her daughter is safe and loved, but I don't have the language to communicate with her. I reach out to touch her, but she is suddenly pulled back into the tide of people crossing the street, one woman among the millions.

I thought of her constantly, always imagining her looking just over my shoulder, wondering what she would think as I played with Annie at the park, fed her lunch, or sang her to sleep. Perhaps I couldn't quite accept the fact that we would never meet, that I could never let her know that her daughter was safe and loved, that her longing would never be relieved with the photographs and letters we could send to the foster mother. Perhaps I was driven by the same impulse as anyone who invents and tells stories, a desire for connection and solace with something that's been lost—a mother, a place, a history.

I continued to ask questions whenever I could. We had a Chinese baby-sitter named Li Li. She had been in the country for only three years; in Beijing, she had been a math professor. Li Li told me that the shape of Annie's eyes was considered very beautiful in China. I had actually heard the same comment from other Chinese women. Before we left for China to adopt Annie, I passed her picture around to my classes, and all the Chinese students remarked upon the beautiful shape of her eyes. Li Li explained that no woman in China would want to give up a daughter with such rare and beautiful eyes, and that no doubt the birth father gave the orders. Li Li said all this without a trace of conjecture; she knew my daughter's eyes, and she knew China. Li Li told me that her grandfather had ten sons, and when his eleventh child turned out to be a girl he was bitterly disappointed. "He have ten boy," Li Li exclaimed, "and he still upset about girl!"

In the meantime, we had written to Annie's foster mother. We thanked her for loving our daughter and expressed our hope that she would always be part of Annie's life. We asked her to tell us anything she could about Annie before we adopted her. Her reply stunned us. "When she came to my house," the foster mother wrote, "she was so skinny that she was like a skin-wrapped skeleton. She had bronchitis. The hospital issued a notice of critical illness, stating that the child's condition was fatal." The foster mother tramped from one hospital to the next with Annie, and at every one the doctors said they could do nothing to save the child's life. But Annie did live, of course. Her foster mother said in her letter that Annie's life was "snatched back from the hand of the God of Death." That's one explanation. But I know my strong-minded, iron-willed little girl, and I think that she had a resolve to live that no doctor could have guessed at as they looked at her frail, skeletal body.

The letter from Annie's foster mother enabled me to complete the story I had been trying to construct about her abandonment—the first of many stories I hope to tell my daughter. I believe that Annie was given up because her birth parents did not have the means to care for such a sickly and malnourished child. Her birth mother left her on the steps of the school because she wanted to give her a chance at life. Perhaps she hoped that Guyue would be cared for by someone like her good-hearted foster mother; I doubt she imagined that in a year's time her daughter would be on the other side of the world, celebrating the Jewish New Year.

I hope my daughter keeps the God of Death at arm's length for another one hundred and twenty years, and that she leaves behind many daughters and granddaughters and great-granddaughters, some of whom might trace their own beginnings to the predawn hours of September 16, 1995, in a Chinese city of eight million, when a woman left her small bundle on the steps of a school and then hurried away into the darkness.

2

Early Childhood

A Prayer for Connection

Samuel Shem

AT CHRISTMASTIME 1991 Janet and I were searching the shops in Harvard Square for a card to welcome home two friends who were adopting a baby in China. We too were in the process of adopting—we'd filed our papers and were awaiting a referral from the orphanage. We chanced upon a card with a Chinese character called *chun*. The caption of the card, from the *I Ching* (The Book of Change), Hexagram 3, read:

> ### New Beginnings
> Times of birth and growth start unseen, yet below the surface. Everything is dark and still unformed, yet teeming with motion. Difficulties and chaos loom. Despite this struggle, energy and resources are collected and form begins to take shape. The young plant takes root, rises above the ground, and is brought to light.

We liked this card so much that we kept it, finding another for our friends. We made a poster of this character, and put it beside our bed, to sustain us until we left for China. In our forties, we felt old for first-time parents. New beginnings.

Five weeks later, just after the new year, we got a call from the agency. Our referral had been made. There were two facts available about the baby waiting for us in China: she had been born on October 20, 1991, and her name was Chun.

"Daddy, what time do you go to the dentist?" Katie Chun asks. She's five and three-quarters, and into jokes.

"I dunno, what time?"

"Tooth-hurty." She and I burst out laughing. She wants to be sure I get it, and she says, "See, your tooth hurtys and it's two-thirty."

"Great joke, I love it."

She and I are buddies, driving home in the convertible from her summer camp as organized and crisp as boot camp. The camp is from nine to four. Yet the ethos is such that when I showed up at nine the first day to let her off, everyone was gone and I had to park and trudge guilt-ily to the camp office to explain why we were late. I showed up precisely at four to find her, again, sitting in the office, all the other kids picked up.

I say to Katie, "And I've got a joke for you."

"Yeah?"

"I've got a dog, and he has no nose, no nose at all."

"Oh yeah?"

"Yeah. You have to ask me how with no nose he smells?"

"How with no nose he smells?" she asks.

"Terrible! He smells terrible."

"Heeee!"

I ask about her day at camp. She talks about her new friend, Suzy. "Suzy's shy, and I have to help her."

Katie is in an all-girls' group at camp. It is the happiest we have ever seen her. Last week she talked about boys.

"Boys don't listen really well, and they're impatient and always mess-ing things up, and sometimes they're mean, and sometimes they push girls, and sometimes they yell at them. I like being with all girls."

"Why?"

"All girls can do more fun things and boys can't ruin it."

It has begun, the separation across gender. In fact, it is firmly in place by age five and three-quarters, and will continue for several years until, at puberty, girls and boys try to connect. Janet's and my work on gender in schools has shown us that there is no such thing as true co-educa-tion. At best it is separate but unequal. From preschool through about eighth grade boys and girls are on their own separate paths, like infants in parallel play.

On our third day in China, we were able to take our babies out of the orphanage and back to our hotel. All eight couples and their babies would be staying in the Xiang Xiang Hotel for a week, waiting for our documents to be processed. Carrying our four-month-old Katie in my arms I said:

"Katie Chun, this is your hotel!"

The eight little girl babies—there are no boy babies in the orphanage—had been swaddled tightly with many layers of clothes to keep them warm. They lay on their backs as if in straitjackets. The hair on the backs of their head was worn off, or never had a chance to grow. Each baby's hands were at its sides, so that they never touch their fingers together. That first night in the hotel we watched Katie's delight at the discovery of her fingers touching her fingers. Over and over again she ran her fingertips over each other, amazed. In the three days we had seen her in the orphanage, she never made a sound. We worried that she couldn't. Only when we put her in the sink for a bath did she start to cry.

Back in the hotel, all of us couples unwrapped our girls in layers held together by string, and dressed them in the American clothes we had brought.

Three and a half years later, we are at a picnic before the start of the cooperative preschool in which we've enrolled Katie. Parents serve as helpers several times a month. The picnic is held in the backyard of the parent president of the preschool. Everyone is having a great time, parents getting to know each other, kids running around. Katie loves animals, especially horses. There is a rocking horse in the backyard. Our eyes, of course, are always flittering back and forth to her. As I watch, she spots the rocking horse, runs to it, and with delight climbs up on it and starts to rock. A little boy runs over to the horse and knocks her off it into the grass. She doesn't cry, but on her face is a look of astonishment, moderating to puzzlement: "Why did you do *that*?" The little boy rocks. He will be in her class. What do we say to his parents? And is Katie supposed to learn to fight back?

This pattern—boys "knocking her off her horse" during play dates, preschool, and playground encounters—will be repeated over and over again as she grows. By the middle of the first year at preschool, at age four, the girls and the boys mostly play separately, and the girls do not want the boys to come to their birthday parties; the boys sometimes want a girl or two at their birthday parties.

What is going on here?

Luckily, our work lives, Janet Surrey's and mine, have been partly devoted to understanding human development. Janet has focused her attention on women, I on men, and together, both of us on gender differences. We are clinicians, I a psychiatrist, Janet a clinical psychologist. Our focus is on helping people to grow. From the Stone Center Relational Model developed by Janet and others at Wellesley College, we have come to understand that the primary motivation in both boy and girl babies is the desire for "connection." (Freud's sex and aggression have been shown, by neonatal studies by the psychologist Daniel Stern and others, to be pure Freudian fantasy.) We have also seen, from our work with children of all ages as well as in our clinical practices, that healthy human growth takes place through and toward mutuality. This may seem obvious, but it is in fact a radically different view from that of the culture, at least of Western culture.

In America, healthy growth has been traditionally that of a strong, self-sufficient, independent self. The idea is that once you have a strong self, at some later date you will be ready for a mature relationship. There are many problems with this dominant view, among which are that that date may never come, and that the worst thing for a mature (mutual) relationship may be a strong, self-sufficient self. It's the Woody Allen falsity: through self-analysis for several decades you may come to understand every nook and cranny of yourself, and yet you may have no connection in a mature, healthy, mutual—and moral—relationship.

This dominant self/other model is a primarily male model, men being the dominant force, in political and economic terms, in our culture. The world is split into two parts. Difference between "I" and "you" implies comparison, and comparison almost inevitably translates into power—one person is better or worse, or has more power or less. When we talk about gender, we have to talk about power. The talk has been dominated by the world experts, so far almost all men. The self/other model, an adversarial model, has created a field-day for lawyers.

The connection model is a paradigm shift, from self as the focus to connection as the focus. That is, there is a third element in human interactions called "the connection" or "the relationship." Connection encompasses self; self cannot encompass connection. In addition to "I" and "you," there is a "we." The "we" informs and reflects the "I" and "you."

This may seem obvious, but it is an elusive obvious. To fully understand this is to change your view of the world. It has changed mine.

What does this mean for our daughter? How does this shape my prayers for her?

As we look at the psychological development of girls and boys it is obvious that there are two different pathways of relational development, and that Katie's repeated encounters with the headlong self-focused rush of boys her age—such as being knocked off her horse by a boy at the picnic—are the result of the collision of those two pathways. Despite anatomical differences, boys and girls for the first few years of life grow in relation, usually, with the mother. I applaud the part that fathers play in this process, but in terms of empathic growth, and the fostering of mutual attention and response, mothers still, in our culture, mostly are preferred. For Janet and me this has been something of a struggle. Despite the fact that we spend about equal time—and equal quality time—with Katie, she has a different sense of connection with each of us. Despite my having sung to her and rocked her to sleep every night for her first year, Katie shifted to prefer "Momma" soon thereafter, insisting that Janet do just about everything for her and with her. At one point she said, quite emphatically, when I offered to read her to sleep one night:

"No, I don't want you! I want Momma. I don't like you! I never want you to read to me again!"

I had heard this several times before, and had said nothing, but this time I said, "You know, Katie, I feel bad when you say that."

She thought a minute. Janet and I stood there. We didn't know a solution to this either/or moment. And then Katie came through:

"I want Mommy *and* Daddy to read to me tonight."

And yet it continued—and continues to be hard. One of the low points was one day when Janet and I were coming home from being away a night. We walked in, I leading. Katie spotted us, yelped with joy, and started running across the room towards us in the doorway. I bent down to welcome her into my arms. She ran straight towards me, and at the last minute made a zigzag around me and jumped into Janet's arms. I felt crushed. What to do about this? I didn't want to lay on her the guilt laid on me. From time to time I tell her that I feel bad in those kinds of situations, and she responds. Now, thank God, she might reflexively say "Momma," but then might add "—and Daddy." I've come to see this not as any judgment on me, but rather on the different qualities of her connection with Janet and with me. She can sense, in relationship, how Janet has spent her whole life being rewarded and valued for her empathy, sensitivity, back-and-forth attending and responding, and her easy manner of fostering the development of another *with* herself, *in relation to* herself.

I, as a "normal" man, have been valued for something quite different, and despite whatever I've learned, I give off the "vibes" which Katie senses, as if they were made of steel cable, of a less easy empathy, a more edged "self," a "self" which for many decades has been bought at the expense of relationship.

Living with Katie is like living with a twenty-four-hours-a-day Zen master: a laser gaze, an iron whim, a continual inquiry into "What's real? What's true? What's authentic?" And the quintessential: "What's our connection right now?"

Katie is almost four, having her first play date with a boy. He will be coming to her house. She has had many play dates with girls, but for days this has been different.

"What should I wear?" she has been asking. "What can we play?"

On the morning of the play date she asked: "Should I wear my pretty dress?" "What shall we play?"

Janet and I look at each other, amazed at how differently she is acting from how she acts when the date is with a girl. We tell her she can wear whatever she wants. She chooses a dress—she never wears dresses—and waits expectantly.

The play date does not go well. Katie continues to try to get the boy's attention, but the boy is interested in doing his own thing. At one point the boy is playing with blocks, and Katie is sitting beside him, moving a block, looking at him for a reaction, sometimes even talking to him. He does not respond, but stays focused on what he is making with his blocks. Katie is constantly turning to him, trying to engage him. No dice. The boy's mother sits with us and rolls her eyes, and, finally, says:

"Why won't he talk? Why won't he pay attention to her?"

In a sense, we know why. Even at this age, what is going on in our living room is a clash of two developmental paths. What we see is not at all unusual, for we have seen it over and over again with many boys and girls we've worked with.

Simply put, although boys and girls both start out with a primary desire to be in relation, at age three or four there is a fork in the path: girls continue to grow in relation, boys—under pressure of cultural forces—shift to focus on the growth of themselves, at the expense of relationship. Mothers of boys of that age notice this, and put it this way: "I feel as if my son is spiraling out." "It's as if a wall is going up between me and my son."

One almost never hears a mother talk that way about a daughter. Girls learn and are valued for paying attention to—and taking care of—the relationship. Katie plays it out, over and over, with her stuffed animals and dolls.

Boys more often tend to sacrifice relationship for self. At that age the culture does not demand that girls make this sacrifice, and so girls continue to grow in a relational way—with mother, father, girls, and boys.

Not that Katie's play dates with girls are all rosy. If there are two girls, often things go well. Adding a third girl results in one girl being left out, and in fact the most pain she feels with her girlfriends are when she has a sense of being excluded. The girl-girl relationships get too intense, too complex for the girls to handle; the girl-boy relationship just doesn't seem to be there at all. And yet while—with our help—Katie did work out the conflicts in the girl-girl play dates, there was nothing to be done about that with the boys. Every boy play date has been a variation on the theme. For example, Katie was excited about another boy in her class riding in our convertible this summer. He got in next to her, we put on Bob Marley, and we took off. Blue sky, warm sun, Bob Marley. She looked at him to share her excitement. His head was in a book. He didn't acknowledge her or the convertible.

One day, when Katie was about three, the same age as when she was knocked off the rocking horse, I came home from work and asked her:

"How was your day, Katie?"

"Good." She smiled at me.

"Great, great," I said.

"And how was *your* day, daddy?"

Taken aback, I smile and say, "Good."

This is "normal" for a girl in our culture, and rarely would a boy respond that way. Rarely would a boy say, "Suzy's shy, and I have to help her." If he did respond that way, he would not be encouraged by the culture. The pressure of self would dilute the primacy of relationship.

This difference in early relational development helps us to understand what we see in Katie's encounters with boys, and her puzzled responses to it. It is as if she is encountering a system that is foreign. Boys are already shifting to valuing self over relationship, while she is still on the path of relational development: self-in-relationship.

But not for long. The work of Carol Gilligan about girls in adolescence is scary. After this period of self-assured growth-in-connection, girls at puberty, under all the pressures of the culture, start to change. Given the choice between remaining authentic to themselves, or twisting themselves to fit into false relationships, over and over again girls choose the latter. If at age three boys choose self over relationship, at age eleven girls choose inauthentic relationship over self. The literature and newspapers are filled with the disastrous results: a national epi-

demic of girls at puberty becoming withdrawn, depressed—even sui-
cidal—school failures, drug and alcohol users, anorexics. Girls give up
themselves, their authentic self and relationship to others, to perform
a sick dance of false connection.

To understand this fully, we have to shift the paradigm of our discussion. This is not about Katie's role as a girl, or Katie's identity as a girl.
It is about Katie's relationships with others, boys and girls both. Relating is not much in the boys' awareness, while relating is at the center of
Katie's awareness. If we worry in terms of our daughters' roles and identities and hope for equal opportunity on the soccer field and in the
classroom rather than for *mutual* encounters on the soccer field and in
the classroom, we are sunk. Katie and that boy had equal opportunity
to use that rocking horse at the picnic; what was missing was mutuality,
a shared awareness and valuation of relating and helping the other person to grow, rather than a sharp-eyed aim at self. If we encourage Katie
to be every bit as aggressive in getting to and staying on that horse—
perhaps teaching her to get back up and push that boy off the horse and
maybe stomp him a little—we will fail. It will be like preparing Katie to
become a lawyer who is just as vicious and sleazy and adversarial as a
man lawyer, so that she too can get paid a fortune to work for proof,
not truth.

In a gender dialogue with eighth grade girls, to the question "What
do you most want boys to understand about you?" the girls said: "We
can be every bit as violent as you boys." This is a sick solution to the
stresses these girls feel. It is like women in the workplace mimicking the
male role and self-values, giving up their relational strengths. But
"self" and "relationship" is a false opposition, for in a good relationship
each person is *more* themselves.

We have to put our shoulders against the status quo, with the faith
that if we create mutual connections, all good will accrue to the selves
in that connection. This is what both girls and boys have experienced
in the first years of life, and what all of us, boys and girls and men and
women, want.

Yes, boys and men, too. It is not by choice that boys devalue relationship. When we ask eighth grade boys what they want girls to understand about them, they say: "Don't believe my actions—I'm really a nice guy underneath." "I may act like a macho jerk but I really care." "Please see my heart." Boys' deepest wishes are similar to girls: good connections with others. We as a society value that much less in boys.

"Let's go on our adventure, daddy."

This, our ritual at our beach in the summer, is to take the most difficult way from our beach towel to the lighthouse. Even when the tide is low and we could walk on the sand, Katie insists that we climb the rocks together to get there. She leads. I cheer her spirit as I follow her, she lithe and daring, I creaky and wondering which little piece of my musculoskeletal system will betray me first, compiling a list not only of what hurts at present but of just how far along the healing process are my injuries from the near and more distant past. What about that ankle sprain from stepping in a hole running for a cab in Boston at night last April? What about the old lateral meniscus tear from my first running experiences in the Dordogne in 1975? She pops along ahead; I follow, full of admiration.

We have tried to share with her, our Zen master, whatever awareness we have of the realm of the spirit—which we don't understand, of course, but which we conceive of as something else, some power greater than ourselves. For instance, every night at dinner we join hands and close eyes and she says, "Peace." We squeeze hands and eat. But we haven't really spoken about prayer. And so one day at the lighthouse, overlooking the expanse of sea and sky, I suggest to Katie that she and I offer a prayer. I start to explain what a prayer is. She interrupts:

"Daddy, I *know*. We pray to the Goddess."

"The 'goddess'?"

"Yeah. Momma told me all about her." She sighs, and says, resignedly, "Ohh-kay."

With mixed delight I realize that Janet has gotten there slightly ahead of me. Katie leads the prayer:

"To the Goddess who made everything and all the animals."

"Amen," I say.

"What's that mean?"

"That's how you end a prayer, you say 'amen.'"

"Do you think I can have french fries for dinner?" she asks, as she starts down the rocks.

I sit in the balcony looking down at Katie in gymnastics class. Up here, distanced, it is suddenly as if I'm watching a group of five year olds whom I don't know, Katie among them. She is the only Asian. I notice her trim, lithe body with long legs and not an ounce of fat, her coordination, her popping energy. I bring her back to being ours for a second, remembering how, after our being with her for the first several months, Caucasian babies' eyes seemed strange to us, too round, foreign. Our world was China, Chinese, eyes shaped like teardrops on their sides, pupils dark as history. We became a family of color. We felt the joy and encountered the racism.

Looking at her once again now as someone else's child down there, I watch her race with a graceful yet controlled stride down a runway, launch herself into the air and without using her hands do a perfect forward flip, landing on her feet. It takes my breath away! Such bravery, such daring and balance, and, yes, such spirit!

Suddenly I am overwhelmed with sorrow, with a sense that this perfect, lithe spirit who will dare everything in this suburban gym will have to face the dimly or perhaps deeply sensed fact of her birth, the forever hole in her soul where her birth mother and father and country are. In an instant my sorrow fills all the space of that bandbox gym. What would make a woman and man give up this perfect spirit? What will she understand? What will she do with her own sorrow as she tries? What if we are no longer there with her when she does? For we are old, and soon older.

All in an instant, this, for now she is turning to look up at me and with pride sending me a "thumbs up!" and I, tears in my eyes, on my cheeks, the salt just starting to sting my lips, respond to her with a silent "thumbs up!," glad that she can't see my crying or hear that I can't speak. She will need all of that brave spirit to walk through the sorrow that awaits her.

Katie, we pray to be with you in whatever sorrow. Pray that we will not be incapacitated at the time. And that together we will tilt your sorrow to compassion and understanding.

We hope for your connections with all the goddesses and the gods, for they are forever and ever and will help you when we are gone.

May our connection continue to grow, us two, us three—and your connection with a community of like-minded others.

And I pray that you will hold the spirit of connection so tightly and lightly that when the forces of disconnection wash over you with all the killing power of acid rain from Ohio or all the unnatural busy destructive garbage of TV and the Internet, you will be aware of its solidity, for that spirit of mutual connection is the only comfort in the whole world.

And I pray that when the hormones flow like sap you don't twist yourself out of your authentic self for the sake of anyone, boy or girl, and that you never mutilate yourself for anyone else or with tattoos and body piercings. I pray for your relational integrity which can't help but assure your marvelous self, just as our love assures your growth.

And—because so far, you may recall, your total intake of vegetables has been seven sprigs of broccoli in five and three-quarter years—I pray you learn to eat green leafy vegetables.

And I pray for your spiritedness that makes you act like you already know everything, like when you were not yet three and you were talking on and on about something and I said to you, "Katie, you're perseverating," and you said, "Yeah, daddy, I know."

And I pray for your laughter, for one thing I have come to understand in my life of fifty-three years is that divinity resides in shared laughter, especially the guileless laughter of a child; so that once, when you were about two and a half and we were in a cab coming home from an airport and I asked you if your nose was running and you said, "No, it's walking!" in that screech of joy from you and the clatters of laughter from me and Momma and the African-American cabby were all the goddesses and gods a person could ever want, and they were laughing, too.

And I pray to the divinity that casts the spell of water and earth and fire and air and maybe does really throw the sun around the earth and not vice versa, I pray to that divinity that—and of course honey this is *my* fantasy, one of my fantasies, and only that and only mine—that when the moment comes when your soul opens up and you realize the power of the strange history that demanded your birth mother and father rise just before dawn and swaddle you and in the dark walk to the police station in their town wherever it was and in the dark secretly place you on the doorstep of the police station with a note that said you were born October 20 and your name was Chun, that when your soul opens and all the matter in the universe suddenly seems to rush in faster than you can scoop it out like dry sand into our holes dug at the beach at low tide at the start of our adventures, that at that moment you will take the hand of the Divinity, the Divine Intelligence which absolutely will be there for you even if we're not, and walk through the suffering with someone divine enough, walk through it far enough so that one day your steps will be transformed to the healing essence of shared sorrow, and I pray that you sense Momma and Daddy there to walk through it with you with the love you brought to our lives, to life, and to all our laughing with.

The Mistake Game

Rodger Kamenetz

I SPOKE to my daughter, Anya, in complete sentences when she was a conceptee and I listened for a response in her earliest cries. Some books recommended baby talk, and that was my wife, Moira's, language with Anya, but I preferred plain English. Why offer her ears a blurry target?

When it didn't drive me over the edge, her cry intrigued me. She had only one word to express every need and fantasy, from the inner world to the outer. Once, in the depths of their despair, certain Jewish kabbalists in medieval Europe made a similar cry, a magical name of God of enormous length—a thousand Hebrew letters jumbled together for pages. Properly intoned, this jumbo word—blessing or curse—promised magical powers. This dream was shared by white and black magicians, Jewish and Christian, throughout the Middle Ages up to the Renaissance. But their ancient predecessors, mystics less entranced by literacy, found God immediate in their own breath. They yowled the primal vowels A-E-I-O-U, rapidly "aah-eh-eee-ohh-oooh," producing the lost name of YHWH, known only to the high priest in the holy of holies. I heard a latter-day kabbalist perform this once at a poetry reading in New York. His chant was very like the full-throated, unconsonanted cry of the baby.

For most of us, language is utilitarian, but a baby in the house restores a sense of poetry. Like the early Romantic Jean Jacques Rousseau, I came to believe that "the first invention of speech is due not to need, but passion."

Later, Rousseau theorized, as agriculture develops, needs multiply, and "affairs become complicated": "Language changes its character. It becomes more regular and less passionate. It substitutes ideas for feelings. It no longer speaks to the heart, but to reason. Language becomes more exact and clearer, but more prolix, duller and colder."

Rousseau wrote in an age of happy speculation before our science of linguistics, also "exact and clearer . . . prolix, duller and colder," took over the field he opened. The first order of business was to dismiss unanswerable questions. When the Linguistic Society of Paris was founded in 1866, its bylaws forbade discussion of the origin of language.

Logically, we can never know precisely how speech began, for its invention is hidden in silence. Or could I hear its traces in a crib? With Anya's first cries, I gained entrée into the subject, not as a scientist, but as an amateur and a father. I listened for the speech in Anya's cry, for if ontogeny recapitulates phylogeny, as the old dictum goes, I was delighting in the growth and development of human language compressed from millennia to thirty months.

In her very first days, she learned to modulate her cries. Very quickly a parent learns the difference between the absolute pitch of "I'm in deep shit" and the warble that simply declares discontent, or the more subtle mewling of "A little more milk would be just dandy." The baby is a practical philosopher: she knows her cry works. It speaks worlds—and moves them.

Need or passion? Clearly her cry was both, all-encompassing, a formless chaos of spirit and matter, energy and need, light and darkness mixed.

Then consonants come to divide the primal vowel, to separate firmament from fundament, and night from day. The hour of cooing is first light. One morning, when Anya was about six months old, I lay awake, watching the minute hand move, dreading the hour of breakfast and work. I heard from her nursery a distinct burbling. She was shaping it into syllables: "bu-bu-bu-bu-*bo*."

She repeated the sounds, singer and listener, delighted and delighting. After that, I made it my business to wake early, just to hear her song. It was like a fountain bubbling from the depths of the earth with perfect clarity: bu-bu-bu-bu-*bo*.

If the vowels are nature, the consonants are culture, all cultures, for the infant speaks Urdu, Swahili, and something that resembles very much the glossolalia in a Free Will Baptist church, where I heard an old man on the altar produce "a-ka-ka-la-ka" for fifteen minutes, slapping his knees hard for punctuation. He said it was Japanese.

The baby speaks in tongues, too; her early morning Pentecost is a descent of the spirit, an entry into a more human language. At first she rehearses these new consonants for her own entertainment. It takes a while for this solipsistic cooing to evolve into genuine babbling. But after a time, I thought I heard inflections of my Baltimorese and Moira's softer North Carolina drawl. Anya was rehearsing the characteristic songs of her tribe.

That these patterns of stress and pitch are more primary than actual vocabulary or pronunciation can be illustrated by listening to distraught speech. The wrong syllables get emphasized: we hear severe "dis-stress": Please pass *the* su*gar*. We feel the emotion in the underlying music—we know something is wrong.

Yet there's also the clear legato of well-being, though the music of language is often lost to us because we are intent on words, not sounds. We forget that the stresses and intonations of every sentence we utter are not only expressive, but sometimes beautiful in themselves. Our needs have multiplied more than Rousseau dreamed: legalese, bureaucratese, computerese; languages frozen shut, with clauses stiff as ice; all need, no passion.

Some parents can't get excited about a child's babble until the first words roll out. The competitive urge is enormous and in our culture we love anything we can count: "My child can say ten words." This stress on acquiring vocabulary overlooks a greater achievement: the melodies a baby can babble by the time she gets around to inserting *Dada* or *car-car* into the tune. Actually, the first words emerge singularly from the flow—like rocks jutting from a stream, around which melodies continue to swirl. A toddler's musical abilities outpace her vocabulary by far and this is as it should be.

Still, when Anya first spoke words, not sounds, I admit Moira and I were proud. Anya's first word uttered in Baton Rouge was recorded dutifully in her baby album. "Ball" seemed to have universal application: my head was a ball, so was a head of lettuce in the A&P.

After "ball" came "No"; after "No," "Mama" and "Dada." I remember her sitting in the corner of the bedroom going, "Mama, Dada, Mama, Dada," looking left then right as if trying to place these important nouns properly in the universe.

By January, when she was sixteen months, she could say ball, bird, bottle, tee-tee (TV), bow-wow (dog), door, book, Mama, Ieeovu (I love you), car, bapu (apple), Dada, bath, bye-bye.

With this tiny vocabulary, Anya could already play what the philosopher Ludwig Wittgenstein calls a "language game."

"Ball," I said, and Anya motored off to her room, and returned with the ball. "Good," I said. "Car." She raced off and brought her toy car. "Anya," I said. She puzzled for a minute, then laughed. I couldn't help myself: I had to tease her a little.

Our language game had an ancient lineage, going back to St. Augustine, as Wittgenstein notes in the opening of his *Philosophical Investigations:*

> When they [my elders] named some object, and accordingly moved towards something, I saw this and I grasped that the thing was called by the sound they uttered when they meant to point it out. Their intention was shewn by their bodily movements, as it were the natural language of all peoples: the expressions of the face, the play of the eyes, the movement of other parts of the body, and the tone of voice which expresses our state of mind in seeking, having, rejecting or avoiding something. Thus, as I heard words repeatedly used in their proper places in various sentences, I gradually learnt to understand what objects they signified; and after I had trained my mouth to form these signs, I used them to express my own desires.

Augustine writes as if all the words he learned were like nouns, whose meaning came to him ostensively, that is, by pointing. The concept seems simple enough: you say *apple* and point to an apple. But observing Anya learn to talk I share Wittgenstein's sense that the obvious is not obvious.

For one thing, Anya's first words included "Ieeovu"—I love you—clearly passion and not at all the name of a thing pointed to. "No" was also not ostensive. It not only does not point to a thing, it negates things, and therefore seems to imply a whole concept of thingness. Yet

"No" was her second word. If "ball" represented the universe, "not-*ball*," or "No," was its shadow.

How does a child learn language? Augustine suggests gestures: "the natural language of all peoples: the expressions of the face, the play of the eyes, the movement of other parts of the body, and the tone of voice," but how do you point to "no" or "I love you"? For that matter, as Wittgenstein asks, how do you point to pointing?

For instance, if I point to a dog and say "bow-wow," how does the child know which way to follow my finger? For Wittgenstein to ask such a question seems absurd, but when you realize there is no particular answer—beyond "convention"—you reel in the chaos of the child. She doesn't have conventions yet. She's sorting sounds and words and categories without a clue.

When he was about two, one of Anya's playmates, Carl, shook his head no when he clearly meant yes. "Do you want some ice cream?" his father asked him. The boy shook his head and smiled. Should Stan give Carl the ice cream or not? He didn't want to teach him that shaking his head meant yes. But he didn't want to frustrate the boy either.

Whoever studies the child's use of the word "No" will see immediately a hole in Augustine's argument. "No" has never been the name of anything. Language cannot merely be ostensive, or strictly utilitarian. It's more as Rousseau has it: the terrible fury and poetry of *No* carries all the charge of an emerging personality.

Anya's *No* came when she was about one and a half, both a blessing and a curse. Her tantrums had a story line. She could shout *No* while she pushed her cereal bowl off the table. Yet her language also gave her parents an advantage. For language bonds in both directions, and her acquiring it allowed us to do terrible parental things, like manipulate and deceive.

Apart from the metaphysical "No" and the lovely "Ieeovu," most of Anya's basic vocabulary was ostensive and arose out of gestures that are very here and now. For her, almost magically, the word was the thing named, and problems emerged whenever words named things that weren't present. This became most clear to me one afternoon when Anya and I were driving home from the hardware store and the child went stark, raving cranky. Already at eighteen months she could con-centrate on television for an hour at a time, a talent we found somewhat disturbing, but which some of our friends assured us was remarkable.

Her favorite television show was *The Muppet Hour.* Hoping to dis-tract her, I said, "When we get home, after dinner, you can watch the Muppets."

"Muppets," Anya said, from the backseat.

"Yes," I said. "The Muppets will be on at six."

"Muppets," she repeated sharply.

"At six." Unfortunately, the hour was four.

"Muppets, Muppets, Muppets . . ." She let it rip, syllables ratcheting into a scream. My mistake. Muppets meant *Muppets now.*

I was trapped at close quarters with an outraged infant—there is no howl like the howl of outrage. Seemingly, I had deceived her with her most precious acquisition, the word. Once we got home, she ran to the set, still bawling, and pointed indignantly at the empty screen. There was something wonderful in that gesture, in her face—this was not only frustration, but the kind of righteous anger adults have when they feel they have been tricked. I turned the set on and spun through the channels, hoping to demonstrate, in vain, the existence of time, the nonexistence of Muppets.

Yet despite the moral risks, as her ability to speak in sentences devel-oped our second fall in Baton Rouge, I often used language to distract her. One morning, she spotted a piece of chocolate on the breakfast ta-ble. Her oatmeal lost its savor. "I want candy," she said. "Candy, candy, candy." Who taught her that word?

"Oh yes," I answered, "you can certainly have the candy"—though I had no intention of giving it to her and while I was talking was secretly palming it, an old magician's sleight that came in handy. "But before you have *it*"—another trick of the trade is to veil the object of desire with a pronoun—"wouldn't you like some *apple juice* first?" She nod-ded her head, and as her tears dried, I made a long ceremony of finding the bottle—"Oh, here it is"—and getting the glass, narrating the whole time: "The glass is on the top shelf, Anya, isn't it pretty, I think it has *Bert* and *Ernie* on it—is that *Bert*?" and I gave her the glass to inspect.

She said, "No, that's *Ernie.*" "Oh," I said, slowly pouring the juice. "Here you go—the *juice,*" and by this time, she'd forgotten all about the chocolate.

This cowardly technique often seemed preferable to the head-to-head confrontation, and Moira and I, without being aware of it, fell into this pattern as Anya entered the terrible twos.

But who were we fooling? I am sure if I had more moral fiber I would have faced some of these issues straight on, and not caused my child's desires to divagate down so many trickling paths. But the chicanery worked.

Children are mirrors, and the great moral lesson they teach, sooner or later, is that they will do as they were done to. They have the annoying habit of always witnessing our most embarrassing errors and bouncing them right back to us. In that light, I could not entirely applaud my method of dealing with what I considered her unreasonable desires.

I was using her own gifts against her, but for her own good. Yet I don't know if I was entirely wrong to avoid confrontations with my child. If I wanted to dress Anya for nursery school, so I could get my own day started, this wasn't a moral issue. What is moral or immoral about a kid kicking like mad and refusing to let me slip a sock on her when I have exactly a minute to get her out of the house so I can make a nine o'clock class? She wasn't being bad. Her refusal around age two came from her need to express herself. She—*Anya*—was the person who did not put her sock on when I asked her. As she wriggled and screamed, all her being was invested in this. How could I possibly match her in will? I have seen parents who force their children to knuckle under in every confrontation because they view each challenge as a threat to their overall authority. I suppose there are lock breakers for every lock, but I didn't want to break Anya.

She was fighting for her life, in a way. On my side, I had patience and guile. True, sometimes, there was no other way: grab her foot and stuff the sock on and let her answer the indignity with a cloudburst tantrum. But if I could distract her with mere words, wasn't that preferable? "No, you don't have to put your sock on right now," I'd say. "It's okay. Here, sit down in my lap. Let's look at the tee-tee." And while she relaxed, I'd slip the sock on without her noticing. With baby's attention, the rule was divide and conquer.

With two verbal maniacs all to herself, she acquired adult habits of conversation early. Her pronunciation was flawless. She quickly outgrew baby words and often her vocabulary outstripped other developments. Sometimes she astonished us with her early pronouncements: "I had a good time at the restaurant. *Actually*, I made pee-pee in the booster."

Or, listening to jazz on the radio, "That piano has a clown in it."

Other parents sometimes became anxious around Anya because of her rapid development. Seething with pride, we tried to downplay it. Anyway, I could see things to admire in other kids besides their ability to produce sentences. They had means of communication just as effective as Anya's. Undistracted by the lies of language, they may have established a more primal relation to their own desires.

Once, when they were both about two, Carl, the head shaker, stayed with us one weekend while Stan and Molly went on a trip. Though he could barely speak, it was a pleasure how well he could communicate.

That Saturday morning, the children woke early to watch cartoons. I turned them on and crawled back into bed.

We must have overslept, because about ten, I woke to the sound of Carl toddling into our bedroom, holding an empty cereal bowl which he'd grabbed off the kitchen table. (Anya had forsaken her stomach for *Smurfs*.) Carl didn't say a word, but I got the messages: Breakfast. Feed me. Now.

I called him Harpo after that. Carl, I decided, was deliberately avoiding speech. He was a second-born child, and wisely seeing that he couldn't compete with his parents and older sister, he refined ostensive language to sheer wordless pointing, like the Zen master who defined Buddha by pointing at the moon. Hadn't Wittgenstein himself written, "Whereof one cannot speak, thereof one must be silent?"

In our house, speech and bantering were the rule between Moira, me, and Anya. Classically, we speak of a mother tongue and father time, which seems to imply that the child learns her language exclusively from the mother—and learns the demands of the world from father. I know that's exactly how I conceived it as a boy. I wonder which was the greater aberration, the rigid apportioning of gender roles in my parents' generation, or the more fluid arrangements today.

With both of us working full-time, teaching and writing, Moira and I became nearly interchangeable as parents. We couldn't afford to divide childrearing responsibilities into neat categories. Anyway, teaching a child to speak is so natural and successful an enterprise that it was more game than chore.

Anya and I invented our own talking games as soon as Anya could talk. These were far more complex than Wittgenstein's "language games"—they were for pleasure only, and turned the world upside down. The most important one was the "mistake game."

"I woke up this morning and brushed my face, then I washed my teeth with soap. Was that a mistake?"

"Yes," she answered. "You should brush your teeth and wash your face with soap."

"Oh, I see. Then I put on my shoes and tied my socks. Was that a mistake?"

"Yes, Daddy. You should put on your socks and tie your shoes."

"I see."

I don't know how it started, exactly. The mistake game flew out of nowhere, a time filler at meals, a distraction while getting her dressed. The game mixed logic with the absurd, inflicting my sensibility on Anya. It also gave her a taste of role reversal, a chance, for once, to correct her illogical father.

It's wrong to tease children overmuch. I've been guilty of it, going too far with the game, taking advantage of their sweet willingness to believe what an adult says.

A few times I drove Anya into screaming fits with my silly wordplay, forgetting she was still a child, in spite of her complex sentences and adult vocabulary. Other times, she'd laugh so hard we had to stop for fear of choking her.

"You're not Mommy, are you?" I'd say.

"No."

"I'm not Mommy either, am I?"

"Right." She'd nod her head sagely, knowing a new game was afoot.

"Well, if I'm 'not-Mommy,' and you're 'not-Mommy,' I must be you because we're both 'not-Mommy.'"

She'd splutter and laugh. "No, you're Daddy."

"I though you said I was not-Mommy . . ."

Soon "not-Mommy" replaced the mistake game, hilarious to her and to me, too.

Teasing is a father's game of distance and closeness, a verbal shadow-boxing or peekaboo. I'm here, I'm not here; I mean it, I don't. Whether the teasing heals or hurts probably depends on how secure the child is in that difficult quality, her father's love.

The hardest thing to learn in any language is irony. When I lived in Mexico for six months, I mastered Spanish vocabulary and grammar, but never learned when a declarative sentence was intended in its opposite sense. I drank in every word like a child.

Young children have absolutely no taste for irony. It shakes a child's bare grasp of language. Teasing Anya was a big mistake—an adult game she was not ready to play.

Once, at the dinner table, carried away by the spirit of absurdity, I said, "You know, Anya, we've been feeding you all these years, and you still haven't gotten any bigger." The remark was true enough, by the way. Anya reached thirty pounds by her second year and stayed there, getting taller, like a round piece of clay pinched thinner.

As soon as the words slipped out, Anya turned red and threw her fork down on the floor. "That's not funny," she shouted, slid out of her chair, and ran out of the kitchen. Despite our mistake game, she was still a language fundamentalist and I had violated her sense of fair play. I hadn't meant to be cruel, just forgotten that she took my joke quite literally. If I didn't want to damage the bond between us, I had to be very careful not to import adult irony into her world.

A father witnesses crucial developments in his children they themselves would otherwise never be conscious of. In two and a half years, Anya moved from "bu-bu-bu-*bo*" to "Actually, I made pee-pee in the booster" to the serrated edge of adult irony. She progressed from vowels to consonants to melodies to words, phrases, and sentences. I can't help thinking that somewhere within her story is a clue to the broader historical question about the evolution of language and consciousness.

But that is probably my delusion. History, and time itself, is an adult deception. Young children know that every when is now, every tense is present. "Did you have a nice day at Carl's?" I once asked Anya when she was barely two. "Gapes," she answered positively, and while I tried to puzzle out who gaped at what, she pointed to green grapes in a bowl. The past is a wispy illusion, but "gapes" are sweet.

My Daughters

Rick Bass

I ALWAYS wanted children, and I always wanted daughters. There hadn't been any girls born into my father's side of the family in over seventy-five years—and though I love those boys and men, I was starving for daughters. I was starving for that beauty, strength, fierceness, and, well, I have to say, for the *exoticness* of it. I pretty much had the guys—cousins, brothers, father, uncles, grandfather, nephews—figured out.

When Mom—Mary Lucy—was sick with leukemia, and my wife Elizabeth and I told her in the early autumn that we were expecting our first child that next spring, and that the sonogram had indicated it might be a girl, Mom had looked out the hospital window in amazement and said, "*Imagine that*—a baby girl."

Perhaps—I want to believe this, and do—she was picturing herself with a granddaughter. Perhaps she was remembering her dues paid— the three sons she and my father raised, all the mud and blood and furor, all the snakes escaped in the house, all the writhing amphibians brought home, the turtles constantly on the loose, the flying squirrels—the whole continuum of boyhood, so extraordinarily short on femininity and its unique companionships.

Mom died a little over a month later. My middle brother and his wife had given birth to their first son, whom she got to see, though not Elizabeth's and my first daughter, Mary Katherine.

To be involved in Mary Katherine's birth six years ago, to be helping Elizabeth with it—to take Mary Katherine as she came out, and hold her to my bare chest, then hand her up to Elizabeth—to see this third person appear—served notice to me, without meaning to sound overly trite, that I should straighten up and enjoy life, and strive to feel the senses more deeply while I still had the opportunity.

What do I want for her, in the world—and for Lowry, our other daughter, three years her junior?

Perhaps it is a measure of the maturity I have not yet reached, and may never reach—I'm thirty-nine and am starting to feel a bit old physically, though with none of the accompanying mental focus that's supposed to come as a trade-off with age—but I don't spend much time contemplating what kind of world I want for my daughters. Perhaps I just assume the worst, and try instead to inhale deeply the blessings of the present. When I do think of what future I want for them, I tend to think in terms of those specific things I can control, or at least influence.

The thing I *can* control—or at least have a fair chance of influencing—is what kind of father my daughters have. And that change or alteration cannot be some sleight-of-hand trick, some artistic performance done on the surface, or they'll see right through it and end up resenting those very values I am trying to instill or promote.

Rather than faking the right thing to do in a given circumstance, the actions—or reactions—must come from within me with a kind of suppleness and confidence that I have not yet achieved. I usually know, as do any of us, what the right thing to do is, but I don't think it's good for the girls to see how often I still labor at making that choice. Forty years ago, John Kennedy called it courage: "A man does what he must—in spite of personal consequences, in spite of obstacles and dangers and pressures—and that is the basis of all human morality."

Too often, though, I hesitate. What I want the girls to see in me instead is someone who pins his ears back and dives ahead, always unblinking. I have learned that the right thing is easy to discern—it's almost always the most expensive, the most time-consuming, or the most uncomfortable—or all of the above. But that's a surface kind of checklist. I want to learn how to act—how to behave—with more surety; to not just do the right thing, but to do it without that graceless hesitancy. In some ways I feel like a dog that is being trained: a dog that loves and wants to serve, but which has certain awkward failings.

So I have to learn, or relearn, values at the cell level, to make them alive and fresh within me again. I have to remember, and protect, the idealism and wonder of childhood. Any strong points that I've developed over the years, or, more likely, which have somehow avoided becoming excessively diminished within me since childhood, are going to come through unconsciously, through the repetitions of daily manifestations. And any of these strong points that their mother and I still retain will, I believe, be inherently attractive to the girls—will stand prominent among the general background of our more abundant mediocre ones.

And while I'm attempting to learn, or relearn, what I believe are good points—courtesy, patience, good listening skills, stoicism (no whiners!)—I'm simultaneously trying to dump or at least hide the awful seething vat of negative attributes that I've accumulated and nurtured as I nose toward half a century. Profanity without reason; profanity with reason; quickness of temper; a tendency to interrupt, even in the midst of listening; the cheap indulgence of unearned descents into moroseness; the uttering of angry words, the thinking of angry thoughts . . .

Sometimes I almost tremble when I consider the enormity and newness of my blessing. *Girls; daughters!* It's all so new; not just to my experience, but to my blood's experience, my paternal lineage. It's a wonderful feeling—like soaring.

But there is groundwork to be done. They are growing fast. *Repetition*; that's how things are taught and learned and refined.

It's sexist, of course, but inescapable; I do believe certain traits are masculine, while others are feminine. And I believe each sex can benefit from the gifts or qualities of the other. Certainly neither gender corners the market on, say, nurturing, or stamina, or endurance, or creativity. But often I find myself thinking about the mix of male-dominated beliefs and observations I present to my daughters, and how they may view the world as a result. (I'm glad they have a mother—glad they have both of us living with them daily.)

Often, already, the two girls seem to have a blood affinity for accepting certain values and tastes while promptly and assertively rejecting those which do not seem to fit some profile. So that's a relief: the feeling that much of it has already been decided since conception. But still, almost as if baiting them, I'll offer up, ever so cautiously, little teases of value. Every morning when I leave to go out to my cabin, both girls, with whom I've been playing, will say, "Why do you have to go to work?" And I'll raise my finger and say what I always say: "Because" (uttering it like a mantra), "*Work is Good.*" And this explanation always works: they always let me leave, then, though not before much leg clinging and good-bye hugging and kissing—as if, rather than walking a few hundred yards down the trail, I am instead going off to war.

I'm not saying little boys can't be equally affectionate, sweet, and loving. I'm just saying that I have fallen into the pie.

I want them to believe in work. I want them to believe in the power of linearity: the ability to drive ahead, bullheaded, through certain obstacles and drudgeries, and to believe in the achieved power of accumulated repetitions: a power that is almost ritualistic in its nature.

There is within us all a wonderful and yet awful yearning to procrastinate. I want to nurture in them to the full extent that I can—to the full extent to which they may be receptive—an understanding and appreciation of this other type of work, this other way of being: of working at things incrementally, in almost a hunter-gatherer fashion—its own kind of organic intelligence—rather than waiting, as is so often our wont, till the last minute for some miracle so dependent upon the grace of another.

And yet: I also want them to believe in the grace of the arc of the circle. I do not want them to ever be shy about departing from the linear, if they feel like it.

If I sound confused, it's because I am. Confused and happy.

We live way back in the woods, up in the mountains. To us, a city is a wilderness. There's a wonderful two-room log schoolhouse, grades kindergarten through eight, that usually enrolls a dozen or so students, so that for those children it's more like constant tutoring than the schools I remember from youth. Deer, elk, and moose wander the playground yard among the apple trees.

The school is heated with a wood stove. Beyond eighth grade, we'll have to search out town, forty miles distant, but in the meantime I am grateful for the good teachers in the little schoolhouse, and the sense of community we have, and I like to think often of what a gift and source of strength this will be for the girls to take with them into the twenty-first century: having had that opportunity, that experience. Bald eagles fly up and down the river. The scent of fir forests sweeps in through the open windows. The eighth graders learn to help the sixth graders, the sixth graders learn to help the fourth graders, and so on. When people ask what we intend to do for a school, living so far away from the city, we tell them that we'll just have to try and make do.

It strikes me that a father's job is to provide constancy and stability—though I have met countless wonderful and admirable women who were raised by fathers and mothers who were anything but that. Nonetheless, it's what I believe—or what I want to believe. Certainly amid that desire to provide constancy is the notion of being not just a good father, but a good husband. I know or believe that constancy and repetitiveness can teach almost anything. I know to show by specific example, too, rather than by speaking in general abstractions. And again the problem seems to be not so much what to teach the girls. To encourage them, for instance, to celebrate freedom and wildness is easy. But do I teach them to deal with stress, for example, as I do—by trying to avoid it? You want your daughters to loathe injustice, but do you want them to burn as erratically and out-of-control as you do—with that much bitterness?

And do I have any say in the matter anyway?

Constancy. I take pains to show them the constancy of the seasons up here—a kind of constancy-in-change, which my hunch tells me will be one of the most valuable lessons for the future: to appreciate constancy, yet adapt to change as it comes—to have a supple strength, rather than a rigid or brittle one.

Certain elements are bedrock in our lives: dried flowers hanging around the cabin, picked from each walk through the woods in summer; the gathering of berries, fish, meat, and mushrooms from the woods and streams; the gathering of each autumn's firewood. . . . I try to engage them in all of these cycles, and though it will be a long time

before they can go hunting with me if they want to, they help me pluck
and clean the birds I come home with. Right after Mary Katherine was
born I had to take a teaching job for several weeks—all three of us went
to Wisconsin—and I remember asking my young women students for
tips and advice about being a father to daughters.

It amazed me how common their response was: that their fathers
never spent quite enough time with them (the more beloved the father,
the greater the desire was for more time); how their fathers never took
them hunting or fishing enough. Only the boys got to go on those trips.
The daughters I talked to had had a smattering of father-daughter
camping trips, and then that was it, they turned eighteen, and were out
of there.

It wasn't that the girls wanted so much to hunt or fish, it seemed, as
they wanted to spend more time with their fathers watching their fathers be themselves.

It seems a simple thing to commit to; it seems like stating the obvious. But the commonality of my students' responses was so over-
whelming that I resolved to do everything I could to keep my daughters
from being able one day to say such a thing. It chilled me to imagine my
daughters being eighteen, nineteen, twenty years old, and saying to
someone that they felt like they didn't get to spend enough time with
me when they were growing up.

We have three young bird dogs, whom we train: Colter, Point, and
Superman. We were going to have just two, but Mary Katherine fell in
love with the little spotted one—Point—and so, well, that was that:
now we have three. Certainly I need to work daily on saying *no*—constancy—but yielding to her desire for the little spotted Point-dog was a
good decision, a joyful one. She and I train him together, and it gives us
a language all our own, I think—one that is slightly separate from, in
a complementary way, the father-and-daughter relationship. We have
shared responsibility for the pup, and try to teach him, through repetition and constancy, his various lessons: sit, come, stay; stop-to-flush,
steady-to-wing, steady-to-shot, steady-to-wing-and-shot . . .

I may have it all wrong. I may be the most sexist father left in this century. I can see hyperfeminists wondering to themselves, *Daughters as bird dogs?*

But it feels right. It feels joyful, working the little Point-man with her each evening. Talking with her about him as if she and I are partners. "He is going to be a *great* bird dog," Mary Katherine will tell me, each night when we're through.

Work is good.

What a relief—what a thrill—to be both told by the experts as well as informed by one's own instinct that, miracle of miracles, one's basic character—a tad masculine; plodding, linear, constant—is the very thing needed for the nurturing of one's children—one's daughters. What a miracle of fit.

Other notes to myself: being full aware, or nearly full aware, of my propensity for those linear kinds of movements, I try to re-educate, re-form myself as best as I can—to offer them constancy, but also possibility and imagination. When, as is often the case, Mary Katherine asks me at ten o'clock at night if we can go camping—when I'm tired and about to go to bed—I don't always tell her, "Yes, sure," but I try to limit the "Nos" or "I'm tired, how about tomorrow nights?" to somewhere around the fifty percent mark, so that there will always be the possibility of a *yes;* and I rouse myself and load the backpack. We hike down through the woods and set up the tent, get in our sleeping bags, and read by flashlight, and it is good for me to step away from plans and learn instead to react; and good for them, I hope, to see how it is just as easy to do a thing as it is to avoid doing it.

When Lowry points to moths at night and cries "Birds," I instinctively tell her, "No, moths." She does not have to learn, however. I have to learn to be amazed by moths, and by the possibility of the existence of night-birds that hurl themselves at the lights.

Knowing also my immense unease at social gatherings of any kind—I am a pathological wallflower—I think also that I tend to give them a bit of a loose rein in public. Whenever Elizabeth or I ask something of them, we expect immediate compliance—but in public, as at home, I am conscious of the distance and freedom of their movements, and I probably encourage them to err on the side of wildness—an attribute which can flee so quickly—rather than domesticity, which can come on so early in life, and stay so completely.

At a writer's conference up at a ski lodge last summer—warm yellow light, thin air, a lazy grasshopper clicking heat-sounds—Mary Katherine was hanging out with some older children—all boys. She has a few little friends in the valley, but I wouldn't say we're overrun with playmates her own age, and so I was glad to see her having fun and socializing—not in the least bit shy, and actually, well, a little wild.

There was a big splashing fountain—a coin-toss fountain—and as it was a hot day, I was glad for her to splash around in it, wetting her long hair and pink summer dress—and glad that the other children had joined her, and that there was much shrieking and splashing. A fountain with laughing children is surely the peak of what any designer hopes for in his or her faraway architectural sketches.

There was a little plastic playground at some distance—one of those Fisher-Price sandbox kind of setups—that had as one of its parts a giant, brightly colored plastic tugboat that looked as if it would barely fit in that fountain; and it did.

It pleased me to see that Mary Katherine was more than holding her own, concerning who would be captaining the ship. It seemed in fact that though there was good-natured mutiny going on, she was ably repelling would-be captains with forearm shivers (the other hand gripping the steering wheel as she shrieked and sang), while those drenched mutineers whom she had previously dispatched seemed now relegated to trudging along behind the boat, pushing, propelling her around and around.

It was so hot. It was so good to see children laughing and playing.

I haven't done this before. I want her to have a soaring heart. We live in the woods and someday soon I need to teach her social restraint, but that sunny afternoon I enjoyed watching her whoop and shout with the older children, being pushed in the bobbing boat. It was only when she leapt out of the boat and wrenched the brass water-spouting centerpiece loose from the fountain and began brandishing it like a scimitar that I waded in to do damage control—though I was careful not to appear disapproving or negative, only concerned and corrective.

I do not intend to raise wild savages. I want, however, to always consider not just their happiness (which can come just as easily from discipline and regimen as from wildness)—but to consider their joy as well, and their ability to feel it fully, deeply, purely. To engage.

I worry about raising eco-bores similar to myself. I do not want so much to hide my momentary despairs from my daughters, in an effort to keep them from developing similar ones, as I want to shed my own, or learn to keep them in perspective, while still managing to nurture unbridled joy. And again and again, for me, a possible solution seems to be found in the natural world, in wilderness, which is a commodity, a natural resource, whose future in this country is extremely suspect.

Without knowing exactly why, I know deeply that I want my daughters to be able to know vast forests and uncut mountain ranges: to know sanctuaries, or whole systems, of ecological health and sanity.

A friend's daughter, a thirteen year old—that age!—had trouble at home, trouble with herself, and ran away. We helped collect her and then kept her in our home for four months, trying to help calm her struggles. We tried to home-school her, and I took her with me on my travels for work, but she would have none of the learning. She descended into self-pity and then from there into true pain.

She, S., was with us for four months, bored out of her mind, back in the woods. In the end, when she went back home, she ran off again, but returned finally, a year later, to her mother's. Did we make any difference—were we of any help, simply by trying to anchor ourselves and call "bullshit" when she said things we knew she didn't believe?

It was hard on all of us. We kept telling one another that it was only a phase. We told each other stories of our own rebellions. It was not until after S. had gone back to her mother's, and Elizabeth and I felt some lightness, some guilty peace, return to us, that we really realized how hard it had been, day after day, to have her with us—the daughter-who-was-not-a-daughter. She felt imprisoned, which in turn made us feel imprisoned.

Mary Katherine was three then. She had gone overnight from being the oldest to being a middle sister. She had to watch each time as S. and I headed off to another airport, another city. And when we would return home, Mary Katherine would ask, "I'm still your daughter, aren't I?" I would hug her and tell her yes, again and again, but still she kept asking it, and I kept telling her.

I do not know how to staunch against the coming tides. I work at being more receptive to the joys of the moment—to inhaling them deeply. I try to be as constant as I can. I am firm and try, in the beautiful heat of my love, not to become manipulated. I try to stand firm.

Mary Katherine and Lowry and I are building a rock wall. It appears to have no rhyme or reason in the path it travels through the woods. We build it with certain rocks that we find along roadsides or in the woods—good squared-off sturdy rocks that won't get frost heaved in the transition between winter and spring each year, as the ground contracts and then swells, giving birth each year to new life.

The rock wall wanders—almost staggers, in places—through the woods, enclosing nothing, bounding and imprisoning nothing. We build it only because we like the beauty of it, and the durability of stone, and the way it fits the forest as it wanders up and down the hills, stable and secure, like a spine, or an earth anchor.

Both girls have their little work gloves. They trudge along behind me as I wrestle with some flat granite behemoth, sweat pouring off of me. ("Sun-water," Mary Katherine calls it.) Sometimes we work deep into the evenings, beyond sunset. The stars begin to shine, and we keep working. "Look," Mary Katherine says, "the sky is all dressed up." Lowry points to the largest rocks, points to me, and says "Up," and then points to the wall.

We stack the rocks carefully. It feels good to be working with such heavy weight. The wall just keeps getting longer each year. It fits where it is. We lean against it and rest when we're tired. It's so strong—so stable. We could stare at it for hours. It's not going anywhere. It feels good to be building something real: a physical model, a representation, of the thing between us. It is like a map of our blood—of who and what we are to each other.

We work on it a little each day. It adds up, accumulating a mass that is dizzying to look at. It speaks not so much to who we are, as to who we would like to, or can, become. Every morning when I wake up and look out the window it lies there, within reach: a thing we have crafted together. The rock wall speaks to more than happiness. The rock wall is a leap of joy.

3

Girlhood
and Adolescence

Prayers for My Daughter

Howard Junker

I ENVY my wife all the womanly things she can teach our daughter. Sewing and gardening are Rozanne's major crafts, and I believe in them, partly because I can't do them myself and partly because I want Madison to be able to provide for herself. Beyond food and clothing, there's shelter, and I hope she picks up the ethos of good housekeeping her mother learned growing up in that foreign land, North Dakota.

Then there are simple girl things, like hair care, whose theory I certainly understand—a hundred strokes a night—but whose daily practice—the variety of arrangements and deployments that Madison seems to enjoy so much—would find me at a loss. I pray that she grows up to be as beautiful as she is now, as beautiful as her mother has always been.

About men, I want my daughter to understand that there are some of good will. I agree with her current view that all boys under sixty-five are "immature." I don't mind that she and one of her third-grade classmates in a single-sex school have declared themselves married. "James," her husband, seems to be a nice girl, from a nice family, fairly good-looking and reasonably intelligent and ambitious. Also, she lives near by, which makes the chauffeuring a lot easier than it might be.

For my part, not so much as an example, more just out of necessity, I try to be modern in practicing the fungibility of many role-chores: I clean the bathroom, shop for bagels and chocolate milk, fetch pizza, take her to piano on Wednesdays . . . Every night, I read her a Popsicle story, which is the one that precedes tooth brushing, which precedes her real good-night story. I'm delighted rather than bored that for the past two years we've been reading and rereading the *Magic School Bus* series, about a weird science teacher, her all-too-normal students, and the weird field trips they go on. Last year, when I went on a two-week Earthwatch expedition to the Rockies to study wildflowers, I made the group leader stop the van one afternoon so I could take a picture of a water treatment plant—to show Madison that Eke, Ms. Frizzle, et alia, and I, too, had explored the way water gets to the faucet.

I certainly want Madison to be at home in the world of science and technology, where I feel so much like an alien. I may have been a bit crude at times in my efforts to keep these options open for her, insisting all too frequently on playing counting games—how many steps will it take to reach the corner? How many blue houses will we pass?

I've always encouraged her to collect specimens and artifacts, Eke pebbles, pinecones, pennies (it shocks me that it is now impossible to find the ones I found so easily as a boy), and rubber bands. (I think she has way too many stuffed animals, and yet more arrive day after day.) Before they became either too boring or too complicated, we used to do a lot of those kitchen science "experiments" you can find in so many books. Now that she's graduated—I suppose there's a progression—to computer games, like building a town, or like retracing the steps of Lewis and Clark, I am happy to supply her with CD-ROMs. (I wish I had had a computer to create thank-you notes, the way she does.)

My main hobby is playing games, and I have tried to teach her to throw a ball not-like-a-girl. I wrote a letter to her phys ed teacher declaring that Madison had always hit with power from the left side and that insisting that the correct answer on a quiz was that the batter should stand on the *left* side of the plate was not just wrong, it was oppressive.

Our favorite board game—although I am promoting chess as avidly as she will permit—has been The Farm Game (partly because her grandfather is a wheat farmer). This Monopolyesque game is so complicated and we began to play so long before she could read much, that we have always made up our own rules, putting as much hay and cattle and wheat on our acres as we wanted, taking as much money from the bank as we wanted, paying whatever penalties we wanted. I like the free-formness of this way of playing; the notion that the important thing is to play the game according to your own needs, not its demands. I want her to remain undaunted by how much she doesn't—and may never—understand.

The main craft that I can teach Madison is carpentry, although I am embarrassingly unskilled. I did belong to the union in my early thirties and actually worked a few months with concrete forms and a few months with framing and a few months with remodeling. But I can't even use a router, that basic tool of finer woodworking.

So far my skills have managed to measure up to Madison's requirements, although my days are surely numbered. Her latest project, a "chest," terrified me when she first proposed it, because I had no idea how we might build drawers that worked. What she really wanted, it turned out, was a clothes closet for Felicity, her Williamsburg-era American Girl doll, the series that is her generation's politically—and historically—correct Barbie.

Usually, to start, I ask her to show me a drawing of what she wants to make. This time, the first things she wrote were two dimensions:

18 ft
10 inch

Eighteen feet, I said. That's very large.

She got the point, of course, immediately, but being a jerk, I was not to be deterred from seizing the tape measure and running it out for eighteen feet.

In a drawing, she then amended her demands for a "chest" to something that looked more like an armoire, something I thought we could handle. Two doors, and two—she insisted on two—clothes rods.

I brought her out to where we store a bunch of empty cardboard boxes.

Measure this, I suggested.

But I wanted it wood.

Try it, I insisted, knowing it would be easy to cut doors in a cardboard box.

She graciously allowed that a box would do; under pressure, she is amazingly willing to believe in my transformative powers.

The best part was cutting up an old mop handle for the rods. I set up my miter box, which holds the saw in two slots for an accurate cut, and let her saw away. It was the first time she was actually able to saw by herself. I stood behind her, leaning around her, holding the broomstick. It was slow and frustrating, but she kept at it. My father, who in his day was a high school shop teacher—he had let me use a hatchet when I was four—smiled down upon us.

The project continued with more advances in technique—gold-spraying a cut-off Kleenex box (for Felicity's accessories); cutting and bending electrical wire to make clothes hangers. . . . She danced with joy when we finished.

I want her to be able to realize her dreams. To have the confidence to know she can make it happen.

I'd also like her to learn self-defense. In the corner of my shop I have a punching bag I picked up at a garage sale. I hit it every once in a while; it's a good workout, much more fun—and relaxing and quickly exhausting—than jogging. Madison has tried it, but she doesn't see the point. I'm glad; I don't want her to see the world as something she has to batter against.

My best friend is Madison's godmother; last spring she gave Madison a swing that her own kids had outgrown. Madison was almost too big for the swing herself, but feeling that it would be ungrateful to suppress the gift, I put it up under the garage overhang. It worked well. All the neighbor kids loved it, too.

One day after school, a classmate of Madison's was swinging when her mother came to pick her up. Her family had fled from Ethiopia; her sister has diabetes; she is the largest kid in the class. She was swinging one last swing when Madison got in the way and was knocked down. Her head bounced off the concrete driveway. I saw it. She got up. She had not lost consciousness. She was crying, her head ached, and she was dizzy.

We tried ice and rest, but it was the weekend, her pediatrician was out of reach, and we were afraid to wait and see, so we brought her in, first to the advice nurse and then, since she had vomited in the car, to the emergency room. The MRI showed no damage.

I pray that she will always be able to bounce back from disaster, although I would prefer that she be absolutely, eternally invincible.

I also pray, with almost equal fervor, that whatever forms of outrage her generation devises to torment—and sadden—their parents, it will not be tattoos and piercings. I am hoping, although I do not dare pray specifically for any special outcome, that the teenagers of the next millennium will adopt some really fiendish retro-tactic, like dressing like (but, Lord preserve us, not acting like) neo-neo-preppies. I will thereby be on familiar ground and capable, I hope, of staying in touch with my daughter forever.

The Driving Lesson

Gerald Early

ABOUT EIGHTEEN MONTHS ago, I taught my oldest teenage daughter how to drive. It was at the same time that I read to both my daughters J. D. Salinger's *Catcher in the Rye,* which I did largely because I was teaching it to a class and I thought my children would be interested in a book about growing up absurd, so to speak. Not to say that I was trying to rear them that way. Naturally, I had not thought that a book about an upper-class, White teenage boy written in the late 1940s would not be especially relevant. I always assume that people should be interested in learning about two things: themselves and everything that is not themselves.

Teaching Linnet how to drive is, I firmly believe, one of the great accomplishments of my life as a parent, not because it was difficult, although it had its challenging moments, but because I learned a great deal about myself and about my daughter, as well. And even this *Catcher in the Rye* business turned out to be more useful than it seemed at first.

When my daughter turned fifteen and a half, she applied for and received her learner's permit. She had thought of little else since she turned fifteen except learning how to drive. It meant a great deal to her, which struck me, at the time, as odd. When I was her age, I did not know how to drive, and did not apply for a learner's permit to take driver's education at my high school, as I thought it would do me very little good. My mother was too poor to own a car. Besides, she did not know how to drive and I lived in the middle of South Philadelphia, where public transportation was readily available and in many instances more convenient than owning a car. (Where in heaven's name could you park it?) My oldest sister, who has lived in Philadelphia most of her life, still does not know how to drive. But my daughter was living in decidedly different circumstances, in a two-car, middle-class family, and in a sub-urb where public transportation is sporadic and far from convenient. It certainly doesn't take you anywhere you want to go. In a sense, she understood very rightly that if she were to have a period of her adoles-cence independent of her parents, she needed to learn to drive. She told me this in no uncertain terms and cut me short when I began to remi-nisce about growing up in Philadelphia. "I'm not growing up in some cold-water, coal-burning flat in an inner-city neighborhood. I'm not living your childhood and I don't care about it." Well, that's telling me, I thought.

My wife had given Linnet her first driving lesson and came back en-tirely bemused and out of sorts. Linnet came in crying, marched up-stairs, and slammed the door to her room.

"I can't teach that girl to drive," my wife said. "She scares me too much behind a wheel. Why don't you take her out? You're much better at teaching than I am. Remember, you taught me how to drive. Besides, this is something a father should do with his daughter."

My wife was exaggerating for effect and because she wanted to get out of something she found disagreeable. I had not really taught her how to drive. When we began dating, she owned a Nova, a new car at the time with an automatic transmission, and I was driving my moth-er's Toyota, a somewhat less-than-new car with a standard transmis-sion. She expressed an interest in wanting to learn how to drive a car with a standard transmission, so I taught her. As my wife is a very good driver, and she did, after all, already know how to drive, it was easy to teach her, and I think she was driving my mother's car on the street in a matter of two or three days. For the first ten years of our marriage, we owned nothing but standard transmission cars. And she thought I was the greatest teacher in the world because I was so relaxed and patient, was never the least concerned that she couldn't master the stick shift, was never upset when she made a mistake, and explained things thoroughly and clearly. This was all an act. I was terrified to my toenails the whole time, but I suspected that she thought that, as a man, I should exhibit a certain coolness.

The one prolonged teaching session I had with my mother was when she taught me to drive when I was eighteen. My mother had learned to drive only two years earlier and she seemed very keen that I should learn as well. I don't remember having much enthusiasm for it. To this day, I hate to drive. What compounded my situation was that my mother's car had a manual transmission. The lessons were tense. My mother was extremely nervous and extremely angry, although I picked up driving with relative ease. She kept thinking I would strip the gears, run into something, or get run into, normal fears but in her case pitched at high frequency.

After three lessons, I could drive the car, a Volkswagen Beetle, fairly well. But I hated the lessons. Then, suddenly, one day, she decided to have a male friend continue the instruction. The change was dramatic. He was very laid-back, patient, and had endless confidence, or pretended confidence, in my ability. The lessons were no longer an ordeal. I learned two things from this switch, which I think in part my mother effected because she wanted me to receive instruction from a man. First, I decided I wanted very much to teach people things in the manner of a middle-aged Black man, because I thought all middle-aged Black men taught like my new driving instructor, and all of my life, I have associated good teaching with being middle-aged, Black, and a man. I wanted to be patient, assured, relaxed, with boundless confidence in my student and in my ability to teach him or her. Second, paradoxically, is that I missed my mother as an instructor. I thought there was something in this cross-gender moment of instruction that helped me understand what being a man was. Perhaps this is why my wife was able, very easily, to talk me into teaching my daughter how to drive. "Men are better teachers at mechanical things than women are," my wife told me in an appeal to my ego. I don't believe it. I am the most hapless man with mechanical contrivances that I know. But it meant something to my male ego to teach my daughter to drive, especially because my wife felt unable to do it.

I went upstairs and talked to Linnet.

"Didn't go too well today, huh?" I asked.

"Daddy," she turned to me with her tear-streaked face, "teach me how to drive. Mommy thinks I can't do it. I know I can learn to drive if you teach me. I think you're the best teacher in the world. Remember how you taught me to play checkers and Monopoly and stuff like that. You always explain stuff well and never get mad if I need to have it explained again. I think most of the stuff I remember you taught me."

It is a terrible weight put on any parent to hear that suddenly and so sincerely from a child, as if the dreadful responsibility of childrearing appears in such vivid relief at such a moment.

I have been a terrible parent, I thought. This kid can't believe what she is saying. Immediately, it struck me that the last thing I wanted to do was teach my daughter to drive. I felt dizzy from the sheer immensity of it, as if, in some surreal moment, I was assigned to teach her the most important task a human being ever could be taught and feeling myself insufficient for the undertaking. After all, I secretly thought that perhaps because of a learning disability, Linnet couldn't learn how to drive. I remember trying to dissuade her from getting her learner's permit, telling her there was "no rush," that she had plenty of time. "You don't know how much time I have," she responded angrily. "Driving isn't everything," I would tell her at other times. "It is to me," she would answer. I felt like a fraud bearing a sickening guilt.

"I'll teach you how to drive," I said.

We went out early every Sunday during early spring. We would drive around the huge empty parking lot on the Washington University campus in St. Louis for about an hour. Turn left. Turn right. Pull into a parking stall. Keep the car straight. Keep your eyes on the road. Check your rearview mirror. The usual instructions. I was calm, collected, coolly explaining everything and giving her tips about various complications that could arise when she actually would drive in traffic, which I promised her week after week but always found some excuse not to fulfill. So, she wound up driving around the parking lot for far longer than most drivers-ed students. After a bit, she wanted to drive on the street, but she never became impatient about it, believing that her father knew best.

One very cold, very sunny Sunday, I decided to have her drive from one parking lot to another. This involved going up a winding, tricky stretch of road. I thought she could handle it. We went up without too much difficulty. But when we returned, matters became very dicey very quickly. Going down the winding road meant hugging a high brick wall that abutted the road. The car started going faster than Linnet could control, the nearness of the wall unnerved her and she couldn't keep the car straight. She turned the steering wheel and it seemed we were going to hit the wall. Maybe she had better control of the car than I thought. Maybe she wasn't going to hit the wall. Until that point, I had been, against my inner urges, very cool, but when I thought she was going to hit the wall, I panicked and grabbed the wheel.

"Goddamnit," I yelled, "you're going to get us killed."

I pushed her out of the way and guided the car down the road, virtually sitting on top of her. When we reached the bottom of the hill, I stopped the car.

"Look," I said, a bit sheepishly, "I'm sorry about that, but it looked like you were about to . . ."

Her head was down. She was crying quietly.

"I wasn't going to crash into the wall," she said. "You don't think I can learn how to drive, do you? You never did. You think I'm too dumb to learn to drive, don't you?"

I was silent for a moment. I didn't quite know what to say. I stammered something, but she wasn't listening. She got out of the car and opened the door on the passenger side.

"I guess you better drive us home," she said.

"Listen, Linnet, I'm sorry. I didn't mean . . ."

"Drive," she yelled at me. I was so startled that I simply obeyed her and got behind the wheel.

I started the car, but I didn't move it. I was trying to formulate something to say, an apology of some sort. I felt so exposed. She knew she had hit a nerve when she said I did not think she could learn to drive. But before I could say anything, she spoke to me in a quiet, choked voice, wiping her face with the heel of her hand.

"Do you know I got out of the Resource Room this year?" she said.

"Yes," I said, "I know that. That's very good for you."

"Hardly any kid gets out of Resource," she said, ignoring my interjection. "Once you get in special education, you stay there. And everybody thinks you're dumb. Even the teachers think you're dumb and they don't help you. They just do the work for you. It's awful to have everybody think you're dumb. I wanted to get out of there so bad. I worked and worked and got out. I'm not dumb, and I was tired of people thinking I was dumb."

"I never thought you were dumb, Linnet," I said.

"You know, there are a lot of Black kids in Resource. I didn't want to be there because I thought, everybody will think I'm dumb because I'm Black."

This was becoming too painful. What goes on in the minds of children is something adults don't want to know about. I didn't want to hear anymore. What was I supposed to say, some trite, unconvincing thing about your great Black ancestry, the wonders of Africa? People who think those recitations make a difference are afraid to plumb the awful and contradictory depths of the human soul. There was no escaping racial pride, in the end, as that was what motivated her to get out of the Resource Room. And there was no escaping race as a burden, a stigma, a form of shame. A Black person is forever caught between a kind of heroism and simply being the nigger. I pressed the accelerator.

"We don't have to go through this now, Linnet," I said.

"It's hard to go to school. A lot of the White kids are racist and can't stand most of the Black kids. And most of the Blacks think you're a sellout if you have White friends and they go around in some kind of clan. They think like their parents. All of them do. I don't want to like something just to make the Black kids happy, make them think I'm Black. They say I act White, but I'm just trying to be myself. What is this being Black? Hanging around complaining about White people all the time. Thinking about your color all the time and how different you're supposed to be? Just being part of a clan? But a lot of White kids do dope, come from messed-up homes, and just act crazy. I don't act like that. I sure don't want to be White. I want to be myself. That's why I wanted to learn to drive. To help me be myself," she said.

I had driven a few blocks, but pulled the car over. I looked at my daughter for a moment and realized that God does indeed give only ironic gifts.

"You know something?" Linnet continued, "I kind of liked the *Catcher in the Rye*. I mean, some of it. But Holden Caulfield was just too crazy. Sometimes I think he's right, though. I think sometimes everybody in the world is phony. I know I think the Black kids and their blackness and the White kids and their whiteness are all phony. They just don't know how to be themselves."

I got out of the car and went around to the passenger side, opened the door and shoved her gently toward the driver's seat.

"I don't feel like driving," I said.

"I don't want to do this, Daddy," she said. She was now completely in the driver's seat.

"Then, I guess, we're not getting home, because I'm not driving," I said.

"I might mess up the car," she said.

"I'll buy another one and take you out next week. There are plenty of car dealers around. Buying another car is easy. As Hemingway said, the world is 'a good place to buy in.' Go ahead and drive."

Wide-Eyed

....

DeWitt Henry

Young women in America will continue to look for love and excitement
in places that are as dangerous as hell. I salute them for their optimism
and their nerve.

—Kurt Vonnegut, "There's a Maniac Loose Out There,"
Life, July 25, 1969

Unfortunately, in a father's over zealous desire to protect his little girl
from risk and the discomfort of anxiety-provoking situations, he tells
her that she is incapable, incompetent, and in need of help. His behavior
sends a message that that is what he thinks of her, so she comes to believe
it herself.

—Mickey Marone, *How to Father a Successful Daughter*, 1992

1.

NEITHER MY MOTHER, nor my sister, nor possibly my wife felt that
their fathers prayed for them. Nor have most of the important women
friends in my life. What is a father's prayer? And why is it different for a
daughter than for a son? Or is it?

My daughter, Ruth, is now a remarkable young woman of the millennium.

I love her, and I fear for her well-being and pray for her future, but I
have had to struggle with deep-seated instincts from my background in
my regard for her. I was a WASP man-child in the 1950s, a sexist bachelor in the 1970s, and a husband confronted with a wife's awakening during the women's movement in the 1980s, a time when divorce seemed

epidemic in my generation. I have rallied, personally and culturally, to social progress in many ways and grown as a person in the process; but I have also, to be honest, often retreated to irony, casting a skeptical eyebrow. The civil rights movement, resistance to the Vietnam War, the sexual revolution: all certainly bettered our world, but that was then. What quality of thinking now, I wonder, is involved in my personal efforts at recycling? Does returning empties amount to more than a gesture of morale, like my mother's saving bacon grease during World War II? Or take language: here I am politely vigilant about pronouns and gender (at a recent seder one of my wife's friends went laboriously through the Haggadah revising all sexist references to God), while grudgingly permissive about "it (or she or he) sucks" becoming acceptable usage for children. In my heart of hearts, the former seems to me humorless, the latter corrupt.

Thanks to my wife, Connie, my daughter's upbringing has been progressive. Connie has supported and advocated Ruth's full flowering as a woman and a person. Since 1983, Connie has taught at an independent K through 6 school devoted to progressive principles, and my daughter was one of the first graduates. For years, in cranky silence, I saw my wife's school as the Academy of Aunty Mame, whimsical and utopian in endeavor. I was preoccupied with my struggles as a writer and as a college teacher. I couldn't help patronizing my wife and her career, which seemed so opposed to mine.

During the process of adopting our second child, our son David, Ruth combined with her mother to overcome my selfish fears about my ability to provide an adequate livelihood, fears postulated on my ambitions as a writer. In our application for the adoption, we characterized Ruth, at seven, in second grade, as "a happy, sensitive, unusually curious and creative child. She has a good sense of humor. She has wanted a brother or sister for a long time."

In describing myself, I wrote that "Pretty much I would be proud to bring my children up as well as I feel I was raised. I'd like to incorporate more of my mother into my fathering than I would my father, but as time passes I appreciate more his own practical insistence and the bulwark of his providing."

Concerning our marriage, we wrote: "As Ruth grew to school age,

Connie put her energies into volunteer political activities at first and more recently into earning accreditation as an elementary school teacher. . . . The ordeal of infertility has strengthened our marriage, and has made us surer of each other and ourselves, of what each of us means and wants. . . . We have a sound marriage, sound values, and a low-key, love-oriented lifestyle (people first)."

Perhaps predictably, the area of my greatest uncertainty and discomfort as Ruth has matured, and as the cultural mores of America have changed utterly, has been that of her sexuality. In reading recent feminist literature about fathering, I have been perhaps overly credulous, receptive to, and concerned about the charges of "distance." From Patricia Reis, for instance (*Daughters of Saturn*, 1995): "A father's inability to speak about certain things, especially his emotional realities, can later become a woman's silence." Also from Reis: "[The] internalized, vigilant father may also curtail a daughter's creative energies, especially if they are in conflict with his wishes or belief system." And from Victoria Secunda (*Women and Their Fathers*, 1992):

> Fathers—not being female—compute a daughter's womanly body, not her immature emotions. . . . Most fathers don't see the war within the daughter, her temptation both to retreat to Daddy's lap and protection and to push out of his embrace to that of beau and of the world beyond home. . . . When a father gives his daughter an emotional visa to strike out on her own, he is always with her. Such a daughter has her encouraging, understanding daddy in her head, cheering her on—not simply as a woman, but as a whole, unique human being with unlimited possibilities.

2.

There I am, the fifty-five-year-old father, wide-eyed, heart racing at 5:02 A.M. on the Sunday of Memorial Day weekend. Outside songbirds twitter and chirp. I am in bed, beside my wife, safe in our three-bedroom cape house in Watertown, Massachusetts, ten miles west of Boston. A noise has awakened me. A click. A familiar click. At 4:36 A.M. I know that what I have heard is the closing of the back door downstairs. That telltale whump. After a moment's listening, I hear the scrape of steps. This is no thief, no intruder. This is my nineteen-year-old daughter, Ruth, and her Hampshire College sidekick, Cassy, back from whatever adventure they had left for at 10:30 last night. I stare at the clock. I try to wake my wife. "It's 4:36, for chrissake. They've just come in!"

My wife remains intent on sleep.

Downstairs, water runs in the bathroom. For ten, fifteen, twenty minutes. What is going on? What could she, my daughter, have found in Boston or in Jamaica Plain? Or at salsa dance clubs, or in Greater Boston?

I am mindful of respect, of trust, but I already know too much.

I think of myself at nineteen or twenty, the summer after sophomore year. For me as a young man, an Amherst man, after all the deprivation of the hard school year, I had been out all night from my home in suburban Philadelphia, and I had come home drunk at dawn. I had come home and vomited in my family's downstairs lavatory, and the next day my mother had tactfully told me, here were my glasses, which she'd found in the toilet. How, my mother had wondered, had they gotten into the toilet? Had I been out with my old girlfriend, the Bad Influence, Kathie (home pregnant from Duke)? Had I found a party of all-night booze and dancing at some suburban friend's house?

For my daughter, Ruth, now, I consider and fear the worst, while the poppa in me—the heart racing and troubled poppa of love and responsibility, Conscience personified—churns over possibilities, discretions, indiscretions. I will talk to her tomorrow, after she wakes up in eight or ten or twelve hours, in the early afternoon. This isn't civilized, I will say. This isn't healthy. What are you trying to prove? This isn't hot-blooded youth, this is contempt for the whole normal world. This isn't partying in any sense but the defying of society, in this case the family you live with, us.

I can't get back to sleep. The daylight greatens. Distant crows or starlings now caww-cawww along with the sursurrus of distant cars. Meaning not to disturb my wife, I get up and cross to my son's room, empty since eleven-year-old David is sleeping over at a friend's. I sit on David's bed (once Ruth's, as this room had been Ruth's, and later had been shared by Ruth with David, from the time David arrived from Korea as an infant). I look out the window at a deserted playground.

I imagine . . . yet stop: what *right* have I to imagine or to care? She is an adult. She has lived whatever private life she lives at college. She has held down her job clerking in a Northampton arts gallery. When she has overreached, the year before, and before, the instances have been those of what her mother calls "poor judgment." As Connie put it: "We are concerned about your having good judgment, for your safety." A year and a half ago, Ruth had made an offhand statement to me, as the father, that she had an appointment at Harvard Health for an AIDS test. I had let that pass as worldly, until a few hours later, when it dawned on me, on the poppa in me—the poppa especially helpless and perplexed and guilty in the face of seeking to control or regulate her sex life among the predatory males that mirror his own worst dating years—that she was telling me she was having sex at college.

In such terms, I turn to my wife as Ruth's counterpart, the woman, the mother, the friend who projects her own overly sheltered girlhood and champions Ruth's right to adventure, while also condemning her beforehand for provocative dressing (a charge that Ruth denies). My wife briefly and without further explanation confirmed the fact. I groaned.

Where do my responsibilities lie? I wonder. Again, now, this adult dawn, I go back and try to wake my wife. The water downstairs is still running—for what? To scour the taste of kisses or worse? To cover the sound of vomiting? A word or two passes between Ruth and Cassy. My wife mumbles, "No. I don't think there's a problem. Let me sleep." Which has always been her modus operandi.

Except for the bad times.

I remember December 16, 1994, two days before Ruth's seventeenth birthday. Ruth had just passed her driving test, and, newly licensed, had permission to take our station wagon, the newer of two used cars, to a party at a girl's house west of Boston, where she was sleeping over. The phone had rung shortly after one A.M., while I was still up writing at my desk in the basement and drinking vodka (an unhappy habit I have since quit). I did not answer my wall extension because my wife, who had finally gotten our son to sleep in Ruth's room, answered in the living room right above me. First I heard my wife's gasps and wails, then her calling down the basement stairs to me. That had been the police.

The state police in Connecticut. Ruth had been in an accident. She was all right, but she'd broken her arm and the car was totaled. She was in a hospital in Rockville, Connecticut. When I got the gist of this, I shouted: "NONONONO!" and threw a coffee cup at the wall: dregs from it splattered everything, student papers, family pictures on my bulletin board, and the stains are still there to this day.

I was enraged, less at the prospect of physical harm to Ruth than at her messing up. Her abuse of privilege. Her lie to us as a family. That in supposed innocence she was going to a sleep-over, when in fact, or on impulse, she was driving to Connecticut to pick up an underage boy-friend she had known in summer camp, a boy fourteen years old, and to bring him to the sleep-over, knowing that we, her parents, would never approve, let alone dream of such a thing in our philosophy.

At word of the accident, Connie never thought twice. She wailed and wept, but leapt to action. David was awake from the commotion, and Connie just dismissed the raving poppa and took David with a blanket and pillows and set off in our second car to go rescue Ruth and bring her home. I was left bereft, confused, guilty, and worried. They arrived back later that morning, the three of them. Ruth with her arm in a sling. Connie glad to have her safe and alive. Police photos of the crumpled Taurus station wagon.

Temporarily, Ruth decided to stop driving, so that I worried and en-couraged her to. The arm healed. Insurance on the book value allowed us almost overnight to buy a better car.

But the issue was her double life, much of which I trace to Rowe Camp in the Berkshires, an earlier way station into adult independence and license. My wife's friends had recommended it. They were social progressives and the parents of Gerry, the female Falstaff of Ruth's life since girlhood; where I have often felt cast as Conscience personified in Ruth's life, I feel Gerry personifies Id. In any case, Gerry was going, and the mother joked, to answer Connie's fears that the camp might be too conservative, that campers there, instead of burning crosses, burned question marks on the lawn. My wife championed the notion, and I went along with it.

Ruth, of course, had loved the camp, went back a second year as a camper, and a third and fourth as a counselor, from when she was age thirteen to sixteen. That first year Gerry had gone with her, but for Gerry the license had proven disastrous, I concluded, hearing of her sequel in drugs and truancy and runaway life in the Harvard Square underground, where a number of Rowe kids seem connected. Gerry did not go back.

The second year, Ruth found her first serious boyfriend, also named Jerry, by psychological happenstance. He was three years older, and after camp, Ruth wanted him to visit Boston and to stay overnight in our house, the way a girlfriend would. As Poppa, I had tried to object. I harked back to my family's standards. You don't bring temporary boys home (or if a boy, girls), especially at age sixteen. You don't waste your family's attention on learning experiences. My wife thinks, however, that this complicity with Ruth is healthy. She polarizes my misgivings—a pattern in our parenting. Ruth and Connie win, of course. Jerry boy arrives. Cooks vegetarian fare. Plays guitar and sings protest folk songs. Connie likes the boy. I, as Poppa, am civil with the boy, but guarded, and put off by the sentimentality and political activism. I am looking for irony. For intellectual edge, for questioning and alacrity. Also the boy does not appeal to me physically. Has a mealy, tubercular quality. He chats and entertains us all, especially David, whom he charms like an older brother. Bedtime approaches. Connie and Ruth make up the couch turned to double-bed-sized futon in the family room off the kitchen, where we've all been watching TV and Jerry has lounged with his arm around Ruth. He "is not a virgin," Ruth has let Connie know, and Connie has told me.

They all set out for bed, good night, good night. Poppa, Connie, and David settle down upstairs; Ruth in her room; Jerry, after using the downstairs bathroom, snug in his bed in the family room. Connie, playing hostess, is the last one up. Lights out, upstairs and down, silence. Connie sinks into sleep, but the Poppa lies wideawake, listening, too aware of myself at sixteen, too skeptical ever to believe Ruth's depiction of girls and boys at camp as living in some Peaceable Kingdom, transcending hormones. Was that a step, creaking? Yes, definitely. I try to wake Connie, unsuccessfully. Hear whispers, creaking. I am outraged. This isn't right. This is disrespectful. I can't ignore this, even if I wanted to. I have to go down. I have to let them know I know.

I don't sneak, but I don't call out either. Still not sure they are together. Just down the stairs, heart pounding, wearing T-shirt and
sweatpants. Seeing light then, around corners, a glimpse through the
kitchen into the family room: she is in Jerry's bed; they are making out.
I don't want to see. I don't rage, but do say loudly, "Excuse me. With
freedom goes responsibility! I just want you to hear that."

Ruth jumps up, flustered.

"I'm sorry, Daddy. We were just talking. We're going to bed now."

I don't wait for the final lights out, or her return to her room and
shutting of her door, though all that happens as I turn angrily and retreat upstairs. Lie awake still, ever vigilant, no more creaks or whispers.

Still later, long after Jerry boy has become history (has gone to college in Florida, written and called, but gradually been replaced in Ruth's
attentions by local boys), despite the Poppa's sense of becoming ludi-
crous, I will rehearse the principle: "Not under my roof you don't"—
don't flaunt your behavior, which you know instinctively upsets me,
while you enjoy my hospitality and protection—and Ruth will counter
with the ideology, supported now by intellect, reading, and her peers:
Only truth! Love me as I am!

6:04 A.M. Sounds again downstairs. More vomiting?

Was this some crazed orgy, I wonder, raving even as I allow for such
thoughts to be irrational, unjust. If so, what? Have she and Cassy been
loving physically with boys/men? If so, what sort? Dudes? Descendants
of my bachelor pals? Drugs? What sort of parties would last from eleven
P.M. to four-thirty A.M. on Saturday night? What nightlife crowd in
Boston's jazz or dance or nightclubs has she found and explored? The
innocent version doesn't compute, the version she gives of hard dancing for hours which is no prelude to sex. The version which is not the
ritual of oblivion, doped and drunk. (The summer before I have felt my
worst fears confirmed by the unsolved au pair murder in Boston, where
the top half of a twenty-year-old Swedish nanny was found in a dump-
ster and investigation placed her late-night dancing with a fast crowd at
a club called Zanzibar.)

She provokes me, of course; provokes the foolish skeptic, the repressive Superego. This is my punishment for harboring suspicions and guilts.

As Dad, I helplessly project my own shadow self, a self denied and avoided by my wife, much as my own mother had supposedly avoided or hidden my father's alcoholism. The libertine Henry passion for extremes.

Three years ago, on her way to camp, she wrote me a note for my birthday:

"I hope you have a wonderful birthday, with lots of peace and quiet—maybe I'll stay off the phone, or something. I really appreciate everything you do for me. . . . I also have a lot of respect for your integrity, as a writer, a person, a father. You have a certain dignity which is difficult to emulate. Perhaps we can spend some more time?"

Me? Dignity? With the backstage confusions and pathologies of my midlife psyche? In my own notebook I am writing letters to myself about indignity.

College at Hampshire, some three hours away (rather than at nearby Emerson, where my faculty fringe benefit would let her go tuition free), has taken some pressure off. She has her own roof there, her life. It is a family-financed and -supported progress into independence and responsibility. Ruth does well academically, although now I am skeptical about her choice of courses, primarily creative writing and courses in various Third World studies. She seems sadly unfamiliar with literature by white males, living or dead. She assumes that most of her liberal arts learning was covered by advanced placement from high school. Cassy, the roommate, is her best friend, and although Gerry remains her best friend at home, Ruth appears to me now to be primarily under Cassy's influence. Cassy lives with her mother now in Santa Fe and must badger her divorced father for money for college. Most vacations Cassy comes to Boston with Ruth, so we never have time to visit alone with Ruth, as family; the Poppa assumes this is deliberate, a kind of buffer against intimacy. When visiting, of course, Cassy is restless, so they must go out. They sleep late together behind Ruth's closed door;

Cassy may go off alone, briefly in the afternoon, but then after dinner they are showering, trying on outfits, full of nervous energy, Cassy's platform shoes clomping impatiently on the hardwood floors.

When Ruth has gone back to school I miss her. I hear, usually after the fact, offhandedly, or as a foregone conclusion, about her impulsive trips from college alone sometimes or with friends to Manhattan, say, or New Orleans. Besides the salsa dancing, in which she has taken a course, her evident passion is for jazz. Jazz clubs in Boston begin their sets late and run into wee hours. Home without Cassy last spring, and lacking local friends who share her passion, she has taken to going out alone late to various clubs. I of course object. See again, I think, her blindness to ways of the world, her lack of suspicion and guard in "the cultural jungle of America" (as Robert Stone puts it); even when one night she takes me along. We sit cross-legged in a loft, listening to earnest young musicians, who play with eyes closed and faces twisted soulfully, reaching for an authority of experience that is still beyond them. The nightlife crowd is randy, high, and hip, some paired, most prowling, on the make. I think I recognize one of my students.

Our father-and-daughter sharing this past sophomore year has been primarily financial—the tuition bill, loans, our refinanced mortgage, contingencies about transferring to Emerson (free), worry about having any money for David's private middle and high schooling, let alone his college. I am again the practically concerned, world-fact rehearsing Dad (like my own father).

In regard to finances, Ruth has demanded recently why I need a $500,000 life insurance policy with a $1440 premium due this month. I fume, the Poppa provoked and pulling rank:

"Because it is my place to protect you. People die."

And Connie huffs: "It's Walt Tolman, the financial advisor. My dad never had insurance and I turned out okay."

Me: "Your dad was a domestic disaster and besides you were a tough cookie."

Ruth: "I'm a tough cookie!"

Me: "No, you aren't; you haven't even had a taxable job in the world . . ."

This is unfair, inaccurate, and what are we shouting about really?

Everything else is between her mother and herself; and between her and her friends. During the school year, Connie calls long-distance several times each week and has long, rambling, whispering conversations, girl to girl. I don't want to know Ruth's private life, perhaps, and haven't wanted to know, pretty much, from Rowe Camp onward.

"Did you know I had my heart broken this year?" she asks me suddenly, in another recent exchange.

"No," I say, "nobody said anything to me. You talk to your mother all the time, but it doesn't get to me."

Connie, listening to us, adds, "No, he doesn't know."

"I did," Ruth says. "I really loved this boy, but he cheated on me."

"Oh," I say, not pursuing it.

I want to respect her now at this adult distance.

Am I a jerk? A Stone Age patriarch unable to look past my father's saying? Or am I too permissive? Am I abdicating where in fact I owe? Am I too distant? Is her maverick nightlife an attempt to get a rise out of me, to challenge the distance? Am I sexist in the worst ways? Are those behaviors that I pride myself on in my own adventuring, my own bold explorations as a teenager coming to adulthood, reserved in my instincts only for males? If my daughter were a son, how and why would I feel easier?

Yes, no, to such questions. These are the torments, the dialectic of best intentions and uncertainties.

I feel awkward and reluctant to read her fiction in progress, however highly praised by teachers. I can and have read it, of course, at her insistence, especially when she is writing at the computer and in her excitement calls for me to see this paragraph or page. She is writing a novel more or less about Gerry girl, whom she calls Jorrie. In the section she shows me, both the narrator girl, based transparently on herself, and Jorrie, are intent on losing their respective virginities.

But then I am the cold professional, more exacting about artistic flaws than encouraging or proud. I would feel better about reading published work, I tell her, work that has signified publicly rather than privately. I don't want her to short-circuit art by using it as a way to communicate with me, the parent, as a private audience.

Is this felt by Ruth as disapproval? I consider now that in writing she is in part competing with and taking on for herself my own ambition in the world; and in part communicating news of her private life and especially her adult sexuality to me (and in that sense, attempting to take her sexuality out of secrecy and asking for respect). I need to account for and examine my avoidance, especially since my own writing is confessional.

When my work is published, she is happy and, I hope, proud to read it, for this is my sharing, my human side. At the same time, I have warned her against reading accounts of my own coming of age or the follies and explorations of my bachelorhood as any kind of precedent.

I do not go downstairs until 7:30, when the day has mounted in earnest, streets are busy, planes passing. Her door is closed. I open the front door and take in the newspaper. I mute my noises. I make my coffee, shower, dress.

She apologizes later that afternoon for waking me up. She and Cassy are up at last and showered, David is home, Connie cooking, life in full swing, all normal. Phone rings. Family bustle and chatter. I nod and grimace ruefully, "Right," I say.

There will be other wakings, I know.

3.

Such are this father's fevers. Vapors.

In present time, this summer's end, I apologize to Ruth, as she reads this writing; likewise, to Connie, who feels that discussing our daughter's personal life in print might be in itself a parental abuse. But a deeper form of trust, regard, and love is meant here.

Culturally Ruth's options, meaning path-trodden, recognized, supported, and progressive choices for women, are wider and more various and demand more free will than the options available for my mother in 1929 (when, having dropped out of college and begun work in commercial art and social work, she married at age 23), for my sister in 1955 (when, pregnant, she dropped out of college and married at age 20), for Connie in 1973 (when having finished college and begun teaching in Head Start, she married me at age 24).

With such apparent liberty, I hope for Ruth that it may continue to prove the liberty of pastoral rather than of decadence, Arden rather than Vienna, folly rather than vice, and that it may lead, as it does in the Shakespeare comedies that I teach, to self-knowledge and to the union of ardor and intelligence.

Ironically, she, her mother, and I have enjoyed watching the series of recent Jane Austen movies together, not only as romantic comedies, but with some yearning, I think, for a world of coherent manners, of measurable character and spiritual value linked to privilege and property; indeed, a racist, classist, patriarchal world to which the challenges and prospects of contemporary America stand in necessary contrast.

I pray that Ruth never feels "silenced" in Tillie Olsen's sense; never feels that her potential has been compromised by life and that, again, in Olsen's words, she "is a destroyed woman."

In terms of lovers and friends, also, and of the life partner that I hope she finds, may she have the luck and judgment to avoid the wasters, the self-defeaters, the thieves, the liars and pretenders.

May she resolve her own balance between ambition, love, and parenting. May she live whole and full, her inner life reconciled to the social roles that exemplify at least the fictions of our best. Our mutual support. Our pledge to futures. May she never lose her appetite for life, her joy, relish, and savor of living, sweet and sour.

May she inherit from her mother, and from my sister, what my sister inherited from my mother, a bravery of love, sheer love over betrayal, loss, and aging.

I have come to appreciate Ruth's commitments with deepening pride. Her love of her younger brother. Her natural gift for teaching children. Her counseling and loyalty to troubled friends. Her inquisitive and even contentious nature, aspiring to equal ground. Her questioning of authority. Her concern for social justice. Her quick mind and good heart; her passion for experience; her omnivorous reading; her writing, acting, photography, and drawing. Her resourcefulness.

This midsummer saw Ruth's boldest departure yet. She traveled alone to Tuscany, Italy, where she baby-sat for parents from Connie's school for one week, then spent another three weeks touring on her own, hostel to hostel, we thought, until on her return she told us stories of sleeping in parks. She furiously studied Italian from a travelers' textbook beforehand (building on her knowledge of Spanish and French). She called around for bargain airfares on her own. She obtained her passport. She packed one huge duffel bag. We spoke sporadically long-distance while she was there, six hours ahead. She was able, she said, to have philosophical conversations in Italian with kids she met.

The family that had hired her returned home before she did and showed us photographs of her there, playing with their children: our Ruth, *there*, on cathedral steps. She herself took no photographs, but wrote in her journal and drew miniature pictures with art pencils. Her drawings were full of gaiety and color, celebrating ordinary people. In her journal she wrote:

> Here in Agropoli on a stone wall by a littered beach, trying to be incon-spicuous so this old fellow pushing an accordion does not notice that I have been following his music for some time now. He has stopped to talk with a couple who are having a midnight picnic on a bench and I am ly-ing here on this wall waiting for the music to start back up. Some ra-gazzo comes by and tries to sweet-talk me and my halting Italian but I wish silence upon us and get it, stare past him at the water and savor si-lence: "Lasciame sola . . . Lasciame avere questo momento sola."

Suddenly, I was proud of her adventure. I had never had one at her age to compare. I envied her the European experience. Envied her com-petence. I had forgotten my own pattern of departures from my family, and recognize now that Ruth's departures from her background, and from me, are part of that pattern too.

Of course, when it comes to her plan to take a leave from college next spring and study land reform in Nicaragua . . .

Perhaps I have come far enough now, from jealousy and fear, to admit to genuine curiosity. What will she see there? What will she ex-perience? How will she grow?

Daughter and father, both, are awake.

Aviva's World

REASON, RACE, AND SOME
DEGREES OF SEPARATION

···

Fred Viebahn

"BY THE WAY, guys, I've joined the BSA."

"You've joined what?"

"The BSA. The Black Student Alliance."

Why? I'm about to ask, but I bite my tongue. It's our first phone conversation since she's left for college, and my wife and I have braced ourselves for a few surprises.

"Great," I say. "So what do they do—I mean, what do you do there?"

I'm about to begin inquiries into the concept, the mission, the engagement, but I quickly manage to rein in my tendency to probe whatever she says and does, while she excitedly launches into descriptions of her new acquaintances. After all, I think, it's a predominantly white Southern liberal arts college for women, and she has grown up and acted "white," whatever that means, all her childhood, with only occasional black friends. Of course, her mother is African American, she has black grandparents, uncles, aunts, cousins . . . but most of her life my daughter—biracial (an expression I don't particularly like to use because it's fraught with vagueness and simplification), binational, bilingual—has been immersed in environments where race was not an issue, at least not overtly—from her Jewish preschool in Arizona to her public school honors classes stocked with kids of white university professors. (Black professors in our town tend to send their sons and daughters to an expensive private school.) She was shielded from racism by her parents' social status, and she had never given us indications that race mattered to her in any concrete sense.

Compared to the stereotypes presented in the media and sometimes witnessed secondhand through relatives and friends, we live a rather charmed life. Sure, there were a few racially motivated insults and minor threats in the more than two decades that my wife and I have been together, but they never happened in our daughter's presence. And on both sides of her family she has experienced nothing but acceptance and affection, making her feel as comfortable at Midwestern Thanksgiving dinners where her father is the only white person, as in my tiny home village near Cologne where her mother is the only black. A true story that has met with incredulity when told to Americans: When we took her to Germany for the first time, at half a year of age, one of my aunts pointed to her blond hair, blue eyes, and fair skin and said with an undertone of disappointment: "But she looks so German!" Other relatives assembled around the baby also expressed their bafflement.

Instead of desiring similarity and fearing the unknown, these relatives were hoping for the thrill of difference, the excitement of the new; they were happy to allow, acknowledge, and embrace this offspring of one of theirs, no matter how "strange" she might be. My daughter's hair turned dark and frizzy before she was ten, her eyes took on a green tinge, and her skin, now a light golden brown, proved more resistant to sunburn than her mother's much darker complexion. And yet for many years she seemed oblivious to race; only lately, inspired by literature and films and maybe her parents' political dinner chatter, has she begun to relate herself to matters of race in the bipolar black-and-white American sense.

Although in elementary and middle school her close friends were exclusively white, recently my daughter has been finding older friends and role models with whom she can identify—among them an interracial actress who, although more than double her age, at first glance might easily be mistaken for her sister when the two are together: the same skin tone, the same hair, the same height. Another role model is entirely fictional—her favorite character in her favorite TV show, Chief Engineer B'Elanna Torres on the starship *Voyager*, is an "intergalactic" mix between human and Klingon, a bossy scientist played against all female stereotypes by a "mixed"-looking actress.

We had always impressed upon our daughter that she was special—not just because she's our daughter but because, with her dual citizenship and multiple ethnicity (African, German, Czech, Cherokee, Blackfoot, Jewish, Irish), she is a veritable multicultural human being in a society that purports to pride itself on its "melting pot" capabilities, even while it commits endless crimes of ethnic and class separation.

Maybe we were plain lucky that her genetic makeup supported sweetness and compassion, so that our steady diet of positive reinforcements did not lead her down a path of arrogance and superciliousness; still, she turned out to be extraordinary beyond her ancestry of black and white, American and German—which is why now, at age fourteen, she has left for college and within days joined the BSA.

"It's real cool," she says. "Cool kids, really. They know their stuff."

How does a father write about his relationship to his adolescent daughter without wading too deeply through the mush of proud parental hagiography—especially if this daughter has done everything to make him proud for the fourteen years she's been "the light of his life"? (Here I go, about to sink into a bog of clichés!) Well, a father has bragging rights, no?

In April 1997 my daughter Aviva, an eighth grader in public middle school, was accepted into college. There was little forewarning, and therefore not much time to contemplate such a giant step into a world that, only weeks earlier, seemed several high school years away. She had always been at the top of her class; in sixth grade she was identified (more accurately, kind of "certified") as a high achiever by the Center for Talented Youth at Johns Hopkins University. She took the SAT a couple of times—first in seventh grade, when her scores jumped above the average college-bound twelfth grader, and again in eighth grade, when she scored along with entering freshmen at the nation's most prestigious universities.

Six weeks earlier she had received an invitation through Johns Hopkins to apply to the only formal program in the country that allows students (well, just girls) of her age and accomplishments to skip the last four years of secondary education while providing them with a social support system: the Program for the Exceptionally Gifted (PEG) at Mary Baldwin College in Staunton, Virginia, a small, private, all-female liberal arts school in the valley between the Shenandoah and Blue Ridge Mountains. Aviva decided to "check it out for fun," a rather easy undertaking since Staunton is only fifty minutes' driving time from her home town of Charlottesville. She did not exhibit much enthusiasm—which American girl voluntarily decides to forgo her prom, that ritual of preening and mating that's supposed to give her the final push from girlish adolescence into the embrace of womanhood? No matter: She filled out the application form, still "just for fun," wrote the four required essays, and in early April spent a night in the dorm where the thirty or so early-admission freshmen and sophomores, all of them high achievers, had formed their own support group under social supervision while attending classes alongside "traditional" students who'd fought their way through adolescence and the educational system the old-fashioned way.

The next day when I picked Aviva up after her interview with a program administrator, she was ecstatic. "I love it," she said. "If they admit me, I wanna go. Now. This fall. Imagine, I could enter graduate school when I'm eighteen and become a veterinarian four years early! All that's missing is high school geometry so I can take college math, but if you get me a tutor I'll finish it over the summer."

And that's why, for the first time since toddler days, Aviva would not spend the summer with her grandmother in Germany but hunched over a voluminous math book instead. Of course the years when we checked her homework every night were long past; nevertheless, I became painfully aware that we were absolutely helpless when it came to the daunting task of cramming an entire year of honors high school geometry into a few weeks of summer vacation. Having long forgotten concepts like triangle congruence and transformations, we felt worthless—even more so when she made it clear that no help was required on our part, not at all.

She had long passed us by and become her own person, a teenager barreling full steam ahead into an independent future, never to return fully to our triple fold that had once seemed destined to last forever.

For years I had refused to face the fact that the blithe unity of our family nucleus—mother, father, single child—was fated to dissolve one day; recently I had consoled myself that such a day lay somewhere in the foggy future, undefined. The illusions created by happiness threaten to block reason's path; if, however, the child's happiness is our fundamental concern, over time reason must prevail, even though we may fight it in our hearts. Life and literature provide too many horrific examples of what happens whenever reason does not assert itself. On one hand, among relatives I had seen what devastation unreasonable authoritarian pressure can cause in families; on the other hand, I and my sister had also experienced how our parents' love for us and each other had allowed us, with careful offers of guidance and advice, to find our own niche in life. And yet in spite of my parents' example, and regardless of all the intellectual reflections I can muster, I find myself combating the devil in me who yearns for continued control.

"So what did you do today?" I ask on the phone. "Any tests? Any grades back? Did you eat vegetables for dinner? Did you eat dinner at all? You sound tired—are you getting enough sleep?" After all, except for the actual birth and breastfeeding, I have always shared the responsibilities that tradition has assigned to mothers, which gives me the right to ask "motherly" questions.

"Yes, Fred. Don't worry. I'm fine. By the way, if you want me to I can probably install the Ethernet card in my computer myself when it arrives . . . "

"No, I don't want you to. You need a screwdriver to open the case. And you have to watch for static electricity. That's sensitive stuff. It's better I do it."

"Okay." She sighs. She is a good daughter. She lets me have the crumb.

Charlottesville, August 24, 1997

Hallo, meine liebe Aviva,

I've decided to write you a letter from time to time. When you come home you will want to see your friends or tell us about your adventures in PEG-land, and the telephone is mostly good as a conduit for hellos and good-byes, for *wie geht's* and *ich liebe dich,* quick stories and requests. Paper remains my medium of choice for deeper reflections and lasting tales, even if they are first composed on a computer.

Don't fear: I'll avoid lambasting you with parental platitudes like:
"By entering college you've taken the first step out from under our umbrella into a world of your own choosing, a world you will eventually be responsible for."
Most likely I'll just ramble along, speak my mind, see what comes to that mind.

It was bittersweet to leave her that day. Of course, we'd left her before—in the summer with her *Oma* in the German village, in Charlottesville when Rita and I went on trips—but it was quite different to leave her in order to go home without her. The realization weighed on me that this was one of those inevitable Major Passages Without Return we have to negotiate in life. My wife and I have been telling ourselves that this is not a real separation and that it should be easy for us, especially in comparison with the parents of the other girls in the program. After all, Aviva is the only freshman PEG student from Virginia, the only one whose *Heimat* lies within short driving distance: It's a snap for her to return home on weekends, or we can cross the Blue Ridge to see her with an hour's notice.

Well, Heimat. What does that mean for her, for me? Home? Home land? Home area? Is Heimat just the place where we come from, where we grow up, or where we live a good part of our lives? Is it a place one "belongs" to irrevocably, a place that one can claim and that can claim us? Marlene Dietrich, one of my favorite German-Americans, sang: "*Ich hab noch einen Koffer in Berlin . . .*" even though she had left Germany as a young actress and found her fortune in the United States, even though she hated the mob of former countrymen responsible for bringing the Nazis to power with their unspeakable mayhem and mass murder—she kept that suitcase full of memories. It was her indispensable piece of the sort of Heimat we cannot choose but which is given to us whether we want it or not, whose redeeming virtues—holiday rituals, old wives' remedies—we will hold onto and cherish, no matter how far away we have been transplanted. For me, too, that kind of inescapable Heimat is in Germany; for my wife it's in Akron, Ohio; and for Aviva? I guess it's in Charlottesville, since the memory of Phoenix, Arizona, the place of her birth and preschool years (which she vowed, at age five, never ever to leave), has been buried under eight subsequent years of public school bustle in Virginia. Charlottesville became her Heimat through her parents' choice. But from now on (although she will come back many times, at least during the next four years) this Heimat will begin to shrink until the memories are easily packed away, a suitcase full of images from a carefree past.

Lately I've been thinking incessantly about Aviva's early child-hood—often sitting down in front of the tube late at night and playing back the videos I shot then. Of course these years are bound to look different from my perspective than from hers, but both outlooks over the past are happy ones, I trust. Naturally, Aviva's early recollections are vague and sporadic while my memories shine so brightly that calling them up can free me from a sour mood. It helps that I videotaped virtu-ally her every move: playing on the Cookie Monster swing set in our back yard in Tempe; pirouetting in front of the TV while the prima donnas revolved in Giselle and Swan Lake; storming out the front door into the hot desert rain to stomp through steaming puddles in only her underpants, utterly ecstatic; telling stories to her imaginary friends in the bathtub; sulking because she had been chided for pouring oil and vinegar all over a restaurant table; on the run from me along a canal in Venice. And all those joyous afternoons when I lifted her into her child seat (weight limit forty pounds) and we biked the ten minutes to pick up her mom at the university, where our daughter immediately stormed into the office of the English department chairman to play with his collection of tiny wind-up toys . . .

When we plan to have children we implicitly have to accept a whole range of possibilities, from worst to best. The exciting and frightening thing is that those possibilities remain open for a very long time—es-sentially "till death do us part." Aviva was a "planned baby" if ever there was one. From our first months together in Iowa City more than two decades ago (which was a couple of years before we tied the knot for-mally in Oberlin, Ohio), Rita and I planned to have a child as soon as we "settled down." We decided to give ourselves time to "live" and travel and finish a couple of books, so we aimed for the year when Rita turned thirty.

And that's exactly how it happened. As soon as she had settled into her first teaching job at Arizona State University, we set out to create the one child we wanted, and we were immediately "fruitful." Rita wished for a girl, while I pretended not to care—though I secretly also hoped for a girl. The joke in our favor was that we had an easy time agreeing on female names, while we never grew attached to any of the hundreds of boy's names we tested on our tongues and committed to long legal pad columns.

Our daughter was born in Phoenix, Arizona, on January 25, 1983. We named her Aviva Chantal Tamu, meaning "sweet song of spring" in our personal Esperanto of Hebrew, French, and Swahili—none of them languages either of us was familiar with; but in the combination we heard the hopeful music we intended as the clarion call for her life. I cut the umbilical cord and stayed by her incubator the first two hours while Rita was "stitched up"; I placed her on her mother's breast the first time; I slept on a hospital bed beside her acrylic see-through bassinet; and the next morning I learned from a midwife how to bathe her, then bundle her in swaddling the Navajo way—so tightly she would believe she was back in the womb. Oh, those tiny toes!

It's hard to remember why I preferred a daughter over a son, and I would never allow a psycho-plumber to snake through my subconscious only to misinterpret the complexities of that wish. I think I was a pretty good son to my parents, so there was no denial and projecting going on, no fear of my own bad example. I can only speculate: as a boy, I often preferred the company of women. During family gatherings, when my father and my grandfathers and uncles played cards in the living room, my boy cousins had to drag me away from the women folk trading stories in the kitchen so that I would play soccer with them. Even now, half a century old, I frequently feel more comfortable chatting with women at social gatherings. End of speculation.

One question I preferred to skirt for years deals with something that has baffled many of my friends: How is it that someone who had published four novels by his early thirties hasn't finished a single book in the nearly twenty years since? Oh, I can pull a multitude of rational-

izations for my procrastination out of my back pocket—from the radi-
cal changes in my surroundings caused by emigration and the switch
to a "foreign" language as my new everyday idiom, to the distractions
afforded by Rita's prominence and my easygoing, self-absorbed, natural laziness. But the main reason (excuse?) is probably the joy of cod-
dling our human oeuvre day after day, prodding and nudging her on
the path to exploring the world.

All that time spent with her at the stable when she had a horse of her
own—would I trade it for the writing of another novel? I used to take
her out to the stable four, five, six times a week and watch her valiant
attempts to train a tricky, neurotic thoroughbred (renamed "Starfire's
Mystery" by Aviva), a victim of mistreatment at its former racing stable. Although the mare never came around and eventually had to be
sold, I enjoyed the afternoons serving as my daughter's stable boy and
dilettante coach, schlepping buckets full of feed, holding the reins,
stroking the horse's baby-soft nostrils. "On the range" all by themselves, daughter and father trudged through pasture and mud dragging
bales of hay, exchanging horse stories.

"When I was a boy we had a lot of snow in the winter," I would say.
"It was great for skiing and sledding. Once I sledded down the path
from Oma's house . . ."

"Was that when you ended up in the road between the horse's
hooves?"

"Mmmh."

"I love that story! Tell me!"

"But you already know what happened!"

"Who cares? Tell me again!"

And what about the frequent drives to pick Aviva up from school so
that she made it home before the school bus? Whenever I saw her skipping out of the school building and across the lawn, past the flagpole
and towards the car, always chipper, my mood lifted.

"Please take me to school half an hour early tomorrow morning," she
would exclaim. "Mrs. Farmer lets me help her collate papers."

At home I played librarian for her, searching among our books for
material she could draw on for her homework projects, and I was her

technician of choice for various construction projects: geography presentations, French village, science fair.

Ah, forget that unfinished novel, already transferred to its fourth computer and mauled by as many different word processing programs! Who cared? I would read the *Washington Post* or *Kunst und Kultur* while she practiced piano, and then the three of us piled on the couch to watch *Star Trek*.

Do I have regrets about my lapsed literary career? Not really. But now that my daughter is no longer a constant presence in my life, I am a little anxious about having to prove to myself that I can return to the enthusiasms of my younger years and concentrate once again on the grand schemes of longer fiction.

"You may have my cottage if you promise to use it only for your novel," Aviva offered; it was the day before my fiftieth birthday. So that's exactly what I'm doing now—leaving behind my spacious study with its four desks and surround sound, fax and phone, the Internet connection and scanner, video grabber and TV monitor. I move my laptop into my daughter's playhouse and wedge myself between fantasy constellations of Playmobile figures and an extensive trove of trolls who have a choice view of the Blue Ridge Mountains. Yes, I'm getting around to myself again.

Charlottesville, Sunday, September 7, 1997

Meine liebe Aviva,

It's me again, your "old man." Have you digested your daily dose of German reading? Just kidding. A little bit. Please try to find the time. You did it at home for years, you can do it in college for years to come. Sorry, I can't help it; I have to meddle. "Father knows best." Seriously: You're only fourteen; even if you're correcting eighteen year olds in the bio lab, remember that being smart doesn't mean acting smart.

Only a few more months, and she'll qualify for her learner's permit.

I'm looking forward to teaching her. Stick shift first. That's what the Volkswagen Jetta behind the house has been waiting for—the same Volkswagen my father picked up for my wife and me from a German dealership fifteen years ago, three days before he died from a heart attack; ironically, it was the same week Rita's pregnancy was confirmed—but Aviva's grandfather never knew. We drove the Volkswagen to his funeral in my home village, then shipped it to the States where it carried us from New York to Arizona, with my daughter in her mother's womb—the same Volkswagen that took us home from Phoenix Memorial Hospital when she was three days old. Years ago when I bought a new car, Aviva begged me to keep the Jetta. "It's my car," she said. "It's cute. I want to drive it when I grow up." So I've hung on to it for the past six years, keeping plates and insurance up to date and the battery charged, starting it now and then and racing it down the driveway to the mailbox. Aviva and I are a sentimental bunch.

It's Sunday night, and I'm supposed to finish an essay. Instead I'm writing her a letter. Maybe these Sunday letters will become a habit.

My Sunday service. Ersatz worship. After all, we're not exactly a religious family. In fourth grade Aviva balked at reciting the Pledge of Allegiance because of the religious reference. The teacher made her and the two others who refused (a black girl who was a Jehovah's Witness and Aviva's atheist Dutch friend) leave the classroom during the pledge. When I protested, calling it discriminatory, a singling out of the principled, the teacher reasoned it was fine with her if these three girls, based on their convictions, didn't participate, but that their example was threatening to spread to their schoolmates, who had no convictions but were guided by spite and mischief. That same week I heard Aviva recite the full "one nation under God" pledge during the flag ceremony of her Girl Scout troop. "What's the difference?" I asked, flabbergasted. "Girl Scouts is voluntary," she answered. "School's not."

Well, the school she has entered now is voluntary. Her choice. We supported her in her decision, but we did not nudge her. We were and remain torn—thrilled that she loves college life, slightly depressed because she exhibits no signs of homesickness.

Charlottesville, Sunday, September 21, 1997

Meine liebe Aviva,

It was so much fun last weekend when, home for the first time since going off to Mary Baldwin, you invited us to climb into your high bed for the requisite good-night kiss—just like old times. The three of us stretched out up there till three in the morning, trading stories and jokes, and the stuffed animals that overpopulated your bed came tumbling down in twos and threes whenever we laughed.

I built her that bed when she turned seven, her first birthday in Charlottesville—custom designed to accommodate her full-size mattress, with integrated desk and shelves. I could have written a television script in the time it took to construct this aerie, but that would have left nothing of lasting value—just something that would have been "conceptualized" and rewritten to death, and its overproduced corpse broadcast into thin air.

To speed things up, I spray-painted the raw bed frame in front of the garage without covering the driveway; naively, I believed the white acrylic would wash off. It didn't, and the raggedy white lines looked ugly on the black asphalt. Outsmarting myself, I sprayed black acrylic over the white lines, which took care of it—the black covered the white nicely, although it was a bit darker than the grayish asphalt.

These traces are still there. The driveway color has faded under the brunt of weather and the wheels of cars, but those black lines and spots, after all the years in heat and cold, sunshine and rain and snow and ice and run over by rubber tires a thousand times, remain visible.

I can see them from the windows in Aviva's room. White on black, black on white. On her first weekend home, Aviva asked me to take her back to Staunton early—"I don't want to miss the BSA picnic." Most of her second weekend home (one night only) she spent holed up in her room, watching Chief Engineer B'Elanna Torres power the starship *Voyager* through the Delta Quadrant. B'Elanna, who has spent plenty of time lately exploring the Klingon side of her ancestry, might prove to be the main reason for our daughter's coming home on weekends. On Wednesday nights when *Star Trek Voyager* is broadcast, it's "quiet study time" at PEG, with the TV room off limits; so we tape the show for her.

For fourteen years Aviva's identity had been defined by her parents. I don't think that she ever considered us in racial terms; after all, parents are parents, a unique breed who look and sound different to their children than to anybody else. (An example of this special relationship: Aviva is incapable of recognizing my distinct German accent when I speak English, whereas she has a fine ear otherwise and no trouble identifying the accents of Arnold Schwarzenegger and Henry Kissinger.)

Now, however, she is "out in the world," and part of letting her go and her letting go is to define herself, her identity, in her own terms—on her own terms. Although race did not matter throughout her elementary school years (except, perhaps, in some Newbery Medal children's novels she read that dealt with slavery or just growing up nonwhite in America), it became more of an issue in middle school.

There were a few casual remarks by both white and black classmates, mostly curious, never really hostile: "Oh, wow, your mom is black?" or "Hey, your dad's a white man?" And there was, quite simply, the element of learning—learning and reading in social science classes about the dreadful underside of The Land of the Free, comprehending the unbroken chain of injustices from the Middle Passage to the civil rights struggle and the inner-city proletariat.

It is impossible to escape society's urge to categorize, even if those categories relate only marginally to the complexities of someone's individual existence. I understand why Aviva joined the Black Student Alliance, why its social life has become important to her; for the first time since kindergarten she can have black friends with an intellectual affinity, and now that she is very aware of race, she can claim that part of her heritage and identity beyond her mother and her mother's family.

By the way, she's also planning to join the German Club.

A Prayer for the Daughters

Nicholas Delbanco

WHEN OUR first daughter had her first—as I persisted in calling him—"gentleman caller," I harrumphed about the house. I grumbled over unwashed glasses in the sink, complained about the way the two of them left our living room in disarray, noted the way the fellow failed to volunteer assistance while I mowed the lawn. Or better still, he could have offered to mow it himself and then take out the trash and wash and rotate tires on my car. Finally a friend taped the following instruction to our refrigerator door: "Be kind to young Peter."

It hadn't occurred to me, really; I thought young so-and-so should instead be kind to *me*. Surely *I* was the one who required attention and merited constant concern. What happened, I asked my long-suffering wife, to the expectation of manners, the old habits of propriety and formal address; why did he call me "Nick," not "Sir"?

"What happened is you have daughters," she said, "and the rules have changed."

She was right, of course, she's always right, and I try to be kind to young Peter or Paul. I was raised in a family with only sons, and we have only daughters, and the rules have changed. What my parents took for granted—an unquestioning if wholly external obedience, a sense that children should be seen, not heard, and then not until their faces were scrubbed—is no longer ours to take. And what my parents' parents took for granted—an equivalence of race, creed, class amounting nearly to an "arranged" or "brokered" marriage—is the exception now, not the rule.

The fellow who so famously killed King Laius at a crossroads got to sleep with mummy as reward. It didn't turn out all that well for Oedipus, but for some years in Thebes he was royal and respected and obeyed. When *he* suggested to his subjects that they mow the lawn or wash the car they made themselves useful, I'm sure. But his counterpart, Electra, had a harder time of it; she and her brother Orestes did away with their mother and wicked stepfather in order to revenge dear dad and not to share his bed. And then there were all those Furies to contend with, all that atoning to do . . .

Freud writes of this, it seems to me, with a kind of clear-eyed confusion: the Electra complex has been less celebrated in our culture than the Oedipus. The "mother's boy" has been widely assessed, the "father's daughter" less so. Might this not be the case, perhaps, because Dr. Freud and his wife had six children but the famous one is Anna, and it is she who carried on as guardian of his work? So the parable becomes instead the story of Lot with his salt daughters or Lear and Cordelia alone in the cell, chattering cheerfully, playing patty-cake and holding each other, "God's spies."

I'm not being fair here, obviously, and write this tongue-in-cheek. I've donned the robes of Old Mr. Curmudgeon in order to make an obvious point: the parent-child relationship has altered over time. Altered also with the teller's vantage, and mine should be located so that the reader may triangulate perspective—taking a reading, as it were, on the writer's point of view. My own is that of a father who, when young, did what he could to alienate the affections of other men's daughters from their own fathers and must school himself to like it now while others do the same . . .

I do; I like it very much; I've been gracefully instructed in the pleasures of paternity by Francesca Barbara Delbanco and Andrea Katherine Delbanco, now twenty-three and nineteen. In 1985 (our daughters then were eleven and seven) I published an autobiographical essay which contains this paragraph. I'm struck, in fact, by how little has changed—or, rather, by the way what changes is but surface alteration. Deep currents stay the course.

So here is the opening snapshot of this brief family album:

Of late our life is located, and we travel when we can. It's a rushed tranquility, a hurried standing still. Friends die, divorce, remarry, retire, make headlines, quarrel, get fat. The children grow. As one of three sons I find it a daily instruction to be the father of daughters instead. Cesca is meditative, inward—a literate person with poise. She has humor, self-assurance and wants to be an actress. . . . Andrea had a dislocated hip at birth and spent months in a remedial brace, then a cast. Released, she has rocketed everywhere—a passionate, spark-sending imp. I work at home and am distracted often, am often forgetful, abrupt. But I want to take advantage of this moment, these crossroads, the page—want to write what they anyhow know. Their parents love them very much. They are luminous presences, each.

Our elder child came wailing to this world in Cambridge, New York, an upstate village with a hospital so small that she and her mother, Elena, proved the entire population of the maternity ward. I was teaching at Bennington College, fifteen miles across the border in Vermont. Francesca was born on a Sunday, May 26, and my first scheduled class that week took place on Tuesday morning. "Poetic Drama and Dramatic Poetry" was a course in which we focused on those poets (Dylan Thomas, Samuel Beckett, T. S. Eliot, and others) who in this century were also writing plays. What interested *me*, at least, was how a poet throws his voice—how the lyric intensity of first-person utterance changes timbre when the "I" is someone else. Dramatic monologues give way to drama when the monologue enlarges into dialogue, or so I told my students, and the fine line between them is one we must attempt as audience to draw . . .

In Bennington such seminars took place, often as not, in the living rooms of student dorms, and there was unforced informality to the way we met, sat, talked. My students knew about my daughter's birth before I arrived to announce it; in such a community news travels fast. Our final author for the term was William Butler Yeats—whose poetry and verse plays we were studying as the spring wore on. So it seemed right and fitting to offer a toast; I read, at the start of the session, "A Prayer for My Daughter." And brought champagne to class.

I remember it clearly: the overstuffed chairs, the morning light on yellow walls, the stained carpet and the plastic cups and crackers and

pretzels and peanuts and cheese. "'Once more the storm is howling,'"
I began, "'and half-hid, under this cradle-hood and coverlid my child
sleeps on . . .'" Yeats writes of "the great gloom that is in my mind" and
avers that women should be apolitical, subservient—a strange sort of
prayer to read nowadays but commanding then as now in its shapely,
stately form. He dated the poem June 1919, and we talked about what
changes the ensuing years had wrought. Then we proceeded through
the pieties, the poet's canny wish that his daughter should be beautiful
but not possess excessive "beauty to make a stranger's eye distraught,"
the hope she prove "a flourishing hidden tree" and that she would "be
happy still" in the world's "windy quarter." That great rhetorical question of the last stanza—"How but in custom and in ceremony are innocence and beauty born?"—seemed its own answer to us all, and at the
ringing final assertion, "Ceremony's a name for the rich horn, and custom for the spreading laurel tree," the students stood and cheered.

It had been a hard spring for me; my mother died in March. She had
known about the pregnancy and gave a hands-on-blessing to Elena, although she did not live to see the child who would receive her name. In
ways that still astonish her parents, our daughter resembles my mother:
the skin, the shape, the right foot slightly splayed while walking, the
quality of impatient intelligence and sharp wit all argue a sort of transmission. She dislikes bugs and birds the way my mother did; she likes
the same perfume. If there be such a thing as soul and if souls might
transmogrify, then something of the sort has happened here. And
though I did not know it then my mother's death and daughter's birth
would fuse in the heart's calendar; I cannot date the one without recollecting the other.

It's a universal story; the wheel circles for us all. "Whatever is begot-
ten, born, or dies,"—to quote another of the poet's famous plaints—re-
minds us, or ought to, "of what is past, or passing, or to come." Our toddlers are gracious young women today, and both of them live elsewhere.
As do we. I no longer teach at Bennington, and Elena and I have not returned to that hospital in Cambridge for more than twenty years. The
house we took Francesca to (swaddled in blankets, sweating in the late-
May heat) has been long since sold; the blue spruce I planted to com-
memorate her birthday is thirty feet high and the new owners' problem

when it sheds needles on the entrance path; the doctor who delivered her has also moved away. The nurses have no doubt retired and those who were my students then are parents now themselves. But it takes little effort to set that morning's scene again: the sunlight on the carpet, the young people silent in the room, the ice chest and cold-beaded bottles of Mumms, the proud father reading William Butler Yeats, half-drunk and wholly elated, reciting "may she live like some green laurel rooted in one dear perpetual place."

What's rooted is memory; what's perpetual are—great definition of the poet's work—"magnanimities of sound"; what we carry where we wander is the spoor of where we've been. So now that I am older than was Yeats himself when he prayed for his girl, and now that I too may proclaim what I wish for my daughter, our daughters, I'm happy to comply.

But first, a disclaimer. Art is exactness, the naming of names, and I have no thoughts worth writing down that could properly be called abstract. The "smiling public man" Yeats called himself when among schoolchildren could be distracted readily by dancers and the "brightening glance"; he distrusted the political asseveration. So do I. The notion that fathers of the present day bear a separate relation to their daughters than was the case a century or six ago is no doubt accurate; it does not, however, engage me. Patterns of obedience and imitation, matters of preserved virginity and the size of dowries and same-sex partnership and professional aspiration and liberated ambition—all these are more important to the sociologist than to the novelist. An overview provided by statistics or schematics is besides the present point.

I want to write these lines since they limn for me a particular case: I am a father who has daughters, and language is a form of prayer for those with faith in articulate art. Or, to misappropriate Claudius—that lethal stepfather in the great poetic drama by the greatest of our English dramatists and poets—"My words fly up; my thoughts remain below." The usurper's on his knees, and praying, and he admits at soliloquy's end that he failed to find salvation. In *Hamlet,* of course, this describes the king's weakness; I prefer, however, to think of all such wordy earth-bound striving as an essay or assay of strength . . .

And authors—or, at any rate, this particular one—work at home. Almost by professional definition we witness and can daily participate in and thereafter report on our own children's progress; we are more a part of process in the domestic venue than those fathers who earn livelihoods in factory or field. Look for the wayfaring dad in the day care center or fetching daughters after school and you'll find, it well may be, a poet between stanzas or novelist at chapter's break. Too, it seems to me that the absence of household help in most American homes has eradicated distance in a way that ramifies: change your daughter's diapers often enough and you're not likely to be curtseyed to in the drawing room.

I mean by this that the rotogravure ideal of the Victorian or Edwardian gentleman reading papers by the fireplace and noddingly receiving the day's-end account from the governess as to his children's deportment is almost wholly obsolete; Mary Poppins doesn't do the cooking or the cleaning anymore. Those TV situation comedies that feature the family unit now seldom have a maid—or, if they do, the serving role is powered by nostalgia, the "downstairs" turning tables on the "upstairs" while the table's being set. Charles Dickens, Victor Hugo, James Joyce, Leo Tolstoy, Thomas Mann, and Mark Twain—to name only a few authorial "authority" figures with daughters—did not to my knowledge make peanut butter sandwiches or strip beds. And even when Tolstoy near the end of his life embraced simplicity and insisted on sweeping out his parlor, it was not for the sake of a child. These six men span a century and six different countries, but they have in common a privileged aloofness from domestic chores. We may harrumph and grumble, as I do in this essay's opening paragraph, but the yield of such proximity far, far outweighs the cost.

"In courtesy I'd have her chiefly learned," writes Yeats, and means by this "the old high ways"—half Castiglione, half coquette. His anger at Maud Gonne seems unattractive here; fine women need not eat "a crazy salad with their meat," or if they choose to do so need not therefore be labeled insane. "What's "peddled in the thoroughfares" as he in his poetical exasperation claims, "are arrogance and hatred"; this is, it scarcely need be said, a constricting and constricted view of women's earned place in the world. But I have to admit to a more than sneaking sympathy for Yeats's wish, and like to think young ladies nearing the millennium need not be wholly ignorant of what was meant by "courtesy"—that our daughters will have suitors and that their suitors will send flowers and hold open doors. I recognize, of course, that this is retrograde if not reactionary, but I was raised in a family where manners mattered, and my formidable grandmother had no greater praise for her grandson than to say "my chevalier." Men left the room to smoke cigars; they stood when she rose from her chair. . . .

So it does seem to me that something has been sacrificed to the ideal of practical equality, lost to our liberated sisterhood while so much else is gained. In many ways, I'd guess, it's more difficult to be a woman now than was the case before and more daunting a challenge to be both female and professional than is the case for men; the job description's broader and the task more various. That scarifying Teutonic definition of a woman's work, *Kuchen, Kirchen, Kinder,* had one virtue only: simplicity, and now that the triad enlarges beyond kitchen, church, and children the equation grows complex. This has been widely noted and reported on, and I veer perilously close to those genre-generalities I promised to avoid. But it's specific, really; I pray our daughters flourish both at home and in the world. May they manage and rest easy with that problematic conjunction of the public and the private life; may they find pleasure and fulfillment turn by turn in each.

In one way or another, we compose such prayers often. In the beginning was the word, and every daughter in my fiction has been created in the image of my actual daughters. Or, to shift the metaphor, these portrayals may be read as variations on a theme. I don't mean by this, of course, that Francesca or Andrea have been characters I've written— and even in a nonfiction account of our family's time together abroad *(Running in Place: Scenes from the South of France)* I gave them lines they never spoke and attitudes they did not entirely espouse. But here, from *Stillness,* a novel I published in 1983, is an articulated prayer that the father of the Sherbrooke children writes down in his journal. His hopes are mine.

March 25. Temperature at six o'clock, forty-two degrees. No wind. I drink my coffee peaceably; train prompt. . . . May my son know just such peace, and may my daughter grow up beloved. It is a worldly prayer but the single thing I pray. Harriet and Judah. May their manners be courtly yet frank. May they have physical health, and long life, and sufficient comeliness to please the eye but not bedazzle. May their learning be solid not showy, and their skills precise. May his work engage him; may they multiply. Let them continue in this house, as I have continued, and after their departure may they welcome the thought of return.

There is much in these lines that echoes Yeats, and consciously—the wish that the children prove "courtly yet frank," the hope for "sufficient comeliness to please the eye but not bedazzle," and the desire that the children "continue in this house . . . and welcome the thought of return." My fictive wild old wicked man does not exist, nor do Harriet and Judah Sherbrooke except insofar as they live on the page, but in that alchemy with which all authors are familiar I found myself able to dream about my own two children while inventing his.

Such transposition is routine; we write out of experience, but experience includes the act of writing and incorporates Yeats's notion of the anti-self or mask. Although I come from a household of sons, my offspring are female and each has a sister. The terms of sibling rivalry or mutual supportiveness are different therefore, somehow, and the terms of aspiration also change. No matter how assiduously we worked to eradicate gender-specific behavior, our girls hoped to be ballerinas, not baseball players; they preferred finery to fishing and shrieked at the specter of mice. And though it embarrasses me to admit this I still feel somehow *useful* when summoned from my desk to squash a bug or carry a spider outside; when asked to lift something too heavy for them or fix something broken I feel honored by their confidence that I can carry, lift, fix. . . .

May their learning be solid not showy, and their skills precise, my fictive father prays. In this regard also I share his hopes and in this context have labored hard; unnumbered hours of homework, of visits to museums and bookstores and concert halls, have been logged in the ledger called "learning"; my wife and I have been committed to the notion of instructedness as another set of parents might teach survival skills. They have had no lessons in what we used to call "home ec," or the "finishing schools" called "deportment," but they can tell the difference at fifty paces easily between the real cultural thing and the fraud; I confidently expect for them both an ongoing life of the mind. The idea that "school" can be "finished" has had no currency at home. And the one rider I'd attach to my fond fictive parent's wish is that he now would also say, *May her work engage her,* since no present father dares to think his daughter need not work. . . .

So, yes, I am conditioned by tradition. "And may her bridegroom bring her to a house" the poet writes, and however limited or patriarchal it seems I find myself in sympathy with that future-facing desire. Yes, I want my daughters to walk at some point down some aisle on my arm—though I don't require them to wear white or be married in a building that has aisles. Yes, I want them to be happy in the way their parents have been, and to emulate as women that exemplary woman who nurtured them throughout their youth and continues to do so today. I recognize that married love is neither original nor, perhaps, now fashionable—but it has made their father happy for nearly thirty years. And what I hope for them is not something other or in contrariety but, rather, more of the same.

These verbs *want* and *hope* are not, I trust, imperatives; neither, come to that, is the verb *trust.* Deploy them here as nouns instead, as the conditions of trust and hope and the explicit parental desire to keep children free from want. I would feel the same way about sons if we had had them, would treat them in the same way—both in terms of expectation and the assessment of what's been achieved. But this is moot; I cannot tell; I can only report on the actual. That "horn of plenty" to which Yeats refers—and which he in anger at Maud Gonne transforms to "an old bellows full of angry wind"—pours out upon our table when our daughters sit at it, and the sum and substance of my prayer is that this may continue, not change.

A decade ago, from *Running in Place,* these lines:

Andrea likes to draw. Each morning we gather flowers, arrange them in a vase, and scrupulously she copies what she sees. I work outside, on the tile patio, and she joins me there in the second wicker chair. She has a drawing pad and watercolors and Caran d'Ache crayons and pencils in ranked rows; she places the vase on the table and outlines it lightly in pencil, then fills in the shape.

"Why don't you draw the step?" I say. "Those steps there, by the table."

She shakes her head.

"Why don't you make it blue?"

"It isn't."

"It could be."

"Not this step, Daddy. It's orange."

"If you made it blue it would look that way to anyone who saw the picture."

"They'd be wrong," she says.

"Don't be so certain, darling. How do you know what that painter was seeing—the one we looked at yesterday—when he painted castles. Maybe he was dreaming them."

"He wasn't."

"Maybe he dreamed them so clearly that all these years later we see what he saw the day he shut his eyes."

"This step is orange," she says.

Other parents dote on and record their progeny with cameras and tape decks and videocassettes. Predictably enough my own form of retention was to write an annual letter to our children on or near their birthdays, reporting on the things they'd done and learned. These epistles bulk large in the day-book, and I don't propose to quote from them at length. But here's a sample from the first such letter after the first anniversary of Francesca's birth:

May 29, 1975 . . . You know which one's your nose, though tend to poke your cheek or mouth when we ask you to find it; you can stand a lot more steadily than you pretend, and, when distracted, do so for a minute at a time. You love to dance and shimmy, love to clap your hands when asked how big you are (eliminating as indecorous by now the infant game of raising hands when asked how big is Cesca, since you've got that trick down pat). You think, as do the rest of us, you're lovely to look at, and take most any opportunity to do so—in toasters in particular, or spoons, and the house sprouts mirrors for your special pleasure. Also gates, since you're a wanderer with splinters in your knees to attest to my incompetent floor-sanding.

And when her younger sister arrived, I kept the same sort of log. Here's an extract from a letter to Andrea Katherine Delbanco, turning three:

March 15, 1981 . . . Tootsie Rolls. Last August when we were in England it was Granny Piggott's candy, and there've been intermittent passions for bubblegum and lollipops and cookies and the like. But you're a faithful devotee, the Tootsie-Roll kid king; you fall asleep clutching one in the folds of what you still call "blankety" and wake hunting one on the instant. (You don't do much of the former, by the by—sleeping, I mean— and you're wakefulness incarnate by seven at the latest every day.) We draw pictures of them, sequester them in pockets and plastic bags— and, splendidly, you asked for a Tootsie Roll cake for your birthday. Also a Benjy sleeping bag, much to your tasteful parents' distress. But when Mommy pointed to the selection in the Sears catalog several weeks later, hoping you'd have forgotten, you proved as avid and exact a file cabinet for memory as is your big sister. "I told you already," you announced, with that magisterial impatience you've learned since first attended to by an anxious, waiting world.

Time now to shelve the family album and go out and mow the lawn. Time now to admit that "prayer" comes hard to one whose mode is secular, and superstitious at that; mostly what I hoped for has been granted and mostly what I wish for is that it can be retained. Not preserved in amber or even in such language as this but via that alkahest, memory, so that what was past and passing may remain in what's to come.

For years we were inseparable as a quartet, going everywhere together and sharing one roof. Now time and the river have done their slow work, and we're together only rarely and on pre-arranged occasions. This is as it should be. But always still, as soon as possible—and it delights their parents always—the two of them go off together and, from behind their shared closed door, the sound of laughter comes. "Be kind to young Peter," they say. . . .

What I pray now for my daughters is that they have children whose father will admire them as much as I do mine. And what I pray for those children is that their mothers prove as splendid a mother as is and has been their own. I want them safe. I want them healthy, not ill or at risk. I want them protected from want. I mean them to know what they mean.

Getting It Done

....

Gary Soto

THE END of my teaching career began suddenly when, during a faculty meeting, the faces of my colleagues underwent a frightening metamorphosis. They began to resemble various chicken parts—breast, thighs, wings—muffled behind the sheen of Saran wrap. Neither Dalí nor Man Ray nor an experimental graduate student filmmaker could have envisioned such a moment—thirteen professors with the faces of chicken parts, their jaws moving and the words unraveling from their mouths like yarn. That was the beginning of the end for me, and two years later, after other surrealistic hot flashes and dark cloudlike drifts of depression, I quit teaching altogether. After my last class, I literally jogged off the Cal Berkeley campus, arms hugging bundles of teaching evaluations after thirteen years of rubbing my bottom on hard chairs. Happy that my books were selling, I took the beautifully redneck stance of "Take this job and shove it!"

By this time, my daughter was sixteen and growing into womanhood, and I, previously taut of flesh and bone, was putting on a ring of fat that baffled me. I marveled at the profusion as I peed at the toilet, my belly now in the way of my morning release of coffee. But here I was, heavy and not bright enough to put two and two together and attribute the problem to beer and the heavy sauces that smothered my dinners. I thought of myself when I quit teaching, and thought of my family—my wife and daughter—whom I had to provide for.

But I quit because our daughter was raised—or nearly raised—and she was now five foot even, a hundred and six shapely pounds, bright, kind and thoughtful, well read, and shy as a pony. I did my job of raising a child, and I'm not ashamed to call it a job because one of the largest fears throughout my adult life, perhaps instilled even earlier, was that I had to get this done, that done, that over there done, and even some of yours done if you were lazy soul. I feared not completing whatever people wanted me to do. For sixteen years I felt that this daughter of ours must be raised, that I had to get her "done."

This was particularly urgent because my own father died when I was six, leaving a hole in my soul no bigger than a pinprick. Through this hole something rare was let out, and I suffered because another person—my drunk father under a ladder—did not get his earthly task done. He had more of an effect on my character dead than alive.

I feared this mortal absence for my daughter, that is, that I would die by accident. I spent a good portion of my adult life thinking like this: that Mariko is now nine years old, almost ten, that it's seven years to adulthood and after that I can die and everything would then be OK.

This was surely not my reaction when she was born early morning July 21, 1978, born with her eyes open and seemingly astonished by her appearance, as if a magician had pulled her from a hat. She was flecked with blood but not much, and on a medical scale of ten to zero (zero being dead), she was a nine. She was healthy and ours, and quickly I agreed to a new title: father. I was twenty-five, and although still full of my own childhood, something that I slowly relinquished only after I lost the spring in my legs, I was ready for parenthood.

During Mariko's babyhood, I felt like a flower that had just broken open, full of color and light and maybe even a wonderful scent. Sure, our daughter cried at night, fussed over cereals, filled her diapers with monstrous debris, and demanded time and our money, even the quarters and grimy dimes piled in the ashtray. Sure, we read books about raising a child and monitored her monthly progress, worried that she was unable to roll over in her third month, sit up at six months, waddle bravely from couch to coffee table at eleven months. But her arms and legs were plump as water balloons, and she was growing. As we suspected, everything evened out. She would soon be in her high chair, then out of her high chair and in her proper place at an inherited family table, round and full of creaks and ancient ticks.

I remember her arrival into my life, and my own tenderness toward her—she and I rollicking on the bed, diapers crinkling underneath her pumpkin-colored pajamas. I remember her discovery of the word *pipes,* and her tiny hand clutching my thumb as she led me to the number of pipes in our house—pipes under the sink, behind the washer, in the back of the toilet. I remember when she let go of a balloon and we watched the balloon's flight over a flowering plum tree and beyond the neighbor's roof. She broke down, hands coming to her face and crying, "I'll never see that balloon again!"

And she didn't, of course, but she did see other things—piles and piles of food, clothes, toys, rides to the zoo and park, kiddy concerts, all before she was five years old. She was privileged, mostly privileged because of her mother, who was kinder than me, wiser, and sober in her evaluation of skinned knees and runny noses. My wife and she had a loving regimen—mother and daughter in bed with a book and, just before the lamp was turned off, a made-up singsong:

Sotooda Odooda, Podewda codewda, Ahooh Permew,
Peacock, Penguin, Pegasus, Unicorn Butterfly,
Stuby the best and only goat that we know.

I had clues about what it was to be a man—to provide for family, to build something with one's hands. For a time we lived in a house nearly off its foundations, located on Cowper Street in Berkeley, named after Cowper, the poet who wrote "Variety is the spice of life." I ignored that foolish axiom which only led people astray and into harmful behavior. I tried to put my house in order by whacking at weeds, recementing brick and stone, planting, silencing the neighbor's radio, and seeing the foundation, literally and figuratively, repaired and put back right. I was a no-nonsense Joe, full of vigor, maybe too much vigor because I became obsessed with getting things done. If I first took care of the house, I figured, then I would subsequently please my wife and daughter; I could then look forward to the more telling business of teaching and writing.

During my late twenties I slipped into a depression and I began to think like this: Now I will lie here and sleep and when I wake I will be better. I repeated this every night for three years, repeating to myself that I was asleep, while in truth my eyes were closed and rolling about behind the lids. I felt paralyzed, listless. I prayed that, in time, the body would correct itself, like a hurt knee or a stab of pain near the lower back. Having been raised in a chorus of God Is Punishing You, I believed in waiting, expecting the gloom and confusion inside me to disappear like a scab. What was there to complain about? You had a family, a roof for this family, a job in which your hands only crab-step over typewriter keys. How dare you complain, my older, immigrant relatives might have scolded.

But the cement weight of insomnia left me slow of mind and body. I had a difficult time concentrating as I ghosted through my days, showing my teeth in theatrical attempts to appear jolly. I remember friends showing up at my house and not knowing their names, or what they were doing there. I had to leave rooms and be by myself for a moment, head lowered and a hand rubbing my forehead as I thought, Now who are these people? Are they my friends and Carolyn's? I remember Wolfgang Binder, a German scholar, interviewing me while we still lived on Cowper Street. I felt tired even before he asked me a question. I kept thinking, This man is from Germany. Don't forget that. Germany. He's here because . . . and then the mind went empty as a pail.

Fear overwhelmed me as I realized that the possibility of happiness was beyond me. But I knew enough to try to appear chipper while our daughter was around, say, in my lap or strapped in her car seat. I mustered all my strength into one heave-ho, let's be happy, when our daughter woke, pink faced, in the morning. I had to live up to an image. I knew that fathers were responsible for taking their sons and daughters places. For us, father and daughter, it was a clean park on Cedar Avenue, or a jungle gym in fog-bound San Francisco. While our daughter played with spoon and pail, I sat on the edge of the sandbox, pouring hourglass after hourglass of sand through the funnels of my hands. It wasn't that I was bored, a feeling parents know because of their disconnection—nonparticipation, really—from their children's play. It's just a big, watery yawn watching children play for any length of time.

I anticipated this mental fog would soon lift, and clarity would shine through as if from an open window on a sunny day. I began to dread dusk and see it as a monster that traveled up the street, filling the gaps between the branches of the trees with an ominous symbol. I began to fear evenings, knowing that I would eat dinner, bathe, sit on the couch with a magazine or book, and then glance over to the bedroom, aware that I would have to go there and lie down in a veil of darkness. While our daughter padded about in her pajamas, still squealing, still making the most of her quickly disappearing babyhood, a dread overwhelmed me. Like a child, I didn't want to climb into bed and see the lamp turned off. The night was a monster that pushed itself into my eyes, and I was scared.

It was a dreadful routine. In bed, I convinced myself that I was asleep, though I could hear my breathing and calculate each restless turn. But mornings, my eyes were raw and, I suspect, punishing to look at from almost any distance, especially the distance my wife and I had created because she was living with my moodiness. Daily, over cereal and our daughter's laughter, I feigned happiness, smiling so big that the tops of gums were showing.

Knowing that I was ill, I was obsessed with seeing that my daughter was raised. My days were godless, uninspiring, a rained-on fire sputtering to keep a flame going. Fearing failure, I became cautious and tentative in movements that would risk an accident. I stayed home more and more, and canceled my subscription to the newspaper—why should I read about others falling apart? My hygiene became neurotic. Like a raccoon at a stream, I washed my hands before touching our daughter, say lifting her into or out of her high chair. I opened doors for her because the world was filled with germs that didn't show up in your system until it was too late. Eat public food at school functions? Out of the question. Invite a school chum to sleep over? You must be crazy.

During the height of my depression, I began to write furiously, albeit not brilliantly, and the subjects regarded our daughter. Three years old, she assembled a vocabulary that was inventive, even poetic. I listened to her quasi-philosophical turns of phrases, noting lines like, "The days are filled with air," a line that I later incorporated into a poem. And one day, while passing a chemical plant, she chirped, "The bad air has replaced the good air in my nostrils." When a Buddha-shaped poet friend spent the evening, the ever social Mariko offered him an animal cracker and asked where he was from. He scratched his belly, ho-hoed at her pleasant demeanor, and told her that he was from Fresno, the grape country. This was summer in our backyard. She raised her clear, unspoiled eyes to our plum tree and announced, "I'm from the plum country myself."

It's not uncommon for a writer's children to appear in his or her stories or poems, to become the subjects of his personal essays. Surely children rob writers of precious time. They taketh away days and weeks, if not years, but they also replenish our sterile waters. And it was true for me. Through my depression, I convinced myself that if I wrote about the best things in my life, namely my wife and daughter, I would get better. Ignorant and reluctant to see a doctor, I tried to write myself out of depression, to appear jolly and a crack-up, though there were warnings in my poems, as in "These Days":

> In my dreams
> A child is crying into a steering wheel
> And Omar is holding onto a tree
> And a shot horse is staring me into the next room.
>
> That was last night, and the night before.
> Today the two of us walked
> In a park—cruel place
> With pigeons bickering over spewed popcorn.
> Later I heard on the radio—
> A plane on the water,
> And the gulls pecking the dead into great numbers.
>
> Or so I imagined.
> And so it might be because it's all possible—
> The dead with wings in their hair,
> Another war, the half-lid
> Of the sun going down in dust.
>
> This scares me.
> If we go up in ash we come down as ash.
> And what are we then?
> A dark crescent under a fingernail,
> A smudge in the air?

Believe me daughter, I want to say something true,
That we will get up on time,
That I'll have coffee and you an egg,
Yellow sun on a plate.
But I can't ever say this.
The world is mad.
Dying things show up behind doors.
Soldiers toss severed feet for the TV audience.

Little one, stay where you are,
Hold hands, and don't let go.

I had an unfounded notion that if we went somewhere, especially on drives in the country, that these symptoms of psychic lethargies would dissipate like fog. I had to get out on weekends. So I pushed our daughter's stroller along pebbled paths, jarring her little frame. I pushed this stroller everywhere, putting miles on her bones. We saw geysers, chilly beaches, small-town parades, country museums, cows and goats behind barbed wire, kites crisscrossing the sky, ponds with turd-colored frogs, and petting zoos—common pastimes for families with children. I felt that if I exhausted myself with the riches of the world, then I would sleep at the end of a day, happy for our daughter.

It occurs to me now that my attitude of Let's-get-it-done was also coming from the direction of our daughter, vague hints that said, Father, it is bad now but it will be better later. Perhaps her sweetness kept me from sinking into self-destruction. Perhaps the gloss of her beauty saved me. The more I wrote about her—poems and personal essays by the boatloads—the more the chances that this veil of depression would lift; the monstrous atmosphere inside my head would clear up. Only now do I attribute my release to my daughter, but back then, during this mentally confusing period on Cowper Street, I attributed this change to my study, which I had lined with sheets of cork to deaden the street and neighborhood sounds of kids and bikes. I had even placed a large, expensive Plexiglas over the front window, further deadening the natural and unnatural sounds of the world.

By fall 1983, I was getting better, taking less time to recognize people, becoming slightly more mentally focused. But was I there? No. I was still distracted by depression. I was working on my first prose efforts, recollections that would become *Living Up the Street*. I worked at my typewriter furiously because I was coming up for tenure, which, I felt, was another thing I had to get done. I needed more evidence than poetry and occasional book reviews; also, I was certain that if I kept writing, especially lighter stuff, I would heal myself. This was the real reason for my ferocity of pages and pages of prose and poetry—the effort to write myself out of a funk.

Nights. The house creaked and the plumbing inside the walls howled like the wind. Breathing in our daughter's room. I was living this notion: I'm going to go to bed and when I close my eyes I will sleep. Mind you, I did this with a peculiar pattern of sleeping on the left side of the mattress, legs slightly set apart, blankets up to my chin. The repetition was endless as waves, nearly four years without a sound sleep, convinced that it had to stop. Then the unexpected happened in November 1983. I woke up, groggy, heavy of limb, the corners of my eyes gripped by a squeeze of sludge, hair tousled and yawning, aware that I had slept more than my customary one or two hours. The wait was over, and I rose for my coffee, a different man.

I didn't tinker with my sleep by reading about depression. I was then, as now, not wholly curious about this illness, which can sink people to their knees, utterly destroy them. I would prefer to strangle all the self-help authors or honest-to-goodness psychiatrists than to open a book and discover what had happened. I would prefer to pretend that this episode of eaten-up years didn't occur. My business was a matter of seeing our daughter raised.

My father died when I was six, the rumors of his passing coming to me as I pulled flowers from a bush on the side of my grandmother's house. Interestingly, the day before my father died a bird flew into our house on Braly Street, a symbol of death in many cultures. It occured in our own household as well: I woke to a noise in the living room, a rattle that sounded like papers being stepped on. When I got up to see, a bird was in the living room looking at me with its liquid and soulless eyes. My heart leapt, literally, my upper body jumping of its own accord. This bird was showing me something, mocking me. I felt that it was after our daughter, then age six, the same age I was when my father died. With the front door open and my hands choking a threatening broom, I chased the bird from the house. I stood on the porch, breathing hard, the bird no longer within sight but somewhere hidden in the neighbor's tree. I returned to bed, shaken. I sat on the edge of the bed, then settled back in, only to hear the same fluttering noise. When I got up, the bird was again in the house, this time perched on wadded newspaper in the fireplace. Crazed, I chased the bird out of the house and would have pulled out its feathers, one by one, it if it hadn't flown onto the roof and out of sight.

We raised our daughter, saw that she was loved by not only ourselves but by others. I buried her pets, drove her miles in every direction, bought her a horse, took her hundreds of places, and saw, above all, to get her an education. Moreover, during my time with her, I feigned happiness when, in truth, my depression was as insurmountable as the Himalayas. Wasn't this something? I gave her life and she returned it to me by her presence.

Occasionally I see fathers with their daughters, fathers who, on first glance, might be bored as they hover over them at play. But how many are ill, mentally pulled into themselves, depressed and fraudulent protectors, bad clowns squeezing out their own cajoling laughter? On the surface, these fathers may appear familial magistrates for their children, fathers who loom tall as trees. They are cheerful; they hold pails for them, toys, or upright spilled trikes. They carefully peel back ice cream wrappers and rub a healthy gloss on apples. They are young fathers, not unlike me sixteen years before. What's in the heart? I sometimes wonder. What advice could I, a man walking past, offer? How could I solve the first crisis of a child falling over shoelaces? Or the serious struggles that follow? I walk past, or jog past. What can I say in my injured heart? My friend, the world was ill, and still I got it done.

4

Separations

Disneyland

James Alan McPherson

1.

SEVERAL WEEKS AGO, as a kind of joke, I sent Rachel, my daughter, by E-mail, a line from an old song by Lambert, Hendricks, and Ross and Louis Armstrong:

> If you're king for only a day,
> How'd you go about having your way...?

This is the answer that came back:

If I were king, people couldn't blast their bass players in their cars, and if they did they would be punished by listening to "All Things Considered" on NPR all day long. Except that (if I were King) NPR wouldn't have much to report on the radio. Only good news. And so they would fill up the air time by playing songs backwards and giving $100 to listeners who can name the tune. Everyone would have to smile at least once a day! Band-Aids wouldn't hurt when you yanked them off sores; the walls in dentists' offices would be covered with Waterhouse and Bosetti murals instead of lame, symmetrical, diamond patterns; and no one would have to listen to elevator music while on hold—only Swing. If I were King oranges would grow prepeeled, and pens wouldn't leak, and no one would be named Gertrude. Parks would have giant tree houses with signs that read: People of Any Height May Climb! Anyone could order off a damn kiddy menu, and swivel chairs would be a requirement for every dinner table—so if conversation got really boring people could twirl around instead. Everyone would have their own ideas

about religion and no judgments about anyone else's. . . . [Weddings:]
At twilight everyone would wander around a giant park with spouting
fountains and a double rainbow would streak the sky. A church chime
would ring at 7:00 P.M. (you know, the one that sounds like our door-
bell) and that would be the sign for everybody to make a circle (not caring or even wondering if you're standing next to a bum, a Ph.D., or a
movie star) and do the Hokey Pokey. That's what it's all about.

I was amazed by the reach and vitality of Rachel's imagination as she
attempted to re-order the world according to her own sense of happiness. I sent her another E-mail, one saying this:

You have learned that God created the world in six days, and on the seventh day He rested. But this is not entirely true. I have heard it said that
on the seventh day God was not yet pleased with his creations. So on that
day he created another thing that would be able to celebrate all the work
He had done on the first six days. On the seventh day God created
IMAGINATION, and he gave this thing dominion over all else He had
created. The person who is blessed with this is able to stand in his own
place and at the same time project himself into another person's place,
see from the eyes of that person, and understand the world from that
person's point of view. This gift is called "compassion," and it is a very,
very rare thing.

Rachel, at eighteen, is doubly privileged. She has had imaginative as
well as emotional support, all that I could give her from a great distance, for all her life. She seems to be a very happy and self-directed
young woman. She graduated from high school in Charlottesville, Virginia, on June 5, 1997. She came to Iowa City for ten days, and then went
off to New York to enroll in the Alvin Ailey Summer Dance Workshop.
I supported her eight weeks in New York as a kind of graduation gift to
her. Other friends in New York—Nancy Ramsey, Stanley Crouch, Al-
bert Murray and his family, Faith Childs, Suketu and Sunita Mehta,
Ana Debevoise, Sherman Malone—supported her emotionally. Rachel
has benefited from being "closely held" by impromptu structures of dependability, which can be improvised around friends in any other part
of the United States, as well as in England, Japan, and Australia. Both
her life and my own have been blessed by instances of kindly interfer-

ence which, while renewing our spirits, have taught me that the increase in the range of their possibility depends on one's involvement in the lives of people outside of one's own group. This is the Great Road that Rachel and I have traveled since she was a baby. Now that she is eighteen, and enrolled in college, I think and hope, and even pray, that she is secure and well adjusted and *whole* in the deepest human sense.

In a recent correspondence with a divorced writer, he expressed how extremely painful his isolation from his daughter was. He loved her a great deal; she lived with her mother in Atlanta, while he lived in Baltimore. In writing back to him about this modern condition of alienation between fathers and children, an alienation that results from divorce, I restrained an impulse to quote to him a line from a song in Walt Disney's *Peter Pan*: "You can fly, you can fly, you can fly."

I know the truth of this from my own experience.

I will not give in to the temptation to finger all the details of my own divorce except to say that it was extremely complicated and extremely bitter. All my efforts to negotiate a peaceful end to a very bad marriage failed, and this void was quickly filled by predatory lawyers. Since I had announced publicly that my only goal was to get appropriate time with my daughter and then get out of Charlottesville, Rachel, who was then not quite two years old, became a pawn in the manipulation of lawyers and other, hidden forces that were determined that I would remain "captive." She was withheld from me through a series of devices, even when visitation times had already been scheduled. When I responded in anger, my voice was recorded and used against me at another time. But it was here that an instance of what I have called "kindly interference" took place. I went to see Shirley Porter, a black woman who worked as a nanny for mothers in the Charlottesville community. Shirley was a wise and kindly woman, one who wanted to be fair. Since Rachel spent most of her nights at Shirley's home, while being withheld from me, I would go to Shirley's home in the early evenings, eat dinner with her and Rachel, and help Shirley give Rachel a bath. Then I would sleep on the floor next to Rachel's crib. The next morning, before the other "mommies" brought their children to Shirley's house, I would help Shirley give Rachel breakfast, and even share the meal with her. If any of the "mommies" showed up early, while I was still there, I would hide in Shirley's closet until they left. On those Sundays when Rachel was with me, I would take her to Shirley's church. The two of us would sit, Rachel between us, on the same bench. Shirley Porter risked her own economic well-being to help us in this way.

In the early spring of the following year, 1981, a second small miracle occured. I had been trying my best to heed the advice of friends in other parts of the country: *"Get out of there!"* I saw two jobs being advertised—one at Tucson, by Vance Bourjaily, and another at Iowa, by Jack Leggett. Both men were understanding, but Jack Leggett was especially kind. On a Sunday morning, about one month later, he called me in Charlottesville and said, "Jim, the job is yours in the fall, if you are able to take it. In addition, we want you to teach summer school." Jack had a gentle laugh, an easy, patrician manner. I believe that he was incapable of kicking anyone who was down. It was simply a matter of breeding and habit.

But the most important incident of kindly interference, the one that set Rachel and me on the pathway leading to the Great Road, came in May of that same year. By this time I had secured, through the legal system, some visitation time with Rachel. We had one overnight every other weekend, plus one afternoon together on Wednesdays. One Saturday evening when I brought Rachel to my small apartment, I saw an Express Mail envelope taped to the door. I tore it down, believing it was another notice from one of the credit card companies to which, back then, I owed my future. Rachel and I had worked out certain rituals for her overnights with me: counting off the steps as we walked up them, playing games while she ate her dinner and while she took her bath. We had a plastic windup duck, and this toy would go into the bathtub of water. And then we would splash water, sing songs, and play until the antique clock next to her crib chimed 8:00 P.M. This hour was our Sacred Time: the eight chimes signaled that our play would be transported to Rachel's crib, where it would continue until she fell asleep. But that Saturday night our bath ritual was interrupted by a telephone call. When I answered a voice with great authority in it said, "Young man, I . . ." But I never allowed the voice to continue. I said, "Look, I'm giving my daughter a bath. Call me some other time." Then I hung up. After Rachel and I had finished *Goodnight Moon* and she had fallen asleep, I opened the Express Mail letter. It was from the MacArthur Foundation in Chicago. It informed me that I had been awarded a five-year grant of $192,000. Later that evening the telephone rang again. It was Roderick MacArthur, who had been personally calling up the winners of that very first round of awards. I had hung up on him. I apologized profusely. Then I spoke with Gerald Freund, who was then the director of the Prize Fellows Program. I thanked him, but asked if public news about my selection could be avoided. I tried to explain to him the personal complexities of a situation that must have been a world away from his understanding; what to a white person would be an honor can also be, to a black person, the sense that one is being made a target in a society devoted to white supremacy. Gerald Freund just could not understand why I did not want the news about my recent good fortune to be made public. But I could remember, very well, just why I had avoided all publicity after, less than three years before, I had won a Pulitzer Prize for fiction. I could remember the contempt of a white colleague, who sneered intentionally in my presence, "Somebody around here is getting *too much* attention!" But Gerald Freund said that the news about the awards had already been sent out for publication on Monday morning. He said I should be proud, having been the first choice on the first list of MacArthur Fellows.

On Monday morning, I said to the caller from National Public Radio, "The gods are playful."

Later that week, I told a reporter for the *Washington Post*, who had come to Charlottesville to interview me, "I'm going to give some of the money to my church, I'm going to take Mrs. Julia Smith to visit her relatives more often, and I'm going to be the best father I can be to Rachel."

Mrs. Julia Smith, an elderly black woman whom I had met a little over one year before, had been, in those days, my constant companion. As a matter of fact, part of the interview had taken place at Mrs. Smith's home in Barboursville. Rachel was with me. I was holding Rachel while I talked with the reporter. The reporter later wrote that Mrs. Julia Smith kept saying "Moo" to Rachel. Rachel herself kept repeating "Candy."

Rachel was in my arms holding a lollipop when she said this.

Rachel remembers very little about those early years, but she does retain some emotional clues. She remembers the plastic duck, she remembers the antique clock, and she remembers the crib next to it. She also remembers Mrs. Julia Smith. Some years ago, I asked her who, of all our friends, were the best people. She replied, "Mrs. Julia Smith, Jo-ellen MacDougall, Ellie Simmons, and the man at the Coralville Fruit Stand" (where we buy our Christmas tree each year). A year or so ago, Rachel, in high school, located through a library computer a copy of the old interview in the *Washington Post*. She sent me a decorated picture of a much younger version of myself holding her while she licked a lolli-pop. Through some miracle, Rachel seems to have escaped the extreme pain of that period.

But I did not.

I completed my last classes at Virginia, adjusting my schedule to meet the very powerful legal pressures placed on me. One of them was a list of written interrogatories, one hundred or more, and the very first enquiry was an accounting of all my books by authors, titles, dates pur-chased, places purchased, prices paid. I hired a student named Edward Jones to help me with the list. We spent almost one week listing close to 2,000 books. But I taught well that last semester. The student evalua-tions, which were turned in to the people in the English Department office, were glowing. I know this because, for some reason, they were never filed with the proper university or state officials. Although they were turned over to the English office when my classes ended in May, in the late fall of that same year, when I had begun teaching again, this time in Iowa, some kindly soul placed them in my departmental mail-box and Edward Jones retrieved them for me. The students said, "Excel-lent." "He is the best teacher here." "He knows too much." My heart grew full when I read, almost six months later, these student evalua-tions from my last semester in Charlottesville. And I will thank, for the rest of my life, the person who made this kindly interference on my be-half. This angel must have been familiar with the destructive strategy then at work: hamstring the suspect, and then gossip abroad that he is crazy.

But before this strategy could work its will, I was in Iowa.

Before I left, even before the custody hearings, I took some things I had purchased for Rachel to her mother's house. Some of my former colleagues were there. One of them said, "*Who* do you think you are?

You've *fired* the University of Virginia?" We were standing in the front yard. Rachel was shouting "Jim . . . Jim?" in imitation of my outraged former colleagues. I picked Rachel up and I kissed her. I told my daughter, "I will always come for you. I will always come for you."

Then I drove, nonstop, to St. Louis. I rested there. And then I drove the rest of the way to Iowa.

I flew back three times for the custody hearings during the summer of 1981, while I was teaching two courses at Iowa. Each time I was pressured to return to the marriage and to Charlottesville. I finally asked the judge to get the issue settled. But when his final decree arrived at my apartment in Iowa City, in late July, I decided to not open the envelope until after my summer school classes were over. The envelope lay on my desk for over three weeks. Finally, a friend from New Haven, Sherman Malone, came by bus through Iowa City on her way back from a camping trip with her family. We had lunch, and Sherman pleaded with me to open the envelope. She went home with me and watched as I read the judge's language: full custody to the mother, limited visitation rights, hefty alimony and child support, and lawyers' fees. In addition, in response to the largesse of the MacArthur Foundation, my apartment in Charlottesville, without any formal inspection, was decreed "inferior" to the home of the custodial parent.

Sherman Malone said that I got drunk and raged all night in my bed. She told me that she lay awake all night, in her sleeping bag in the living room, and listened to my ravings. Sherman told me, when I took her the next day to the bus depot, for her trip back to New Haven, that I never expressed any anger toward her. Then she left. In the evening of that same day, I went out to Lone Tree, Iowa, to keep a dinner appointment with Bob Shacochis and Catfish, Bob's companion. A number of young writers from my classes that summer were also at Bob's home in Lone Tree. But I did not feel teacherly that evening. Emotionally unequipped for small talk, I excused myself and went up to Bob and Catfish's bedroom and lay in their bed. Later, Bob came up and asked what was wrong. I disclosed a few facts to him. And it was then, during that bleak evening, that another instance of kindly intervention occurred. Bob Shacochis insisted that I go for a drive with him in his car. We drove slowly along the narrow, dirt roads of Lone Tree, up hillocks and down dales, through the dying summer light. Bob drove aimlessly past tall cornfields, past soybeans begging for harvest. We smelled farmlands and animal manure in the moist breezes of sunset. The heavy smells seemed to be insisting that one form of life was *intended* to sustain another form of life. The bursting crops said that this was Nature's Way, and that all of life was, finally, only an extension of this same blueprint in Nature's Plan. Kindly, cooking-loving Bob Shacochis drove me up and down those roads, desperate to find some way to help, until something renewing from Nature began flowing into me from those fields and I knew that I would not die. When we returned to Bob's house, well after dark, people wondered what had been wrong with me. Bob never said a word to anyone.

This was in mid-August of 1981, when I touched bottom and slowly began to rebuild.

I wrote to the judge, acknowledging his decree, and asked him, as chancellor, if the situation could still be moved toward arbitration instead of remaining in the legal system. He wrote back to me, saying that he was bound by law. He also suggested that I should return to Charlottesville, because the noncustodial parent and the child "tend to lose a great deal." I wrote back that I could not return. I also wrote my resignation from the University of Virginia on the back of the judge's decree. And it was here that my priorities came into clear focus, and it was here that I began to make some firm decisions.

I had about $3,000 each month coming in from the MacArthur Foundation, plus about $29,000 per year coming from the University of Iowa, plus another $6,000 for each summer that I taught summer school. In addition, the MacArthur Foundation awarded, in those days, an institutional grant of $15,000 for a period of five years to the institution with which I was connected. I had an apartment in Charlottesville, and another one in Iowa City, and friends in both places. Most important of all, I still had my imagination. I decided that I would not spend any of the MacArthur money on myself. The institutional grant, amounting to $75,000 over a period of five years, I gave to the University of Iowa Foundation for the support of young writers in the workshop. Jack Leggett and I agreed, over a handshake, that the money would be used to support any talented writer who, because of special circumstances, was not eligible for the usual areas of financial aid. I made a will, one leaving everything I owned to Rachel, and I named my older sister, Mary, Rachel's guardian, just in case something should happen to me. I tried as best I could to strip myself of everything that was a distraction to my focus. I began, then, in my *imagination*, to view the country as one big house. My bedroom was in Iowa City. Rachel's bedroom was in Charlottesville. Friends had guest rooms, for Rachel and for me, in Richmond, in Washington, D.C., in Stamford and in New Haven, in New York, in Boston, in Cambridge, in Chicago, in Oakland, and in Los Angeles. All Rachel and I had to do, with the MacArthur money, and with my own earnings after that largesse had run out, was to move from room to room in this huge house, bonding as we went with each other and with our friends.

It was then that I began to fly.

One weekend each month Rachel and I spent "quality time" together with Edward Jones, my former student, who lived in my old apartment on Little High Street in Charlottesville.

I hired a therapist in Charlottesville, one who expressed outrage over the terms of the judge's decree. He helped me negotiate more time with Rachel. He suggested that, since Rachel was older, she ought to be able to spend one weekend each month, and then one full week each month, with me in Iowa City.

Then Rachel and I began to fly.

The therapist suggested that, because Rachel was still older, she should spend two weeks, then three weeks, then six weeks during the summers with me in Iowa City.

But, later, this same therapist declared that he could no longer do any more for me. He advised me to return to Charlottesville.

In 1986, after a court hearing, the legal system of Charlottesville conceded to me the full summer. I also "won" spring breaks, including Easter, every other Christmas, plus one weekend each month from after Rachel's school on Friday afternoon until school time on Monday mornings. The lawyer who secured this "boon" for me noted, with some theatrical relish, that the long weekend each month made room for me to remain with my daughter until time for her school on Monday morning. This, he said, was the best possible reason for me to return to Charlottesville for good. He told me, with some hint of brotherly love, "Now, don't make yourself such a stranger to Charlottesville."

I made myself a stranger.

Rachel and I met in Washington, D.C. We met in New York. We met in Boston. The United Airlines people at Dulles came to know Rachel through their escort service. She told me that they always said, when she was connecting at Dulles for her flight into Chicago, "There goes Rachel again." The ticket agents and security people at the Cedar Rapids Airport also came to know me and our ritual. One of the security guards, a woman, would always say when she saw me, "There goes that father who loves his daughter." Rachel came to Cedar Rapids; I went to Dulles or to National. When she was still too young to travel unescorted, I *imagined* a pathway for us. I hired Opie Porter, Shirley Porter's son, to drive Rachel from Charlottesville to Dulles or to National. My usual pathway was through St. Louis. To reach St. Louis on the very first flight out of Cedar Rapids, I had to get up early enough to drive from Iowa City to the Cedar Rapids Airport to take the flight at 6:45 A.M. When I reached St. Louis, and was sure that I would be booked on the flight into National or Dulles, I would call up Opie Porter in Charlottesville and tell him to begin his drive. My own flight usually arrived at National at 11:30 A.M. The same flight back to St. Louis, and from there into Cedar Rapids, left National Airport at 12:30 P.M. During this hour, I would arrive at National, Opie would arrive with Rachel in his car; she would be led to me, and then she and I would take the 12:30 P.M. flight back to St. Louis, then back to Cedar Rapids, arriving at 3:30 P.M. or so. Then we would drive in my car directly to my class at 4:30 P.M. Rachel would sit through the class with the grace of the innocent. And then, after class, we would go *home*.

Rachel passed through dangers. Once, during the Persian Gulf War, she told me by telephone that she could not fly anymore because Saddam Hussein had threatened to blow up the airplanes. She, like many other people, was very frightened of the Arabs. I asked her if she actually *knew* any Arabs. She said that she did not. I told her that I knew some Arabs, and that if she found the courage to fly from Charlottesville to Dulles, I would fly there to meet her. And then we would spend the weekend in Washington, D.C., and I would introduce her to an

Arab. She consented. Then I called up Sam Hamod, an old friend, a Lebanese Arab with roots in Detroit, and asked if Rachel and I could meet him and Shirley, his girlfriend, in Washington. After Rachel and I arrived, and after Sam came to our hotel, I told Rachel, "This is Sam Hamod. He is a friend and an Arab." Rachel liked Sam because of his *personality*, but she especially liked Shirley. We spent a number of years, during many trips, exploring Washington with Sam and Shirley.

Just before Christmas, during a visitation period, Rachel called me from O'Hare Airport with quiet hysteria in her voice. A massive snow and ice storm had close down the airport, and all flights in and out of O'Hare had been canceled. And since the cancellations had been due to the weather and not to any mechanical failures, United Airlines would not be responsible for meals and lodging for its stranded passengers. Rachel was then about ten years old. She had no money, and was being obliged to sleep in a chair or else on the floor of the airport with the other children of divorce, tagged like Christmas gifts, who were serving out their obligations to distant parents. I heard in my daughter's voice, that cold December evening, the quiet desperation of the many millions of young people who, through no fault of their own, had become casualties of two decades of gender warfare between selfish adults. In reality, the children had had to assume the responsibilities of adults, while the adults were content to dramatize their own fantasies. During that hard December night, I sat at my table and made telephone calls, like thousands of other anonymous parents, to every possible source of help. I called up Leon Forrest in Evanston. I called up Marshall and Irene Patner in Hyde Park. I called up a former student, Joe Hurka, who lived in a suburb closer to O'Hare than Evanston and Hyde Park. There is a kind of doom-filled desperation, if not hysteria, that comes when one realizes that almost every established structure of dependability—parenting, family, technology—can be rendered useless when the mysterious currents of life, or when the indifferences of Nature, decide to announce themselves. While the old structures still remain defined and intact and viable, the flow of life, which has moved beyond them, looks back at this impotency and laughs at the naïveté of those who once placed all their faith in human inventions of the mind. I learned that night, or perhaps I only *relearned*, that all such dead ends are under the control of the gods of life, and that one must depend on *them* for magic, for instances of kindly intervention.

All of the friends I called offered to drive to O'Hare and rescue Rachel. But Joe Hurka's father had a tractioned car, and his suburb was closest to O'Hare. Joe Hurka and his father went to Rachel, while I waited by the telephone ready to comfort her if, by some miracle, she was able to get through the crowd of hysterical children and use the telephone again. Well after midnight, Joe Hurka called me from his home. They had arrived safely and Rachel was in bed. Joe advised me to also go to bed. He said that Rachel was fine, that she had viewed the experience as an adventure, and that I was much more upset than she was. He said that, before she went to bed, Rachel had gone out to have a snowball fight with his mother, and that the entire family had been struck by her calm, politeness, and good manners. Joe promised that he and his father would drive Rachel back to O'Hare in the morning and put her on the first flight into Cedar Rapids. He advised me to go out to the airport as early as possible so that, when Rachel arrived, mine would be the first face she saw.

I did not go to bed that night. I waited until dawn, and after Joe Hurka called to say that they were leaving for O'Hare, I drove, ahead of the snow plows and the salt spreaders, to the Cedar Rapids Airport. When the flight from O'Hare arrived and when Rachel came down the jetway, I thought my heart would break.

Rachel knows very little about my side of the story.

2.

A belief in the possibility of magic, or of acts of kindly intervention, has been one of the sources of our bond during all these years. I did not want my own pain, my own bitterness, to affect Rachel, so I intentionally grounded our bond in instances of spiritual nurture as a way of calling her attention to the possibility of magic in life, or perhaps I did this in order to heal myself. I just do not know. I know that, like many black males, I had never had a loving bond with a father. The void that this loss left in me was, when I consider it, a kind of opportunity. I was "free" to imagine the kind of father-child bond I would have liked for myself. I knew, from my own experiences as a child, what *I must not do*.

But I did not know exactly what *I should do*. I was thus forced to improvise my way. During all these years, Rachel has not wanted for anything of a material nature. I grew up in extreme poverty, and, as for all other children of poverty, the expatriation of this condition from the lives of our children is the first order of business, the first "Thou shalt not." But I wanted Rachel to exhaust her appetites for material comforts early on, and then I wanted her to look for something beyond the material world. I think I wanted, first of all, to open up a philosophical issue for her.

It is common knowledge that the human spirit has, for its illusion of stability, a sense of being totally encompassed, of being *held*, in a reality that has a structure of dependability. That is, all things *inside* the self and all things *outside* the self, ideally, must cohere, must seem to belong *together*. This is the gift of childhood, the gift of natural integrity that is basic to human equipment. I did not want Rachel to lose this gift, even as I flew with her over a corrupt and uncaring world. I wanted very badly to provide her with something she could hold onto, through childhood and adolescence, and as far into adulthood as she could carry the idea. Simply put, I wanted her to know that something *more* existed beyond the conventional structures of dependability. This thing had to do with, *has* to do with, the frightening vistas that come into focus when all things on which we once depended—family, status, settled orders—erode, and we are left to make a path for ourselves. During such times, when the gods of life seem to be laughing at our mind-based illusions, our only refuge must be in the realm of magic, or religion, or imagination, or in those instances of kindly interference that flow from the coveted goodness in the hearts of other people. This realm is beyond race, or class, or region, or all the other structures of social gradation. It ministers to life itself, to what is best in other people. I had come to learn this the hard way, and I wanted to pass it on, with my approval, to Rachel. *Something is always with us, in the darkness as well as in the light. And if this is true, then one must walk through the world, even in the darkness, by the same light one saw when all was light.* Without really believing this, I tried my best to walk with Rachel through all the dark places as if I could guide us by my concentration on the light. This seems to me the footpath to the Great Road that

would take my daughter toward some absolute meanings. As for myself, I could only approach that road by way of the footpath. Perhaps
this was, finally, my destiny. But I wanted very badly for Rachel to leave
the footpath I had trod for her and get on the Great Road that will lead,
eventually, to transcendent meanings.

Perhaps, for this reason, we began at Disneyland.

The three great revolutions into which my daughter was born—the
one called civil rights, the one called feminist, and the one called technological—had, as one of their consequences, eroded all accepted
structures of dependability, structures which, in much of human history, had helped define what was meaningful in human life. A black
person was *supposed* to be a servant, an inferior. A woman was *supposed*
to be an appendage to a man. A technique was *supposed* to be something linked to ritual, and the ritual itself was *supposed* to be an affir-
mation of ancient, ancestral imperatives. Then, quite suddenly, all of
this changed, and a new generation was left with the responsibility of
walking its way through a broken world, one with no certainties and,
much more crucial, one with no real purchase on the future. The fear
and the anger and the defensivenesses which resulted from this massive
breakdown has caused those who were supposed to be innocents, those
who were supposed to be the saving remnants, the future generations,
to retreat in fear from the world that has been made for them. They
seem to not want that future, because they cannot yet see themselves at
home in it. Newspaper accounts, daily, provide stories about young
people in all regions and groups and classes, acting out this sense of
spiritual impotence. Stories of killings in Iowa, in New Jersey, in New
York, in Mississippi. And closer to home, my daughter tells me that a
young woman she knew, named Elizabeth, hung herself on April 23 of
this year. She was a brilliant young woman, was about to graduate at the
top of her class, had everything going for her. And yet she hung herself,
without telling any of her friends that she was in extreme pain. And it
is here that I want to believe that some of what I have been trying to pass
on to Rachel may have been effective. Rachel tells me that, ever since
Elizabeth's suicide, she had taken it upon herself to write letters to all
her friends, letting them know that she will be there for them if they are
ever in that kind of deep despair. Rachel, I want to believe, has learned

about the magic that derives from instances of kindly intervention. She has learned this, I want to believe, from the sense of magic that has been cultivated between the two of us, over the past eighteen years. We have gone to Disneyland, a place where the established order of dependability soars up into fields of magic. Perhaps Rachel has seen, in that Magic Kingdom, the places at which the rational world, with all its assaults, and the irrational world, with all its potency, meet and dance in some kind of benign compromise about the hidden gods of life and their intentions. I do not know. I do know that I have tried, despite my own pain, to take my daughter along the footpath leading to this Great Road.

We went to Disneyland many times and in many different ways.

We began with fireflies. We began with sitting on the back steps, on the front steps, of our house in Iowa City, always at dusk, and watching motes of light scramble and blink in hurried conversation about their hidden secrets. My girlfriend helped deepen this mood. Her name was Vera. She was less than two feet tall, and she lived under my dining room table. She only came out at night, and even then she disclosed herself only to me. A magic tree soon grew up just outside Rachel's bedroom window. It was in secret communication with a magic rock we found by sheer luck. If one wished sincerely enough for something, while holding the magic rock, that thing wished for sometimes appeared, overnight, on the branches of or under the magic tree. We attended church. Almost every Christmas Eve, when Rachel was with me, Santa would call from some point on his journey to speak with us and to determine whether we were being good. We always wrote letters to him and to Mrs. Claus, wishing them well. Fresh food—carrots, eggnog, peanuts, candies—were left on the windowsill just behind our Frazer Fir, sweet-smelling Christmas tree. Santa and his crew always had a feast. They always left us many great gifts. The only time I was slighted was when I wrote my own letter to Santa in the braggadocio of rap lyrics. I have never, ever repeated this mistake. The Easter Bunny, too, came to our house each spring. He could be counted on to leave bounteous Easter baskets brimming with choice candies. The Iowa Tooth Fairy came, once in a while, usually disguised as a pig. When the accelerating technological revolution produced the VCR, we considered this artifact benign, but only if used for a good purpose. We secured tapes of Disney's *Dumbo, Bambi,* and *Jack and the Beanstalk.* We waited breathlessly for each new Disney release. Once, with this same streak of luck, we secured a copy of Disney's *Song of the South* in a London department store. In a mall in downtown Washington, D.C., we located a store dealing with items for magical acts. We always went there to study the demonstrations, and we secured a great many devices. We spent the winter months planning, by long-distance telephone, our plans for the summer and for vacation trips in late August. Our watchword was, always, *"When the leaves come, we'll go to Iowa."* We flew, on magic carpets, to London, to Paris, to Madrid. We toured the Tower of London, walked the streets of Paris, took a train to the Disneyland in the suburbs of Paris. We took a bus tour from Madrid to Toledo.

But most of all, for at least six summers, we went to Disneyland. At first we went by train across the Rocky Mountains and the Cascades. We flew to Los Angeles from Seattle, and we drove a car from the city into Anaheim. We went to *Dis*-ney Land, diz, diz, diz *Dis*-ney-land. Then we went by airplane directly into the John Wayne Airport. We took friends there with us. Sometimes we stayed for almost a full week. We took Jarilyn Woodard, Yarri Lutz, from Iowa City to the freeways of Los Angeles leading to Anaheim. Driving, I would say to my female passengers, *"Let's go, men!"* And they would answer, *"We're not men!"* We went to *Dis*-neyland, to diz, diz, diz *Dis*-neyland. We met friends from Los Angeles there: Cynthia Kadohata, Jeannette Miyamoto, Adrienna Woodard, Brenda Chadwick. Jarilyn Woodard, Rachel's best friend, always went with us; and her sister, Adrienna, always met us there. Once we went there with the entire Woodard family, Jarilyn's mother, Barbara, included. While the young people explored, Barbara and I would sit and talk about adult things.

The best thing about Disneyland is that the real world is left at the door. Nothing unhappy gets into that place. It is a controlled environment, one strolled and controlled by infectious illusions. Mickey, Goofy, Minnie, and Company are always visible in the crowds to remind people of the possibility of magic. I have a picture of Rachel, when she was four or five years old, trying to pull Arthur's sword from its stone. I have pictures of her hugging Mickey, Goofy, Tinkerbell, Peter Pan, Wendy, Captain Hook. We always stayed late enough to watch the Electric Lights Parade, one in which the entire product of Walt Disney's imagination, waving from lighted floats, would parade through the entire length of Disneyland. Thousands of people stay until closing time just to see this act. The adults among them, from almost every nation in the world, seem, at that special time, to forget that they are adults and glow with the magic of children. In that place, both imaginations and spirits are renewed. It is a place chock-full of kindly interferences. I have heard it said that Walt Disney was inspired by God. I do not know this for a fact, but I do know that we went many times to *Dis*-ney-land, to diz, diz, diz, diz *Dis*-neyland, always looking for something.

Rachel liked the Peter Pan ride and also the Pirates of the Caribbean. I was partial to the Small World tour. It was an old ride, in boats, one that displayed in each carefully crafted exhibit comic hints of a number of cultures. I always considered this Small World tour an optimistic assertion of untested assumptions. The beauty of the ride resided in its stubborn insistence on something—all those nations singing in one accord "It's a small world after all"—that was steadily being called into question by reality. But reality, as I have said, had been banned from the park. Both Rachel and I liked that. We liked to be renewed by the old insistences.

A time of reckoning came, however. When Rachel entered high school, realities began to crowd in. Her peers began to challenge the authenticity of Santa Claus, of her magic rock, of all the good things she kept associating with Iowa. She got into a fight with one critic and was suspended from school for a day. After this she grew depressed. After Christmas of that year she told me that she wanted to come to Iowa to live with me. A month or so later she tried to do harm to herself. I tried, at first, to negotiate a way for her to get out. This effort failed, and so I had to mount a legal fight. I lost this battle. Now both Rachel and I were disillusioned. I was prepared to throw in the towel, to give up on all the flights and on the constant wear on my health and on my resources. I was prepared to let Rachel go. But then, in another instance of kindly intervention, at another point at which an established structure has asserted the dominance of its reality, a wise friend advised me that the currents of life are not, finally, under the control of *any* structure of dependability. She counseled me, in response to my desire to give up the struggle, "I would suggest just the opposite." So the flying continued, through all of Rachel's high school years. And so did the reliance on fields of magic. If *something* magical sensed that Rachel was frightened of the growing expectations and demands of adulthood, as all teenagers are, some magic beads and crystals might just appear on her magic tree outside her bedroom window. This was sent by the gods of life for purposes of reassurance. And so, during those high school years, with the steady optimism of childhood behind us, Rachel and I kept going to *Dis*neyland. We went to *diz* diz diz *Dis*-neyland.

I have no way of knowing, now, whether or not this cushion of unreality has helped or hurt my daughter. The world is an unrelenting enemy of all illusions. But, at the very same time, the world is always in great need of some guarantors of the future. It may well be that Elizabeth, the young woman who this year hung herself, had no such guarantors. It may well be that Rachel did not harm *herself* because she, after being educated into the power of illusions, had something *more* to look forward to. I just do not know. But I do know that something was learned, by Rachel and by her best friend, Jarilyn Woodard, during all those excursions to see the Magic Kingdom.

It was Jarilyn Woodard who taught this thing to me.

We went, on our next-to-last trip to Disneyland, with Jarilyn Woodard and John, her brother, and with Barbara Woodard, their mother. Fred Woodard, Barbara's husband, did not go with us. But all of us had a wonderful time, as an extended family, during those five days. Rachel and Jarilyn had grown up together in Iowa City. Even when Jarilyn was two or three years old, Barbara would allow me to fly with her to O'Hare Airport to meet Rachel's plane coming in from Dulles. Jarilyn's heart would break each time Rachel left, and it pained me to have to inflict this loss on her so periodically. Both girls spent a great deal of time together in my house. We played "Big Bad Wolf" together; I cooked for them; I laughed when they imitated me at my table, mechanically turning pages in books, smoking cigarettes, and drinking beer. They used to write little tomes to me about the dangers of smoking, and many times I chased them down the block, in mock desperation, because they had taken my cigarettes. I loved Jarilyn Woodard as I loved my own daughter. Rachel and Jarilyn grew as close as sisters. They *were* sisters when we went to Disneyland during the 1980s. And they were still sisters when we went there with Barbara Woodard in August of 1988.

But four months later, on January 10, 1989, Barbara Woodard had a heart attack. Fred Woodard called me early that evening and said, "Would you come and get the children. I have to go to the hospital. I think that Barbara has just died." I drove out to their house and found Jarilyn in a state of shock. John was down in the basement, kicking at the wall. I took both children back to my house. I put John in a sofa bed. I put Jarilyn in Rachel's bed. Then I prayed with her until she fell asleep. I sat at my table then, and waited. Around one A.M. Fred came to the house from the hospital to say that Barbara was indeed dead. Then we sat until Barbara's family arrived from another town in Iowa. While we talked, Jarilyn woke up. She came out of Rachel's room and walked to her grandmother and sat on her lap. She never cried.

But for several years after that, whenever she spent time in our house, Jarilyn would, at the least expected time, burst into tears. This happened over and over. Then, one day, purely by accident, I discovered a roll of film that I had neglected to get developed. When the prints came back, I saw a collection of pictures that had been taken at Disneyland in August of 1987. There were many pictures of the children—Rachel and Jarilyn and John—and there was also one of Barbara Woodard, one taken at the Denver Airport just before we boarded our flight back to Cedar Rapids. Barbara looked tired, but she was smiling. Some weeks later, Jarilyn was in our home. I showed this picture to her. Jarilyn looked at her mother, and then she began to laugh. I want to believe that she laughed because, beneath the tragedy of her mother's death, lay an optimism still grounded in the happy time all of us had had the past summer at Disneyland. We went to *Dis*-neyland, to diz-diz-diz-diz *Dis*-neyland.

Rachel will have to tell me, years from now, whether all the things I tried to do have made some difference in her life.

My daughter graduated, as I have said, on June 5 of 1997. I had vowed, years before, that I would not re-enter Charlottesville. But the high school graduation date, as it approached, became a kind of emotional clock tick-tocking inside my heart. It was the old problem, the old deeply *human* problem. It was a commitment to the purity of an abstract commitment that had come to ignore the reality out of which the commitment first grew. It was in essence an emotional structure of dependability that had grown into something just as adamant and just as unyielding as the structure of white supremacy that had first caused me to leave Charlottesville. And it was here that *I* learned something.

The real tragedy of the history of black Americans is that we are shaped in part by the structures that constantly abuse us. We study the sources of those structures, their mental habits, and we learn from them. It is a truism that the prisoner always knows more about the prison keeper than the prison keeper knows about *him*. But the deeper *human* tragedy is that the prisoner, who knows so much about the prison keeper, runs the risk of *becoming like him*. There may be a certain degree of "equality" in this appropriation, but it is always *self-destructive*. And, ultimately, it is the prison keeper who wins because his onetime charge now generalizes his old guard's habits of mind further into the future than the *life* of his former guard. This freezes the flow of human emotions into habits of mind that have already proved to be destructive. The gods of life must expect something *more* from the prescient prisoner. Perhaps this thing is only a refusal to impose on the future the smallnesses of mind that have been imposed on the past and on the present.

Perhaps another way of making this abstraction concrete is to say that I will do for love what no power on earth could make me do if I *did not* love.

Early on the morning of June 5 I drove to the Cedar Rapids Airport and took a flight into Richmond, Virginia. I rented a car in Richmond and drove the sixty or so miles into Charlottesville. I located the building where Rachel's graduation would take place, and then I went to a shopping mall. I found a florist shop and I purchased one rose. Then I went back to the auditorium and watched Rachel's graduation ceremony. This was the first time I had ever seen any aspect of her life in that place. When all the seniors had been awarded their degrees and were marching out of the auditorium, I stood up in the balcony and walked as far down the steps as the railing overlooking the main floor. When I saw my daughter marching in line and approaching a place almost underneath the railing, I shouted "Rachel! Rachel!" She looked up just as I was throwing the rose to her.

Then I walked out to my car and drove straight back to the Richmond Airport.

I took the next flight into Chicago, and from there I returned to Iowa.

Rachel came to Iowa City, two weeks later. She brought the wilted rose with her.

Now that Rachel is growing secure in college, I still want to take her again out to Disneyland. We'll go to *Dis*-neyland, diz-diz-diz-*Dis*-neyland, just for a reminder of something very precious.

Daughters Lost

Mark Pendergrast

In modified form, the following essay and letter to my children appeared in the first edition of Victims of Memory: Incest Accusations and Shattered Lives *(Hinesburg, Vt.: Upper Access, 1995; 800-356-9315), my investigative book on recovered memory therapy and false accusations of sexual abuse.* The Sun, *a literary magazine, also printed it in June 1995. As in this instance, I protected my daughters' anonymity by changing their first names (they have both changed their last names). Many of the resulting letters to the* Sun *editor were surprising and disturbing to me. One typical response called my piece "a self-serving terrorist attack on his daughters," though it is instead a loving plea for reconciliation. Most of the letters— and some reviews of the book—concentrated on "Did he or didn't he molest his daughters?" rather than the scholarly investigative work that constituted the bulk of the book. Because of these attacks and misconceptions, and because it was extremely painful to detail my personal tragedy in print, I removed this material from the second edition of the book (Hinesburg, Vt.: Upper Access, 1996), although I referred to it in the introduction. Also, I figured that if my children were going to read it and the letter to them in the epilogue, they would already have done so.*

Thus, when DeWitt Henry approached me for permission to print a revised version, I was hesitant to comply. Yet I can see that the narrative of how I lost my daughters opens a window into the confusing world of recovered memories that no amount of scholarly discourse could ever achieve. I hope that its publication in the context of this book will inform the examination of the fragile, magical, vital link between fathers and daughters. In

Western culture, fathers have all too often retreated in stumbling confusion from involvement in their daughters' lives. Today, as the "gender wars" further polarize us, and popular authors treat men and women as though they fell from different planets, it is more important than ever that fathers and daughters learn, over and over, to respect and love one another.

I wish that I could report my daughters' reappearance in my life. As time goes by, their absence has become a routine, dull ache rather than an open wound. But the ache will never disappear, and I continue to hope and believe that we will one day find one another again. In the meantime, it is so sad that they are missing out on a wonderful extended family. My two younger brothers and one younger sister now have six children between them, so that I have a new generation to introduce to "feet games." It is heartbreaking that my daughters do not even know their young first cousins, since I know how much they would enjoy them. And, of course, my children's grown-up cousins, aunts, uncles, and grandparents all miss them.

> We gotta get going,
> Where we going?
> What are we gonna do?
> We're on our way to somewhere,
> The three of us—and you (thump).
> —Gabriel Ruiz, "Cuanto le Gusta"

MY KIDS and I are on our way to the dump, jouncing along in my beat-up old Chevy pickup, clouds of unrepentant burned oil punctuating our song like visible whole notes out the exhaust. This song is normally reserved for the beginning of long trips. But Stacey requested it, and on this late spring morning in 1973, with the Vermont sun finally dissolving the last vestiges of dirty snow, and red-winged blackbirds claiming every fence post, the happy, lilting tune, with its promise of action and good times, seems appropriate. On the final beat (thump), we all bang on the dashboard.

> What'll we see there?
> Who will be there?

> What'll be the big surprise?
> There may be caballeros
> With dark and flashing eyes.

How I love these little girls, I think as we sing and bounce along. They are so innocent, so beautiful, so full of life. I can never get over having been part of their creation. I feel graced.

> We're on our way (clap, clap),
> Pack up your pack (clap, clap),
> And if we stay-ay-ay,
> We won't come back.
> We're on our way, hey,
> Though we ain't got a dime,
> But we're going and we're gonna
> have a happy time.
> Cuanto le gusta, le gusta, le gusta,
> Cuanto le gusta, le gusta.

Then the song starts over, because I can't remember any more of the words. In fact, I have no idea whether I'm saying the Spanish correctly or what it means. I learned the song from my parents, all seven of us kids pitching into the chorus as we barreled down the road in our 1950s station wagon. My parents must have been crazy, I reflect, to take seven children on a camping vacation. Stacey and Christina, as wonderful as they are, are handful enough. Still, I enjoy knowing that I am passing on a tradition, and perhaps my children will sing this song to the next generation.

Going to the dump is an adventure that we all look forward to—except my wife, Joanne, who laughingly complains that we bring back more than we dump. It isn't, however, the same stuff, I point out. Why, just look at how we saved money on the pigpen with scrap lumber and posts from the dump! And what about that great-looking old Victrola box we use for the records? Besides, it's fun for the kids. They love dump picking, too, and we take only the best cast-off toys.

Today, we retrieve a real treasure, a small sliding board with a broken ladder. "Hey," I say, "I bet I could make you guys a playhouse and you could slide out of it down this." Five-year-old Stacey thinks that's a great idea and grabs one end to help drag it to the truck, while Christina, a year and a half younger, solemnly regards us, sucking her thumb. She removes it only to shout instructions. "Look out, Stacey, don't step in the mud!" Then pops the thumb back in. "That must be the best-tasting thumb in the world," I say. "Can I try it?" This is a long-standing joke between us. Christina shakes her head emphatically from side to side, stifling a smile, holding her opposing digit firmly in her mouth, while I strive to pull it out. Finally, giggling, she relents and lets me have a taste.

It seems such a short time ago, that spring day, but that was twenty-five years ago, and Stacey and Christina have grown into exceptionally attractive, intelligent, creative, caring young women. Both have graduated with high marks from fine Ivy League schools. And both, through therapy, have retrieved "memories" of sexual abuse which they think I inflicted on them. I don't know exactly what I am supposed to have done, because they will not tell me. In fact, they don't communicate with me at all, and I am forbidden to call or write.

It all started when Stacey and I went to see Christina perform in a college play. By its end, both of us were in tears, since Christina quite convincingly portrayed a damaged young woman. I learned years afterward that Stacey later told Christina that she acted like someone who had been sexually abused. Stacey had recently declared herself a lesbian, which may have had something to do with it. By that time, being a lesbian—particularly on college campuses—was also a political statement about the patriarchal society and generalized male oppression.

I didn't object to Stacey's new status. It was none of my business, and I really liked Mary, her lover. At one point, when my car broke down in New York City, I spent nearly a week in Mary's apartment, along with her male homosexual roommates, and Mary introduced me to the gay bar scene. As we danced among the men, she laughed and said, "We're probably the most unusual couple here—a straight man dancing with a lesbian."

Soon after appearing in the play, Christina, who apparently was already seeing a college counselor, initiated a search for repressed memories of abuse. I didn't know anything about it at the time, though I noticed she began to act very strangely towards me, and when she came home, she examined the family picture gallery with an unusual intensity. Finally, months later, she said that she had something important to tell me, but she didn't want me to ask her any questions about it. She then told me that she had been molested at the age of nine by one of my housemates during a summer stay at my house. She had previously repressed the memory, she said, but now she remembered.

I was completely unprepared for this revelation, which hit me hard. All my life I had tried to protect my children from harm, but I'd always been particularly worried about Christina, who seemed so gentle and vulnerable. Now I found that the most unspeakable horror had occurred years ago, right in my own household. "What are you saying? Who did this to you?" I demanded.

Joanne and I had divorced when the kids were six and four, and, after the divorce, I'd had a number of housemates because I couldn't afford a decent home alone. My mind whirled back to Mack, a heavyset depressive who lived with us that summer. He had told me that he spied on his old girlfriend, pacing outside her window, and I always felt uncomfortable around him, though it would never have occurred to me in those days to worry that he might molest my children.

"Was it Mack? Did Mack do this to you?" Christina nodded. "Oh my God! What did he do to you? Nine years old?! Are you telling me he put his *penis* inside a nine-year-old girl?" This was exactly what Christina did *not* want to hear. "Shut up! Shut up!" she cried. She never did reveal any details, except that it had happened on my bed, and she'd knocked a lamp over in the struggle.

From that point on, my relationship and communication with Christina deteriorated. It seemed that everything I did or said was wrong. "Do you want me to confront him with you?" I asked. "Do you want to sue him? Would you like me to kill the son of a bitch?" "No," she answered. "I want you to find out where he is and tell me, but that's all. This is my concern, and I'll confront him only when I am ready." I tracked down the man's location and informed her, as she requested.

Frantic to help her in any way I could, I bought a book called *The*

Courage to Heal: A Guide for Women Survivors of Child Sexual Abuse, by Ellen Bass and Laura Davis (New York: Harper & Row, 1988), and sent it to her. I skimmed the book, which appeared reasonable enough, discussing how difficult recovery would be, how to build self-esteem, how to seek support. I found a one-page section directed to "Parents Who Didn't Abuse" and began to read it. "Don't allow yourself to be overwhelmed with guilt or regret for what you didn't do before," the authors wrote. "Your feelings need recognition and expression—and for that reason you should seek support for yourself—but don't lose sight of the chance to be an understanding parent to your adult child in the present. Your compassion, courage, and willingness to change are extremely valuable" (pp. 318–19).

All of that made sense to me. God knows I wanted to help Christina in any way I could. I should have read further, however, and more carefully. "If the survivor feels you didn't protect her, she may be very angry at you. Although no one is ever responsible for someone else abusing a child, children have the right to expect to be protected by their parents and other caretakers. . . . Accept the responsibility for not protecting your daughter. Apologize" (p. 319). This should have been my first hint that Ellen Bass and Laura Davis had an agenda against parents—*all* parents—but I didn't get it. Nor did I read the section on "Families of Origin" which was clearly slanted toward cutting off all contact with family.

Even though I wanted desperately to be supportive, nothing I wrote in my letters to her seemed to help, and I could sense her withdrawing. I couldn't understand it, since it seemed that her family should be her biggest support system at a time like this. Christina's letters became formal, cold, almost robotic. She dropped out of college, moved to New York City, and began going to therapy twice a week. I paid the bills.

Confused and upset, I sought out Kate, a therapist who specialized in sexual abuse issues. We explored my mixed feelings of guilt and anger. After three sessions, she encouraged me to clarify why I was paying for all of Christina's therapy. "In many court cases," she pointed out, "the perpetrator is forced to pay for therapy as part of the judgment. It sounds to me as if Christina is blaming you for what happened to her.

And that isn't fair." Subsequently, I wrote to Christina asking why her mother wasn't paying for half of the therapy, making it clear that, one way or another, I would make sure she got as much help as she needed. I let her know that the situation was devastating for me, pointing out that if I had known about the abuse I would have done anything in my power to stop it.

In response, Christina wrote me a letter accusing me of violating her "physical and emotional boundaries" from high school on. She gave only two specific examples, one of which was my pressing her for details of the abuse when she first told me about it. The second was that I had located Mack and told her where to find him, against her wishes. I was mystified by this second charge because I had done only what she had *asked* me to do.

I couldn't clarify any of this, however, because of the final injunction in her letter: I was forbidden to write or call, because it would just upset her. She needed space from me. For the indefinite future, I had lost my daughter.

Distressed, I tried to talk with Stacey about it, but she didn't want to discuss it. "Christina won't have much to do with any of us," she said. "She's not talking to Mom much either. Don't push her. She'll come around." When I asked if she had any idea what "boundaries" Christina was talking about, Stacey said, "Well, you know, Dad, you oversensualized with us when we were little." This stunned me. "What are you talking about?" I asked. But she refused to elaborate. "No, Stacey, I really want to know. What do you mean?" But she wouldn't say and quickly changed the subject.

I couldn't believe this was happening, but I felt sure that Christina would come to her senses soon. She didn't. By the following summer, the only contact I had with her was a request for tuition money—she was enrolling in college again. When I got the endorsed check back, I noticed that she had signed it "Christina Pendergrast / Christina Sloan." What? I called Joanne, my ex-wife, and asked her about it. "Yeah, she changed her last name. Her therapist thinks it will help her somehow."

I was beginning to suspect that Christina's therapist was some sort of quack. Surely, any good counselor would have gently suggested by now that I be brought into a session. Clearly, Christina and I had issues that needed to be addressed. This was an unhealthy situation. I broke the enforced silence, begging Christina in several letters to allow me to come to just one therapy session. There was no response.

Two years after Christina had cut off contact, Stacey, now twenty-four, came home for one of her infrequent visits from Oregon, where she worked as an actress. At her request, I arranged for her to accompany me on a writing assignment to a country inn, followed by a sailing afternoon on a friend's boat. I was excited to see my remaining daughter and catch up. Our time together turned out to be quite strained, though, and I got the distinct impression that she was simply fulfilling an unpleasant familial obligation. After the inn visit, she announced that she wanted to cancel the sail and go back to her mother's house.

On the trip back, I once again asked if we could go to counseling together. (Just before she'd gone to Oregon, Stacey had agreed to attend a session, but had then reneged.) It seemed to me that what Christina was going through had to be seen as part of the family web, that it was like the proverbial elephant in the living room that no one talked about. I wanted to explore what Stacey had meant by the remark about "oversensualizing," to hear any problems she felt she had with me. Now, in the car, I tried again. "There seems to be a kind of wall between us," I said, "and it really bothers me. I know you love me, and I love you, but something is going on here, and we don't seem to be able to talk about it. I think a counseling session might help."

Stacey reacted with fury. "I *hate* it when you say stuff like that. I don't want to go to a stupid counseling session. There are no deep, dark secrets here. I share a lot more about my life with you than most children do with their parents, but you're never satisfied. I'm more like Mom; I just don't want to have all these deep discussions."

Before going back to Oregon, Stacey visited Christina in New York City. I was glad, because their relationship had been strained ever since they had attempted to live together two years earlier. I had been gently trying to convince Stacey to resume contact, and now it was happening.

Three weeks later, Stacey sent me the worst letter of my life. It began:

Dad,

I'm sorry if you aren't ready for this letter, but it must be written. Things are clearer to me now, so I can address the huge problem I have with you more completely. I have recently recalled some memories I have of you. These are things I have always remembered but put them on the back shelf, have never spoken of them before recently. Because they made me sick and upset.

She described skinny-dipping at age seven, and a massage four years later that made her feel "disgusting and horrible." She said that I had discussed sex with her when she was "just too young," telling her that it was "natural" and "healthy."

The letter went on, with statements that were almost too painful for me to read. I had made her and Christina my "surrogate wives." I had cried in her presence too often. "I remember thinking once that if I didn't hold you like you wanted," Stacey wrote, "that you might kill yourself and it would be my fault." Stacey continued by writing that I had no "boundaries," that I often made other people uncomfortable. Though I considered myself open-minded, she said, I was really manipulative and controlling, particularly with women. I had, for instance, insisted on her going hiking when she didn't want to, assuming that it would be a good experience. "Maybe you don't see it in yourself," she wrote. "I'm sure you don't see your relationship with your daughters as abusive and manipulative, but I *do*."

All this was awful enough, but the next paragraph took my breath away. "And I know what you did to my sister." That's all she would say about it. "I am writing to you about me, my memories and my feelings. I will only ever deal with you about me; I will never talk for my sister. You have to recall what happened and deal with this on your own." She advised me to get therapy and not to expect any help from her. "You took it from me when I was a child, but now that I am an adult I don't have to do that anymore." She went on to suggest that I had probably been abused as a child myself by someone who had said it was "healthy" and "natural."

Finally, Stacey forbade me to contact her for a year and a half. At that time, provided neither I nor anyone else in my family tried to contact her before then, and assuming I had changed through therapy, she might resume contact with me. Her last paragraph read: "A closing note: no, no, you weren't the worst father in the world. Of course not. But you did some pretty selfish and destructive things and you need to change. Get professional help." She signed it simply "Stacey"—no "Love" before it, which was hardly surprising, given the contents.

I read and reread this letter, trying to sort out my feelings, trying to understand how Stacey could believe this. How could she recall with such clarity many things that never happened, as far as I could remember? And how could she twist other incidents into something repulsive? The father she spoke of sounded horrible, insensitive, abusive, but he was not someone I recognized. Yet I was supposed to be this person. Was this true? Had I abused and manipulated my children?

Although the letter portrayed a sick person who likely needed years of therapy, the specific allegations weren't all that damning. Though I didn't remember them specifically, some of the incidents Stacey mentioned might well have happened. I'm sure we *did* go skinny-dipping, something I had done both as a child and as an adult. And yes, I thought it was a wonderful, natural thing. But I certainly couldn't imagine forcing her to do so. I might have given her a back rub. But I couldn't imagine massaging my child in a way that was unwelcome, or that could be interpreted as sexual.

With its self-righteous, angry, politically correct tone, the letter didn't sound like Stacey. This was the same daughter who had written me a very funny letter only a year earlier, complaining about an acquaintance who was "knee-jerk, left-wing, dogmatic, and stupid to top it off," and who said that if we could only, you know, like, you know, work all at once together, there'd be no more hunger. "Please help me if I ever say inane things like that," Stacey had concluded.

Now, this accusatory letter came completely out of the blue. We seemed to remember radically different childhoods. Most of my memories of Stacey and Christina were joyful, playful, and open. Also "natural" and "healthy," as Stacey so scathingly put it. I was a child of the sixties, and I wanted my children to grow up with a matter-of-fact attitude towards their bodies. I considered sex a normal part of life, and when the subject came up I would tell them whatever they wanted to know.

There were very few difficult incidents with Stacey and Christina during their childhoods, so I remembered them quite clearly, and I could see the basis for some of what Stacey wrote. When she was twelve or thirteen, I tried to have a "birds and bees" conversation with her, since I didn't know what Joanne might have told her. Stacey blew up before I even got started. "Dad," she said, "you and Mom have already told me all this stuff a million times. Why can't you be like other parents? It's like you *want* me to go out and have sex." I was startled. "No, Stacey, I don't want you to have sex. It's just that your body will mature soon, and I wanted to make sure you understood what your period is, and to know how to prevent pregnancy in case you *did* have sex." Afterwards, I bought a book written for teens about sex, and I asked Stacey to keep it in her room. "You don't have to read it," I said, "but if you want to in private, you can." Now, as her letter made clear, this parental behavior was being interpreted as sexual abuse.

I was distressed by Stacey's statement that she had thought I would kill myself if she didn't hug me. I *was,* in fact, quite depressed during part of their childhoods. In the wake of the divorce, I had a hard time trying to get my life back on track. My former wife was angry at me, I couldn't land a steady job, and I missed my children. I *did* cry easily at times, and I reversed the proper roles by making my children my confidantes and supporters. In retrospect, I certainly deserved criticism for my behavior at that time.

But now, as I read Stacey's accusations over and over, I wondered whether there were additional incidents I just couldn't remember. The most disturbing lines in the letter were the mysterious references to Christina: "You used us (but mostly my sister) physically," she wrote. What was that about? "I know what you did to my sister. . . . You have to recall what happened and deal with this on your own." It was clear that Christina had told Stacey something really *awful* that I had done to her. But what could it be?

Finally, I pieced together what had probably happened: During Stacey's trip to New York City, Christina had told Stacey something terrible that I had done to her, something she must have recently recalled in therapy. Horrified and upset, Stacey had sought a therapist herself when she got back to Oregon—that would explain her writing that she had never spoken of these memories until recently. This therapist must have encouraged her to reinterpret her childhood and had told her that I, too, had probably been abused as a child. At this point, I began to wonder what kind of therapists there were out there. Something odd was going on.

I located Sarah Pagett, a local hypnotist, and made an appointment. Like most people, I thought that hypnosis could tap directly into your subconscious to help unearth long-forgotten memories. I also felt compelled to write Stacey one final letter. I was careful not to deny anything—that would only have exacerbated matters—but I also didn't confess to anything. Mostly, I wanted to tell her that I honestly didn't know what I was supposed to have done to Christina:

Dear Stacey,

I got your letter about my inappropriate behavior. Thank God it's all out in the open now, even though most of it came as a complete shock and surprise. Some things you wrote about I remember; some I don't. I understand clearly now what the unspoken "wall" was that I sensed. I will try to understand how coerced you have felt. I will go to therapy. I'm also going to try to get hypnotized or take sodium pentothal to remember more.

It's clear from your letter that you think/know that I did something truly sexually abusive to Christina, and that you don't want to talk about it. That's understandable. I just want you to know that as of right now, I have no idea what it is that I purportedly did to Christina. I am not lying.

I would very much like to talk about you and me some day, perhaps in a few years. Of course, I also hope that you shorten your year-and-a-half timetable, but that's up to you. You will not hear from me again until March of 1994 unless I'm dying, or a short note to let you know where I am if I move.

And I am infinitely sorry for everything I may have done to screw you up and hope to stop as of now.

Love,
Dad

On the outside of the envelope, I wrote "LAST LETTER FOR 1.5 YEARS. PLEASE READ." Stacey sent the letter back, folded and unopened, along with a curt note: "Don't contact me now for three years. Every time you try the time will increase. Deal with this on your own."

It is impossible to convey the horror of losing your children like this. I found it difficult to sleep, to concentrate. Every night I had beautiful dreams in which my children were young and loving, and every morning I woke up to a reality more like a nightmare. How could this be happening? I wanted so badly to be able to talk it all over. I was more than willing to discuss anything from the past, and I would certainly *never* touch my children again—I wouldn't dare even shake hands—without their requesting it. But I couldn't tell them any of this. I had simply been cut off, surgically and angrily.

I did go to see Dr. Pagett. She told me that hypnotism could sometimes help to enhance memory, but that it was not necessarily a magical way to tap into the personal past. (My subsequent research revealed that hypnosis should *never* be used to enhance memory; the trance state is notorious for producing fantasies that fulfill expectations and fears.) The doctor asked me at great length about my own childhood, in which I recalled no abuse, and about how I had raised my children. She commented that I appeared to have been a good father. Then we had a hypnotic session in which I tried to recall the skinny-dipping incident. During it, I pictured Stacey shivering and clinging to the side of the pool, but I wasn't sure whether it was a real memory or something I pieced together in my effort to explore the statement made in Stacey's letter. Hypnotism wasn't what I envisioned. I felt relaxed and inward looking, but I was certainly aware of what was going on.

I also joined a grief group, many of whose members were mourning a loved one's death. In an odd way, I envied them. At least for them the separation was irrevocable, and no one was blaming them for it. For me, the loss of my children was a constant wound, and it was caused by their apparent hatred for me and what they thought I had done to them. I lived in tortured hopes that they would contact me again, and in dread that this would continue for the rest of my life. I also asked for a session with the Clearness Committee at my local Quaker meeting. It helped but provided no answers.

I tried to keep informed through my ex-wife, Joanne. At first she was polite enough, if cool. She would tell me sketchily how Stacey and Christina were doing. It struck me as ironic that she was now my sole source of information about the kids, since I had longed for the time when our children would be adults and I would no longer have to deal with Joanne's bitterness. I hadn't discussed the abuse allegations with her, on the advice of John, my new therapist. Finally, I couldn't stand it any longer. I wrote Joanne a long letter, explaining everything that had happened, taking as much responsibility as I could, and asking for clarification. I waited a month for a response, then called her.

It was a one-sided conversation, with Joanne simply screaming at me for fifteen minutes. "You trashed those kids' lives!" she yelled. Both children, she said, had told her that I had threatened to commit suicide if they ever told the awful things I was doing to them. I also supposedly had burned Christina with an iron to terrorize her into silence. Although Joanne wouldn't tell me what atrocities I purportedly had committed, she said that both Stacey and Christina were actively recalling more and more memories in therapy. Then she hung up on me. She continued to hang up every time I called after that, so I gave up.

That conversation shook me, but in a strange way, it was a relief to realize that this had gone beyond interpretations of things that I may or may not have done. These were accusations of things that simply had never taken place. I most certainly had never threatened to commit suicide or intentionally burned Christina. I began to move beyond confusion and guilt. Instead, I felt an increasing concern for my children. Something horrible seemed to be happening to them: their minds, their memories, were somehow being twisted, distorted.

But I couldn't shake all of the *good* memories I had. When they were little, I would play "feet games" with the girls, which they loved. They could stand on my hands or sit for "elevator," "roller coaster," or flips. Joanne and I read *Winnie-the-Pooh* and many other children's stories to them. I built a playhouse (with an exit down the sliding board from the dump) and hung a huge horizontal tire swing, held by a chain tripod, from the maple in the front yard. I made a set of blocks out of two-by-fours, with which the kids and I made "monstrosities" that often reached higher than they were. At night, I made up stories about their stuffed animals. We always sang together in the car. They were beautiful, happy children, and our house was the social center for other neighborhood kids. Christina's "Silly Puppy" stories used to make Stacey laugh so hard she got the hiccups.

After the divorce, my children and I continued to see each other almost every weekend, except for one disastrous year when I moved far away and sank into a depression. I realized then that my career was not as important to me as being near my children. I quit and moved back, though I struggled for quite a while to find a decent job. We continued to have wonderful times together, though. They lived with me for half of each summer. They wore out the grooves of old musicals—*Oklahoma, South Pacific, West Side Story*—and we all memorized zany Monty Python records. They made up a dance to the tune of "Eric the 'alf a Bee." They imaginatively filled in elaborate coloring books, wrote poetry, and read young-adult fantasy novels. In the summer, we went swimming in a wild river with deep pools and clambered over boulders until we reached a magical rock formation, a sort of natural whirlpool spa where the water poured through a hole. We named it Pendergrast Dome.

I was unwilling to enter into a relationship that would conflict with my role as parent. I dated several women briefly, but I had fathered children at a young age, and most women near my age were not ready to take on the role of stepmother. Finally, when the children were in their teens, I began a long-term relationship with Betty, a divorced woman with children of her own. Stacey and Christina liked Betty, though they had little in common with her children.

As teenagers and college students, Stacey and Christina continued to seem fond of me. Their friends came over often. We enjoyed a dictionary game in which we made up silly definitions for strange words; we played charades; we watched *Cheers* every Thursday night. Like me, they both enjoyed acting in plays, and I helped them memorize lines. We hosted the postproduction party at my house one year. Stacey became enamored of a cappella singing groups, so we formed our own, aptly named The Lost Keys, with two of her male friends, and practiced once a week.

"Dad, the funniest thing happened last night," Stacey reported while she was in college. "A bunch of us were in this greasy spoon, and it was really late. I got into this *really* interesting conversation with the guy flipping the hamburgers, and my friend just stared at me. When we left, she said, 'Do you always get off on talking to strangers like that?' And I said, 'Well, yeah,' and I realized that I was just like you. Dad, that was a really nice thing you gave me."

When she was a freshman in college, Stacey sent me a single sheet of paper with bright crayons announcing "I LOVE YOU, DAD!" with a small note at the bottom saying "Sudden burst of appreciation." I have similar memories of Christina being caring and thoughtful. The night we went backstage after that fateful play she was in, I was still wiping away tears, and Christina hugged me and said, "Are you OK, Dad?" I kept thinking of the letter of recommendation one of Christina's high school teachers had written for her:

> Miss Pendergrast is a talented, caring lady. She possesses a fine mind, capable of identifying, analyzing, and solving problems both in and out of the classroom. Her mind and logic are tempered with a gentle, empathetic approach to life that continually nurtures the respect and love that her peers hold for her. I have seen Christina help one fellow student on a difficult theoretical problem, then turn to another to provide comfort and support during a time of family crisis. I hope that my son, now seven years old, grows up to become the kind of person that Christina Pendergrast is.

That was true. The Christina I knew was a kind, understanding, intense, empathetic young woman. We used to have wonderful talks about the meaning of life and how to understand and help others.

I had a hard time connecting the Stacey and Christina I knew to the angry young women who had cut off all communication with me. Everything had been utterly changed. So I sought out their old high school friends, looking for answers. I told them about my children's accusations, asking if they recalled anything negative the girls might have said about me. They were dismayed and confused. "No, Mr. Pendergrast, they never said anything bad about you at all," one of Stacey's friends said. "In fact, when the rest of us were bitching about our parents, Stacey would say, 'Not my dad.' She'd always be talking about you: 'my dad' this and 'my dad' that. How you knew all these songs, and how you raised bees, and how you were a writer and how cool you were. I just can't believe this is happening."

One of Christina's friends said, "I know for a fact that Christina adored you. She sometimes had trouble with her mom, but you were a really important person in her life. This doesn't make sense." None of their friends could understand why they, too, had been cut out of Christina's and Stacey's lives.

"Here's something you might be interested in," a lady in my grief group said one night. "I found it in my Unitarian magazine." She handed me an ad. *"Has your grown child falsely accused you as a consequence of repressed 'memories'?"* it began. "You are not alone. Please help us document the scope of this problem. Contact: The False Memory Syndrome Foundation, 1-800-568-8882."

Curious but apprehensive, I called and left my name and phone number. Two days later, a woman from Maine called to welcome me to the loosely knit organization. We talked for two hours. Unlike me, her husband knew exactly what his daughter thought he had done, which included rape from the age of three. She said that my story wasn't unusual, that a third of the parents who had contacted the Foundation didn't know exactly what they were supposed to have done. The only thing all the cases had in common was that the children accused the parents of sexual abuse and completely cut them off, leaving no opportunity for dialogue.

That phone call marked a turning point for me. I got the FMS Foundation packet and devoured its contents. I discovered that *The Courage to Heal* (the book I had sent to Christina when this all started) was quite controversial, implicated in virtually every case in which children had accused their parents of incest. It seemed likely to me that Christina had read it long before I sent it to her. "If you think you were abused and your life shows the symptoms," its authors opined, "then you were." You needed to become enraged, confront and cut off your perpetrator, and consider "getting strong by suing" (p. 290).

I bought my own copy of the book and read it carefully. I was appalled. The authors appeared to be trying to convince women that all of their problems in life stemmed from long-forgotten sexual abuse.

"If you don't remember your abuse, you are not alone," Bass and Davis wrote. "Many women don't have memories, and some never get memories. This doesn't mean they weren't abused." When memories do come, according to the book, they usually arrive as vague dreams or obscure intuitions. "Often in the beginning stages, belief in your memories comes and goes" (pp. 22, 310). With time, rehearsal, and encouragement, however, the "memories" become all too real.

Then I read the section on "Believing It Happened," in which they relate the story of Emily. "When confronted with the abuse, her parents denied everything and her father offered to see a counselor, take a lie-detector test, anything, to prove his innocence." What was wrong with that? Plenty. Whenever Emily talked with her parents, she became ill. "The conflict between what she knew inside and what they presented was too great." The solution? Try to sort all of this out with her parents and a good counselor? Try to understand the pain and confusion her father was experiencing and appreciate his efforts to reconcile? No. "It was only when Emily broke off all communication with her family and established a consistent relationship with a skilled therapist who believed her that she stopped doubting herself and got on with her recovery" (p. 90).

I began collecting other self-help books of the recovery movement. I found that Stacey's letter was filled with the jargon and concepts from these books—*boundaries, manipulative, surrogate wives, inappropriate.* I learned how "memories" were extracted by questionable methods such as hypnotic age regression, dream analysis, obsessing over childhood photographs, guided imagery, automatic writing, or massage, and of how therapists regarded their job as "bearing witness" to their clients' narratives and overcoming any doubts they might have of their validity.

I learned that the process of memory retrieval was often gradual and slow, and that the number of accused molesters in a given case tended to grow over time. (That would explain why it took Christina's therapist over two years to dredge up something concrete against me. Stacey, already prepared by Christina's experience, apparently found her "memories" more quickly.)

Next, I ventured to the library for esoteric tomes on hypnotism, dreams, memory, and anything else I could find that might help me to understand this bizarre phenomenon. Finally, I began to interview other parents in my situation, then some of the accusing children and their therapists. I stopped hand-wringing and immersed myself in an effort to understand what was really happening.

I attended the first national FMS conference in April 1993. I felt a surge of hope as the speakers repeated much of what I already knew about hypnotism, suggestibility, social coercion, group contagion, and memory distortion. Six hundred people listened attentively, furiously taking notes. It struck me as odd that some of the most renowned psychologists and sociologists in the country were presenting their findings to a group of middle-aged and elderly people accused of sexual abuse. The question of repressed memories, which had been merely the arcane subject of academic squabbling a few years before, had now become life-or-death issues for these beleaguered parents and siblings.

Over and over, I heard horror stories from other parents. One man, for instance, following the suggestion of his accusing son's therapist, had checked himself into a psychiatric hospital for what he thought was a two-day evaluation. Then he couldn't get out. Eventually, the therapists convinced him that he was the high priest of a satanic cult. "It's like a vortex that you can't get out of," he told me over lunch. "After a while, the people in my group would have agreed to anything this therapist said."

I began to understand something of what motivated Stacey and Christina to rewrite their pasts and to hate me. In therapy, I learned, manufactured memories of sexual abuse usually incorporated pieces of real memories. For instance, Christina really *did* bump into a hot iron at my house when she was young. For all I know, Christina now thinks that our game with her thumb was part of a satanic ritual, and Stacey may be convinced that the "caballeros with dark and flashing eyes" of our song were molesters.

That sounds flip, but black humor has become a necessary defense for most accused parents. This process is one of the most painful, inexplicable, debilitating things that could happen to anyone. Your own children hate you, convinced that you damaged them irrevocably, stealing their innocence, abusing their trust so terribly that they had to repress all memory of it simply to survive the nightmare of their child-hood. It is a chilling scenario, one which continues to haunt all of the parents. Could it be true? Could we have done something awful to our children without remembering it?

And so I go over and over my memories of Stacey and Christina, re-viewing, trying to listen honestly to my conscious, my subconscious, hoping to find clues to a mystery which threatened the very foundation of who I really was, who my children really were.

During the conference, I listened to a panel of women known as "re-tractors." They had gone through the therapy mill, become "incest sur-vivors," cut off ties with their families, and finally come out the other side. Where once they had directed their anger at their parents, now they raged against the therapists who had led them to believe they were incest victims. It was here that I first understood that the parents' trag-edies were almost minor when compared with those of their children, whose very identities and pasts had been stripped away. Many of the re-tractors had been hospitalized after suicide attempts, had spent their life's savings on therapy, had lost their friends, relationships, and jobs. Gradually, I began to worry more about my children than about myself: What were *they* going through?

Dear Stacey and Christina,

I have worried that writing this book, telling the whole world about our situation, may only push each of you further into a corner. I've ago-nized over this, thinking that maybe you'll interpret this as an attack, a self-justification, or a way to make money off of your pain. I hope, if you've read the text, that you realize it's none of those things. I wrote the book because I am a writer now, and because I couldn't get myself to write or think about anything else. I envisioned a twenty-year-old pick-ing up this book and being a bit more skeptical when her therapist tells her she has "all the classic signs" of a victim of sexual abuse. If she is spared the horror of losing her family and her past, I'll know that this book was worth writing.

But of course, I also desperately hoped I could reach you. I figured I didn't have much to lose—I've already lost you. Maybe, just maybe, this book would bring you back. Maybe you'd read this and figure out what's going on. I'm not saying that you are necessarily miserable in your new identities as "incest survivors." I imagine that you have come to accept the "fact" that you were sexually abused as children, that you have no father any more, and that you must struggle with this legacy for the rest of your lives. *But it's just not true!*

You're so smart, both of you, that I keep thinking that with all this publicity and uproar over "recovered memories," you're bound to call any day and say, "Uh, Dad? It's me. Do you have a minute?" And we'd just start over again.

This whole situation is so crazy! I've written this whole book about it, but I still really don't understand it, can't believe that the two of you would fall for this. How can you be so *angry* at me? I had a fantasy the other day that you two were screaming at me, "Confess! Confess!" And I would say, "Well, I didn't expect a kind of Spanish Inquisition." And you guys would suddenly break up, remembering that stupid Monty Python skit we used to imitate, and you'd say in that high, funny voice, "N-n-nobody expects the Spanish Inquisition. Our principal weapon is fear. Fear and surprise." And we'd all laugh. What happened to your sense of humor? What happened to everything we used to laugh about?

Since you've both cut off contact, I've thought many times that it might have been better if I had just dropped out of your lives, as many fathers do, after the divorce. Then you'd probably be coming to find dear old Dad about now to see what he was like. But that's crazy. I wouldn't have given up those years with you for anything in the world, and I don't think you would, either, if you allow yourselves to recall the *real* memories.

You see—I *know* that I am with you now, both of you, in good ways, and I'll be with you forever, regardless of anything or anyone. If any memories appear to be truly "repressed," it's those wonderful, warm memories you must have of me. I cannot believe that they have disappeared forever. Somewhere, somehow, they will come back to you. They probably do now, when you hear a particular song, when you tell someone about sledding, when you swim in a river, when you watch a child building a monstrous block construction, when you act in a play. But you must bury those fond memories quickly, stuffing them back. One day, I hope you'll let them out. And you'll call or write.

I promise I'll be here waiting for you when you do. Don't worry, I don't want to turn you into infants or teenagers again, and I don't expect we'll see each other all that often. You're adults now, and we're all busy.

I do hope we can re-establish a comfortable, affectionate relationship, though, and that you can call on me when you're down or need money or advice, for what it's worth—or even a zucchini bread recipe, which is the last thing you called me for, Stacey.

I'm a very stubborn person, as you know, and I will never give up hope of reuniting with both of you. Do you remember how much I always liked *King Lear*? I know that Lear was a patriarchal son of a bitch who, as Goneril says, "hath ever but slenderly known himself." That's why I've always found the play so moving. He loses his identity completely—no more king, father, or even man. He is simply a "poor, bare, fork'd animal," like everyone else, and mad to boot. Well, maybe that's what this repressed memory delusion has done to me, and to you, and maybe we'll come out of it in some way wiser. I'm not saying that this is all for the best. I think what you've gone through is horrendous, and I would not wish my suffering on anyone.

But some day I hope we can speak as Cordelia and Lear do near the end of the play. "We are not the first / Who with best meaning have incurr'd the worst," Cordelia tells her father. No, Lear says, don't worry about it. "When thou dost ask me blessing, I'll kneel down / And ask of thee forgiveness."

And so I do, Stacey and Christina, getting down on my knobby knees for you.

I love you,
Dad

Man in the Middle
Visits Daughter at School

Alan Cheuse

THE FLIGHT to Boston turned into an iffy proposition. I'd risen in the chilly early March dark in Washington in order to leave from Dulles Airport in rural Virginia at seven in the morning because it was the cheapest flight around, and in these years of college and high school tuitions, cheap means best. So for forty-eight dollars I boarded the USAir airplane, a DC-9, the smallest in their jet fleet, a plane that I didn't even know they used anymore. Crowds of Veterans of Foreign Wars filed into the cabin along with me, returning to New England after some convention, all of them World War II veterans by the grizzled faces on them, the bloated bellies, the balding heads trimmed with white fringe, fathers who years ago had seen their own children approach middle age. I always rate flights by the amount of reading I get done in the air and this trip did not look promising, not with this boisterous mob of ex-privates turned seventy-plus talking and guffawing and wandering up and down the aisle, not with me squeezed into a middle seat between two of these chattering vets.

And then there was the weather. The winter of 1996 was already a record breaker all up and down the East coast. The rain that was falling when we bounced up into the clouds above northern Virginia turned to ice and sleet by the time we were making our bumpy descent into Logan Airport.

Here we go, I said to myself, always ready to land and always fearful of it, as the icy mix splattered off our wings. Our wheels touched the glazed surface of the runway and we skipped ever so slightly and then got a grip on the ground and rolled through the mess falling from the same sky through which we had only moments before been descending. It was going to be a cold and bleak day in Boston, but now that we had arrived the freeze didn't faze me one bit. As inner weather goes, and by that I mean the climate that happens to prevail in your soul, I was wearing shirt sleeves and going barefoot. I had arrived to spend four and a half days with my older daughter, Emma, a second-year student at Harvard, and found myself with plenty of time to stop off at my hotel room and drop off my bags before meeting her. Our rendezvous was going to begin with me attending one of her classes, and I couldn't have been more pleased.

Well, all right, I could have been more pleased, I admitted to myself as I extricated myself from the airplane, caught a taxi outside the terminal and rolled through the harbor tunnel and along Storrow Drive. These were the kind of thoughts that came up a lot over the years as I made my regular visits with the kids. I could have been more pleased if I hadn't moved out of the house, and a marriage, when Emma was five years old, leaving her and her younger sister behind in the care of their mother. I had already busted one marriage and had parted from a household inhabited by my only son when he was just about five years old himself. That thought became a rubric with me during the years between the end of my second marriage and the beginning of my third and present marriage. *I can't seem to stay in the same house as my children after they reach the age of five,* I'd say upon occasion. The occasion was usually a date with a sympathetic and inquisitive young woman who wanted to try and get to know me. Yuk yuk! Great line, I'd think, good for pronouncing after a couple of shots of vodka or some good limited edition Tennessee sour mash. (And try to get to know me—I dare you—as I try to seduce you.) But if my daughters' mother and I had somehow been able to keep our love together and stay married and raise the girls in a two-parent household, I would have been a happier man.

Or a different man. We both would have had to be extremely different people to make that marriage last. Same for my first marriage. If I had been about twenty years older than I was when I first married—say,

forty-four instead of twenty-four—I might have been better able to negotiate the twisted windy paths on which I had to tread along with my
beautiful and sharp-tongued first wife along the way toward torment
and along the river near the end of it all. (I had a line about her that I
dragged out every once in a while when the occasion—the women, the
drinking—seemed to call for a laugh: *My first wife, yes, she looked like
Tuesday Weld and had a heart like Lucrezia Borgia!* But looking back I
have to admit that the line says more about me than it does about her!)

But experience isn't all it's cracked up to be. I had had the experience
of a tormented first marriage behind me when I married for a second
time, and it didn't help me to understand what I was doing. Boom! you
say to yourself. I've done this once before and messed up. Now I really
know how to proceed! Rather than careful, it makes you all the more
reckless. You plunge ahead at full speed, certain of your powers and
abilities, and when you hit the rocks you yowl even louder than at the
first crack-up. At least back then you had the excuse of inexperience.
The second time around you have only misery.

I don't know for whom the shock of ending a second marriage is
greater, the parent who has been married and divorced before, or the
children. Well, that's hyperbole. Of course it's always more difficult for
the children simply because they are children. But look at it this way
just for an instant—for them at least it's only their first separation and
for you, you believe, rightly or wrongly, it's yet again a disaster of your
own making. So it doesn't surprise me in the least that when disaster
strikes a lot of men run. Or at least withdraw. And they don't even have
to have had a previous marriage behind them to do so. It may be something in our nature; it's certainly something in our culture. Men break
things, women pick up the pieces. Men spill, and women clean it up.
You can add to this list as you like. It's easy to do. Particularly in the case
of broken marriages. First time around or second or whatever the men
leave the scene of the accident—or crime—and women are left with
the furniture, sometimes—mixed blessing—even an entire house,
and, of course, the children. Statistics reveal it. Anecdotal evidence
supports it. Custom makes it so. Men are the ones to leave, and they
often leave on the run.

What they leave behind is the real stuff of modern heartbreak. The hearth fire keeps burning—if the mother has enough cash to pay for the firewood and enough time and strength to haul it inside and enough expertise to make the fire from scratch—but there's no father to sit in front of the grate and help the children with their homework or read to them before bedtime. No one to help with bathing them and tucking them into bed. Or the kitchen chores. No father for the kids to run to in the middle of a fright in the darkest part of the night. No father to help get the kids ready for school. No father to pick them up. No father to meet with their teachers. No father present when they're sick and staying home from school. No father to help with the shopping. No father to help with the cooking. Or the washing. Or the household maintenance. Or with the car. Or with keeping up the spirit of the family in dark times and partaking of—and the making of—the laughter and music the household knew in its best of days. No father to admire and applaud after the first dance class recital. Or to comment with a firm but encouraging voice on a school assignment come back from the teacher with a certain grade. No father to notice the difference it makes to wear a red hair ribbon instead of a green hair ribbon. No father to say how beautiful and handsome these children are when they perform their mighty feats of climbing trees or swinging on swings or shoveling sand or making towers out of blocks. No father to sit with the kids during the feature-length cartoons and ooh and aah with them. No father to hold onto during the scariest part of the carnival ride. No father's hand to grasp in the darkest part of the trail through the woods. No father's voice somewhere in the house, raised in song or humming or reading an article aloud from the morning newspaper. No father to huddle with in front of the television screen on the sofa at night after the homework's done. No father to see embracing the mother in the oldest circle in the world, holding her sweetly as bedtime for the household arrives and the night sweeps up the children into interesting dreams.

It seems that for the majority of divorced fathers with children, life is an either/or proposition, or at least the astronomical percentage of men who default in their child support payments would suggest this. Men are either in the household, or they're out. And once they're out, most of them are far out. Eighty percent of them don't pay their monthly, court-mandated checks for the upkeep of the children they have left behind. Many of them break off contact with the family altogether. Some stay in touch, but, for whatever reason, without sending cash. Some of this group, I think, probably stays away from the household out of the shame of being unable to send a full check every month. But most of the delinquent men are behaving like vengeful, uncaring cowards. They've figured in the breakup of a marriage, and they don't want to be reminded of their failures, even if this means losing touch with their children.

These men are the definition of absent fathers, men for whom, for one reason or another, the bond of parenthood becomes so attenuated that their very humanity becomes stretched to the breaking point. Some of these men go on to make second marriages and form second families, lavishing great affection, love, and attention on their new crop of children without ever maintaining their relations with their earlier families. I met such a man during the past decade, a hale-fellow-well-met Washington hotshot who left behind his first wife and several young children in order to marry one of his assistants. His new wife became insanely jealous, forbidding him to visit his children because she was afraid that this would somehow lead him to get back together again with their mother. He was afraid to challenge his new wife, but since he wasn't visiting his old family he withheld all support payments on the grounds that he wasn't getting his money's worth in visitations. When his ex-wife finally decided to take him to court, he left the East Coast, figuring that what he wasn't missing he didn't need to pay for anyway.

That may seem like an extreme portrait of an absent father, but as the figures show there are a lot of these nonpayers around. They just don't advertise themselves. It doesn't make for cheerful dinner table conversation, or good banter on a date, to say, oh, yes, I have a couple of kids up in New Hampshire, but I never see them and I certainly don't send their mother any money. It certainly won't get you very far at the office.

Much more visible is the middle range of divorced father, the man who pays his child support and tries to keep up his obligations by negotiating with his ex-wife for regular, if widely spaced visits from the children on school holidays and annual vacations. If he has remarried and made a new family, things become quite complicated. Pity this poor man in the middle! Caught between his ties to his old family and to a new household, maybe attempting to integrate or "blend" (as the jargon has it these days) the two sets of children into a single unit over the time that all the kids are together. Better that, he thinks, than visiting the old family and causing all sorts of jealousy among his new brood. But then he doesn't like to imagine the sentiments back up in the old nest, where the kids are terribly resentful of the new offspring with whom he lives and spends most of his time.

This man in the middle is also often stretched, both emotionally and financially, sometimes almost to the breaking point. Unlike the bigamist in the old Alec Guinness film *The Captain's Paradise,* who moves cheerfully back and forth between two households, this man lives with the guilt of not spending enough time with the old family and of having to abandon the new in order to spend what time he does with the old. There's also a painful and destructive element that seeps into his relations with the children from his first marriage. Although in both heart and mind he knows that they are blameless, he comes to associate them with the destruction of the marriage that spawned them and begins to penalize them for that by not paying as much attention to them as he might. When he looks at them, he sees their mother. (God knows, when she looks at them, she sees him!) In the children he sees the very sign of his failure as a younger man to make a home and a marriage that could last. Now and then it makes him wonder if in the long run he can keep his new family together.

On the other extreme is the father who, though he is separated legally from the family, has won a joint custody agreement. He almost always has to live in the same town in order to maintain this, maybe even in the same neighborhood. And in his new house, or household, he sets up a room for the kid, or kids, and they come to his house to live for a few days each week, or every weekend, or every other weekend. In this way he can still easily play a major role in the lives of his children. He may have to give up a large portion of his own new life to be always present when he's needed, showing up for meals, for bedtime, on duty all the time for school car pools and school crises, and he has had to give up a certain amount of potential freedom in order to stay in close proximity if he is going to keep up this joint custody. But he's done this by choice so that he can play the largest possible role in his children's lives while living outside the household.

I've never been that man on either extreme. In twenty-five years of paying child support payments, from those for my son on through those for my two daughters, I think that in the worst of financial times I may have missed one or two payments. But in all that time I have lived in cities and towns apart from the family, called to these other places by reason of work, mostly, or the kind of elements necessary for emotional survival, but I have always kept the closest possible contact with the children, abiding by the spirit if not the usual stipulations of a joint custody agreement. So while I have lived in the middle I have not lived as a man-in-the-middle, if I can make that distinction.

Not that I haven't ever felt stretched. In the time that it takes for the cab to drop me at my hotel, a lot of memories of family life run through my mind, not all of them good. In the time that it takes me to walk through the falling icy rain from the hotel to Harvard Yard, I can count up a lot of torments and failures in this business of trying to be as present and as available a father as I could, though still living at some distance from my children. In the time that it takes me to climb the icy steps of the main library where I am to meet my daughter, I can account for a heartache for every stair. But at least I'm feeling something instead of living like the absent father who must have to deaden himself to this vast aspect of his emotional life and carry on as a sort of zombie. At least I tried, I tried my heart out.

And then as I reach the top of the steps and gaze out through the freezing rain across the Yard I see my tall, lean, hatless older daughter striding along one of the paths, her new short dark haircut exposed to the elements, and she waves, and I wave back, and we meet midway on the slippery stairs and embrace as we have on countless other occasions. Except when you don't live with your children, you do begin to count, and you count each meeting precious—coming to the door of their mothers' various houses (in the beginning houses where you yourself used to live), the day care centers, the school yards, the parks and playgrounds, the restaurants, the movie theaters, the concert halls, the innumerable airport lounges, train and bus stations, and lately the restaurants and street corners and libraries—all of the locations where you have traveled to make these rendezvous so that something broken might seem like something whole. And now we hug and kiss and hurry off to her sociology class on the modern American family.

The lecture room is packed, maybe a hundred or more people gathered there out of the way of the nasty storm, chatting with each other, turning pages in the text, reviewing notes, mostly undergraduates and a sprinkling of older graduate students and some other more mature observers—researchers? other faculty? visitors, parents, like myself? From the raised platform at the front of the hall, the instructor, a rather attractive if somewhat plump graying woman in her early forties, calls the class to attention. She quickly outlines her purposes. Today, she announces, as she commences pacing from one side of the platform to the other, she'll begin by delineating the profile of the modern household: this begins with the fabled nuclear family, but now also includes such new varieties as the "blended" family in which offspring from previous marriages of father and mother live together in a distinctive unit; and the single-parent family, growing each year in big numbers, in which usually the mother carries on the load traditionally borne by two; and such hybrids as the lesbian household in which two women bear the responsibilities traditionally assumed by a woman and a man.

"We're in there somewhere," I say.

Emma has been making notes, writing busily in her pages. But at my remark she looks up from her jotting. Completely unself-conscious in the midst of all this academic sophistication, she leans her head against my shoulder, happy that we're both present for this calling of the roll.

Father and Daughter

M. G. Stephens

The rug bristles with the absence of her dancing feet. The windows glint with the history of her looking. Water rings on the sills recall where her teacup should be. The air lacks a sweet buzz.

—Scott Russell Sanders

MY DAUGHTER prepares to leave home for her final year of college. Her leaving is not as traumatic as it was several years earlier when she left home as a freshman. But since she is about to graduate and become involved in what commencement speakers call "the rest of life," I have to ask myself what I contributed to her sense of what that life is and how she is going to respond to it. What have I contributed to her happiness and spiritual promise? If I write about being a father, don't I have to understand who my daughter is? That being the case, I call her on the telephone. After the usual greetings and small talk about school and friends, I ask my daughter what she thinks a father should be.

"Can I get back to you on that?" she asks.

"I'll call you later this evening," I say, and hang up.

A few hours later, I call again.

Of course, I would like to write her a letter, but time does not allow that. That is not to say I don't write her because I do. Yet even speaking to her on the phone, I can't help think of literary models. After all, I'd rather be a poet than a journalist—a Yeats instead of a Boswell—but time is not on my side. My model for writing letters to Mora—when time does allow—has been F. Scott Fitzgerald's letters to his daughter when she was in college. He wrote her: "All I believe in in life is the rewards for virtue (according to your talents)." Further along in one letter, he tells her to worry about courage, cleanliness, and efficiency, but not to worry about popular opinion, dolls, the past, the future, growing up, anybody getting ahead of you, parents, boys, disappointments, pleasures, and satisfactions. My own letters (needless to say) were nowhere near as brilliant as Fitzgerald's were, nor had I offered any really earthshaking advice to my daughter about life. Still, I thought of Fitzgerald's letters as the ideal communication between a father and a daughter, even to addressing one part of my desires for her happiness and spiritual promise.

Fitzgerald writes his daughter: "I am glad you are happy—but I never believe much in happiness."

That is probably true; happiness is an overrated condition. Contentment might be better. Or consider love itself. Happiness is only a part of it in sappy popular ballads and annoying situation comedies on television. So that left spiritual promise. I asked myself what I had bequeathed my own daughter in this regard. Had I given her any sense of a spiritual life? When I asked her this very question, she said yes, although we had never practiced any kind of formal religion in our household. The closest we had come to a religious institution was during our journeys to Korea where we often visited Buddhist temples. We did not attend services, though. I want to say that my daughter Mora's spiritual life resembles my own transcendentalist sense of nature being a harbinger of a higher power, but I realize that in her case it probably is a combination of her father's Emersonian (via Thoreau) awe of the natural world and her mother's native animism that found spirits in the earth, trees, mountains, and rivers.

Waves on a beach at Cape Cod, a powerful sunset on the Hudson River, a special tree in Central Park, all of these things were what made my daughter reflect on spirituality. She told me that she would even ask herself, at heightened moments of awareness, Who made this?

I don't want to portray either Mora or myself as some kind of New Age nature-loving pantheistic family. But I also don't want to suggest that, because we did not attend church, there was no spirituality in our household. You cannot be a creative person, living and struggling in the world, without being aware of some kind of spiritual force in the universe, but particularly in one's very own life. But what was ours?

When we speak about spirituality—I tell her that my spiritual awakening came after I got out of an alcohol treatment rehab—it is not any kind of organized religion Mora remembers, but rather her own versions of sacred places. We lived for years uptown on the edge of Harlem in Morningside Heights, half a block from Saint John the Divine, the largest Gothic cathedral in the United States. Before the Episcopal Church closed it to build a garish moonfaced bronze statue, Mora spent her early childhood playing in the church's public garden where peacocks called out, opening their colorful plumage; and the Biblical Garden, behind the church, taught her what plants came from the Bible.

We did not attend church, even when I taught writing at Fordham, a Jesuit university. But we walked in New York City's parks and along its beaches. Our family's spirituality was a combination of my lapsed Irish Roman Catholic upbringing, particularly with its stress on Saint Francis of Assisi's simplicity and literal-minded faith, along with my wife's Korean Buddhism, and perhaps our daughter's own American transcendentalist belief in the sun, the sky, the moon, the stars; and especially in a cherry tree in Central Park that Mora and her friend Amy used to visit every spring to hold a meeting of the Cherry Blossom Club.

Mora tells me that in addition to her belief in spiritual places—she mentions Cape Cod, a geography in which we have always had good times—she has a sense of treating others kindly. I think that this idea comes from her maternal relations, an enormous Korean family that she has known since she was a small child, for we often went to visit them in Seoul in her childhood. This idea of cultivating good ways to treat others comes from Buddhism—though I can see how it also relates to the Christian idea of good deeds—and I think of Mora's great-grandmother, a tiny, wrinkled, whiskey-drinking, cigarette-smoking octogenarian who exemplified the virtues of a compassionate Buddhist and who took us to her favorite Buddhist temples when we came to visit her in Seoul.

The first time Mora visited Korea was in 1978 when she was only two and a half years old. We spent the spring, summer, and beginning of the fall there. Prior to that, we lived in New Haven, where I was in a graduate program at the Yale School of Drama. Only weeks before coming to Seoul, we had seen a production of Sam Shepard's *Mad Dog Blues* on a working-class beach in East Haven. One of the characters, coming over a dune, shouted "Yahudi!" at the top of his lungs, and right in the middle of the play, Mora returned the call, shouting back "Yahudi!" The audience broke up laughing, and the actor, a very good one, ad-libbed his way back into the production. It reminded me of an old theatrical adage about animals, naked women, and children upstaging any action or characterization in a play.

In Mora's three years at college, she has acted in plays, written them, and directed her own and other plays. Also, she has written and directed several movie scripts which she shot on video, and one short script was shot on 16mm film. In other words, she still is, like I once was, involved in the mimetic arts, the collaborative ones, of theatre and moviemaking.

That's when I realized, recollecting these events, that probably our deepest spiritual connection was found in the theatre. Yet someone might ask, What is so spiritual about an egotistical pursuit like show business? I can't answer that, simply because I need to go back to Western drama's origins in the Greek choral dances and songs, and suddenly this becomes pedantic. Still, I can see how theatre, my own drunkenness, and spirituality all hook up, and how finally they are all one thing, the life of the spirit and the spirit one brings to a life.

Drama starts with paying homage to the god of wine, Dionysius, the patron of this dissembler's art. Drunkenness was the religion of Dionysius, and he created such a frenzy in his worshipers that they even devoured their own god. Dionysius was the god of frenzy, of extreme feeling, of libations, of complete and utter drunkenness. Fifteen hundred years would pass before the Christian gods entered the theatres in Europe, and that journey began with a bit of improvised dialogue recited by the three Marys at the tomb of the risen Christ on Easter.

Before I came into the theatre myself, I engaged my life in what I heard one writer call "the theatre of the poor," that is, drinking. First I was a drunk, then I became a writer; later, still a drunk and a writer, I became a playwright. I should say that I became a drunken playwright because my most successful play was one called *Our Father* which ran for five years, off and on, at midnight weekend shows in a theatre bar on Forty-Second Street off of Times Square in New York City. Sometimes, instead of getting paid for a performance, I sat at the bar upstairs, drinking myself into oblivion.

Alcohol is where I lost myself, and alcoholism is where I found myself. Although I had twelve plays produced off-off-Broadway in the 1980s, I've had none performed in the 1990s. About the only place where I experience the collision of the sacred and the profane nowadays is at Alcoholics Anonymous meetings. Yet I still see the spiritual connections I passed along to my daughter Mora. She has handled the Dionysian part of the drama more effectively than I ever did, though. For starters, she does not drink. Her sense of tragedy does not need to include her own life; she prefers the tragedies to take place on the stage, where—to this day—Hamlet's definition of the drama is still the best one, "four boards and a passion." Oddly enough or maybe not so oddly, these boards and this passion define the tensions that ultimately create the spiritual legacy of the stage, and what I think I gave my daughter.

But already I am getting ahead of myself; I need to backtrack. Let me go back to the interview I did with her on the telephone.

My daughter's earliest memories of the theatre occurred when she was three and four years old, and I was a graduate student in New Haven. She remembers going to rehearsals for a verse play I wrote called *Cloud-Dream* in which her mother performed the female lead. It was a play about Kim Sakkat, a legendary Korean vagabond poet who supposedly bedded down with thousands of women and who spoke only in improvised verses; his pen name was Rainhat. His wife Solmae, being a shaman, keeps changing herself into other women in order to keep her husband, but eventually he slips away, drinking himself to death. I think what fascinated Mora about this production was the poetry I provided, the operatic voice her mother brought to the part of Solmae, and the delightful improvisational qualities the director and other actors brought to the production. What impressed her most was the spirit of collaboration, the spirituality found in how people worked together to create a unified creative work.

London is another theatre venue my daughter remembers well. After

Our Father had been running at the West Bank Cafe on Theatre Row for a few years, we took the play to the Edinburgh Fringe Festival one summer, and then to a theatre bar in Hampstead, north of London. One of the actors received a callback for the lead in a television situation comedy, and our one extra actor—filling in as a stagehand and theatrical factotum—plugged the hole in the cast, leaving no one to take over the house manager and lighting board jobs in Hampstead.

My wife and daughter arrived in London the day before, shocked to see how dissipated we all had become after a monthlong sojourn in Scotland. Dionysius ruled us in the guise of Budweiser beer, the actual producer of our show in the U.K. After a month of round-the-clock drinking, the spirits had reduced me to a jittery mass of nerve endings in bad need of sleep. It was my then nine-year-old daughter Mora who became house manager/light-board specialist for the rest of the play's run. I remember coming back to the cheap hotel room late one night after drinking with the cast in an after-hours place. Mora lay in bed under the covers, listening to her mother scold me about my drinking and general behavior. My daughter smiled; really, her smile was devilishly angelic.

"Oh, no," I said, "she's got the theatre bug."

"No, she doesn't," my wife said.

But she had it.

Only now, interviewing her, I realize that she had the theatre bug long before coming to London. It started in New Haven, attending rehearsals for my play because we could not find or could not afford a baby-sitter. Then the theatre bug took off for her one summer in Wellfleet—a few years after moving from New Haven—when we rented perhaps the tiniest cottage on Cape Cod. One evening, the humidity thick, we walked via Uncle Tim's Bridge into the town center and saw a community theatre production of Noel Coward's *Blithe Spirit*.

"That's probably when I caught the theatre bug," Mora says.

I need to note, though, that Noel Coward rarely did anything for me, and so I found it hard to imagine that this play and this production did anything to interest her in the theatre. I think this only proves that we find our spirituality in odd places. The monk Basho wanders Japan in search of enlightenment, and returns home years later, only to find the

light in his own yard. I have to remind myself that Mora is utterly perplexed by how much I adore Eddie Murphy's *Nutty Professor* movie, a
work whose comedy I find transcendent, even sublime.

Although Mora, twenty-one years old, is an adult now, I cannot
shake the memory of the first sight I had of her at Saint Luke's Hospital
in Morningside Heights. I say this now because it is one of the most dramatic moments in my own life. Not only that, it was one of the most
spiritual. It was dramatic because her mother had been in a long, painful labor, and although I had been prepared to assist in my child's delivery, I had to leave at the last moment when the doctor decided to perform a Caesarean section.

After I first saw my daughter in the hospital, staring at me with her
dark, ferocious, probing eyes, her tiny hawklike nose, and her little
pursed lips, I ran home to write about this experience:

> Mouth of kiss, rose-puff mouth, high-strung Mora, mother-brine and
> fish-like, she reaches with fish-hand as though still in seaworld of
> mother-womb, Mi-Ok . . .
>
> High-strung Mora, mountain and sea, dragon-girl, florid-cheek Mi-
> Ok. The night, you were born. Night was snow. I walked in white, sing-
> ing in the snow:
>
> > Rose-puff mouth
> > Mouth of kiss
> > Mora, Mora mia
> > Mi-Ok, little love
>
> Earthworld woman and woman. Mother & daughter well, resting.
> Earth-hand Mora. Pink Mora. Cool daughter I love. First beauty, new
> jade. How she suckles and sighs. Pale Mi-Ok, dragon black eyes and hair.

I suppose all fathers, add or subtract the vocabulary, feel this way
when their first child is born. But what made my response different was
the extremity to which I went to celebrate this occasion. Though I did
not think of myself as an alcoholic at the time, I had given up drinking
the year before. Now I wanted to celebrate. Who else better to celebrate

the birth of a daughter with than my old friend Dionysius, the god of fermented grapes, in this case, not wine, but cognac. I drank a bottle of Remy Martin with a friend. Spirited, full of emotion, I consumed a spirit, so that by morning, when I should have been high on the excitement of a new life, I was hung over, miserable with detoxification, full of the shakes and tremors as Dionysius slipped away in the morning shadows to rest himself.

Even in that postdrunken squalor, I could not undo the feelings I had experienced. I recalled how fiercely my daughter Mora stared at me. In those fierce eyes I saw an intelligence filled with questioning and skepticism, demanding to know who I was. I was her father, and it was love at first sight. But unlike her immediate relationship with her mother from whom she had lately sprung, this was a relationship that had to be earned. Mothers get their parts automatically as the receptacle around which a child finds nurturing life. A father must do an audition, bring along an effective monologue to make any sort of relationship worthwhile. What my daughter was getting was a deeply spiritual man who either did not know this fact or else was embarrassed by this condition. Thus he drank. But not just drank. He drank to excess. How Dionysian!

More than two decades after my daughter's birth, I am still learning how to be a father. My human sympathies—particularly ones for women—derive more from being a father than a husband or a lover. Yet what is it I have bequeathed her? Is a love of the stage, of what Hamlet called "four boards and a passion," enough legacy to give her? Yes and no, I have to say. To merely act is to dissemble, as the old preachers and even the ancient Greek politicians said. But to find a spiritual way in the dramatic moment is quite another thing; that is where the theatre becomes transcendent, a paean to the human spirit.

It was Yeats, not in the prayer for his daughter, but in another poem entitled "Lapis Lazuli," who articulated that the tragic moment is not about sadness but joy. Theatre, then, is about the joy of living, not its angst alone, even though that which is dramatic demands tension. I remember a teacher telling us that the tragic condition exists on the stage and nowhere else; we cannot replicate those terms in our lives. And Yeats was right. Tragedy is about the joy of living, even when suffering is involved. Pain is a touchstone of spiritual growth.

Perhaps because I wanted to write Mora wise letters, I still harked back to literary models as some kind of ideals. But maybe I ought to forget the literary models and think about the human condition before me. I need spirits in my life other than Dionysius. If the Christian gods won't help me and the Old Testament god appears too formidable for me, I still have that gentle eastern god, the Buddha, forever a comforting friend when I lived or visited Korea. And I have the spirits in the earth, the sky above, the trees, the flowers, in the rivers and mountains without end. I am delighted that my daughter Mora chose to follow in my footsteps in regard to mimesis, but I also want to bequeath her these other spirits, too.

What do I want for my daughter? I want her to flourish in life, to find, if not answers, then good questions; to live at peace and even find serenity in her life; to be a good person to herself and to others; to understand—another lesson from theatre—that collaboration is a high art, one that involves a deep understanding of human nature, people's foibles, their insecurities, and their fears, but also their dreams, wishes, aspirations, and deepest beliefs. I want her to have true humility, which is not being too small or too large, but just the right size. I want her to express gratitude for her gifts. Yet I am articulating fatherly values here, not daughterly ones.

In the course of my telephone conversation with Mora, I ask her what she thinks a father should be. This is the other side of the spiritual equation. Now I have to listen to my daughter. Sometimes you talk to god (prayer) and sometimes you listen (meditation). What better way to find god than through another person; and what better person to do this with than my own daughter!

Mora tells me that a father should protect his daughter, be a good friend, be playful yet serious. Oh, yes, he must be consistent, at least, he *should be* consistent. It is not a father's job to punish or be severe.

"Be wise," she says, laughing.

We are beginning to sound like koans, like Taoist monks, like Zen masters.

"A father is the man who makes the strongest impression on a daughter," she says, and I scribble this down quickly, trying to keep up with her. What a woman's male relationships will be like depends upon how her own father treats her. What a father does, she says, will be repeated, over and over, in all her relationships with other men. My daughter continued: "A father's actions have consequences for a daughter far down the line."

Finally, she says, a father is "a provider, someone a daughter can trust, someone who does not lie to her, someone who commits to be there."

I am reminded of an old show business adage. Showing up is eighty percent of the work. The rest is about concentration and focus, about being specific, all of which—just being there, just being—are deeply spiritual values. What I want to tell my daughter is to be yourself. Just be yourself. But really I mean that she should just be. Just be. And, conversely, that's what a father has to do, too. Not to be or not to be. Just be. Be, be, be. . . .

5

Wings

To Eva, on Your Marriage

Scott Russell Sanders

SOON YOU'LL WALK down the aisle with a dancer's grace, your hand looped through my arm, and the minister will ask who gives this bride away. I will obey custom and your firm instructions by saying "I do," yet I can't give you away, for you aren't mine to give. You belong only to yourself, and to the power that created you, so beautiful and bright, out of sunlight, food, water, and air.

For me to claim ownership of you, as fathers since time out of mind have claimed ownership of their daughters, would be like a twig on a great oak pretending to have made all by itself the newest bud. You're a sprout of the whole tree; you're the daughter of Earth. Yes, I contributed my share to your making, passing on my genes through an act of delight. But this joining with your mother to set you in motion gives me no right of possession, for the biological memory carried in my genes stretches back, unbroken, through the countless inventions of eye and hand and backbone and brain to the first flicker of life in the primal seas.

I knew you, darling, while you swam and kicked in the small sea of your mother's womb. I knew you from laying my fingers and ear to her taut belly. I knew you from the shining in her eyes and from the catch in her breath when you moved. All that summer and fall of 1972, while you waxed inside her like a secret moon, she and I took long swaying walks every night after supper, brimming with tenderness and anxiety. By the short days of December, we began our walks after dark, so we kept to the lighted streets, not wanting to stumble. Mom was determined to hold out for the full nine months, which would end in January, because in that month Bloomington Hospital would begin allowing fathers into the delivery room, and she wanted me there. I was there, from the earliest pains right through your birth, holding her feverish hand, reminding her to take shallow breaths, mopping her forehead with a damp cloth, murmuring to her steadily all night, then babbling ecstatically when you arrived near dawn.

Nothing I had imagined beforehand prepared me for the sight of you, so perfectly made, so intent on life. Every inch of you pulsed with energy, hands groping, legs churning, and your skin glowed furnace red. I trembled. When your body convulsed for a gulp of our difficult air, I gasped. The sound of your first cry echoed through my bones. I wanted to shout. Maybe I did shout, because the nurses looked at me appraisingly, as if to calculate my need for a sedative or a straitjacket. No matter how old this miracle, no matter how many times it had been repeated through the generations, it was brand new to me. You were the first baby ever born, my heart was sure of it. The birth of the universe could not have been more thrilling.

You were utterly fresh, every toe and finger and eyelash and cell an unprecedented wonder. Done up in a turquoise cap and gown like a refugee from an asylum, I sat in the hospital chair, my feet planted on the floor to make a solid lap, my back tense with responsibility, and for the first time I held you, so fearfully small, barely six pounds. My hands, cradling you, seemed clumsy and huge. Wondering, I bent down to feel your breath against my cheek. You smelled of apples. After a few minutes you started to whimper, so I handed you gingerly to Mom, knowing that only she could satisfy you. I stroked your fuzzy head while you nursed. How avidly you sucked, even before her milk began to flow! No monk in the rapture of meditation could have been more devoutly focused on God than you were on your mother's breast.

When it was time for you to go home, the nurse handed you to me while Mom lowered herself gingerly into a wheelchair. Only your drowsy eyes and tiny dollop of nose showed from an opening in the pink blanket—the inevitable pink blanket—in which you had been wrapped against the January cold. As I clutched you to my chest, a wave of worry swept over me. These experts in babies were actually going to let us take you out the door, as if we knew how to rear a child. What training had we ever had, except watching our own parents carelessly as we grew up? At least my watching had been haphazard; I can't speak for Mom's. Oh, sure, we'd read books on babies, but that's like reading manuals to learn about sex. It seemed outrageous that a hospital would turn over a creature so tiny and precious and new to a pair of rank amateurs. Yet no one blocked our way as I pushed the wheelchair, with you in Mom's lap, down the tiled halls to the entrance, then out to our waiting car, its engine running and the heater on high. An orderly followed to fetch the chair. I half expected him to demand you back; but he only waved and wished us luck. I gave one lingering look at that haven of experts, and away we drove.

In early English, *wife* simply meant woman, as if a girl could not graduate to adulthood except by marrying. Farther back, *wife* sprang from an Indo-European root meaning "to wrap, twist, or turn," a reference to the married woman's veil. To become a wife was to go into hiding from the world.

In most places and most ages where those words have been used, women were chattel, like any other piece of a man's property. Girls were betrothed at birth or in childhood, often married in adolescence, and married not for love but for the father's advantage—to return favors, forge alliances, settle disputes, clear debts, buy land. Daughters were spendable coin. Once given or sold in marriage, the woman became a servant, if she was lucky, otherwise a concubine or slave.

Ancient history? During the week in which I begin this letter to you, dearest Eva, a puritanical faction has emerged victorious in the Afghan civil war. Their first act, after hanging the thugs who preceded them, was to order women off the streets, out of government, out of the professions, and back behind the veil. Any woman caught away from home with her face bare may be summarily whipped. Who would have thought, on the brink of the twenty-first century, that women could still be banished from public life, turned away from the light, wrapped up like packages to be opened only by husbands?

From the moment of your birth, every reference to women in the news, in literature, in jokes and jibes, took on for me a burning importance. I'd read the New Testament several times in childhood, for example, but now suddenly I felt the menace in Paul's advice to Timothy: "Let a woman learn in silence with all submissiveness. I permit no woman to teach or to have authority over men; she is to keep silent. For Adam was formed first, then Eve; and Adam was not deceived, but the woman was deceived and became a transgressor." Suddenly I recognized the danger to women in the Genesis account of that primordial marriage—a "poetical story," as Mary Wollstonecraft called it, which certifies "that woman was created for man." Here was Eve, the original wife, created as an afterthought out of Adam's rib, giving in to the wily snake and her own appetite, plucking the apple, then foisting the forbidden fruit onto her innocent mate. This calumny against woman, the vain temptress, irked me all the more because her name is another form of yours, dear Eva, one that derives from the Hebrew word for "life."

After blaming Eve for our fall from grace, Paul adds, "Yet woman will be saved through bearing children, if she continues in faith and love and holiness, with modesty." Paul reads Genesis selectively, of course, as patriarchs are inclined to do, ignoring the first version of the Creation, which grants Adam no priority: "So God created man in his own image, in the image of God he created him; male and female he created them. And God blessed them." Them, male and female. Jesus appealed to this earlier version when the Pharisees challenged him to see if he would approve of divorce: "Have you not read that he who made them from the beginning made them male and female, and said, 'For this reason a man shall leave his father and mother and be joined to his wife, and the two shall become one'? So they are no longer two but one. What therefore God has joined together, let no man put asunder."

Those words, in turn, have certainly caused much grief, forcing many couples to stay together in misery when they would have been far better off put asunder. But seen in historical context, Jesus' prohibition on divorce appears as a stunning defense of women, for under the laws of Moses only men had the power to break a marriage. "For your hardness of heart," Jesus told the Pharisees, "Moses allowed you to divorce your wives, but from the beginning it was not so." That the abandoning of wives, especially those who failed to produce children, was an affliction in Israel might be surmised from repeated warnings in the Hebrew Bible. "Let none be faithless to the wife of his youth," Malachi insists. And the book of Proverbs offers these instructions to Jewish men:

> Let your fountain be blessed,
>> and rejoice in the wife of your youth,
>> a lovely hind, a graceful doe.
> Let her affection fill you at all times with delight,
>> be infatuated always with her love.

Paul certainly honored love and loyalty in marriage, but not equality. In one of the more notorious passages from his letters, he proclaims: "Wives, be subject to your husbands, as to the Lord. For the husband is the head of the wife as Christ is the head of the church, his body, and is himself its Savior. As the church is subject to Christ, so let wives also be subject in everything to their husbands."

Again, this is not ancient history I'm rehearsing. Paul's words, together with those of Moses and countless other patriarchs through the ages, still influence the prospects for women today. Those who hold power never give it up without a fight. Only recently, Pope John Paul II reaffirmed that women may not become priests within the Catholic Church ("I permit no woman to teach or to have authority over men; she is to keep silent.") and that birth control is a sin ("Yet woman will be saved through bearing children."). Well, I set myself against those ancient prejudices. I oppose any constraints that apply only to women, and my concern for you and your fate adds to the warmth of my opposition.

Multiply this little excursion of thought by a million, and you will begin to see how your birth made the reputation and condition of women personal for me. Statistics on rape, on poverty, on wife beating, on single mothers, on jobs and pay for women, became disturbing facts about the society in which my daughter would grow up. Would you be injured by the sexual fantasies pumped out endlessly by advertisers and filmmakers and rock stars and cranks? Would you be free to pursue your talents, wherever they might lead? Whenever I learned of women being hurt or ridiculed or held back, I thought immediately of you. Would you be scarred or scorned? Would you find men blocking your path, soldiers or bureaucrats or executives? And how was I implicated in the shameful history of men mistreating women?

Even falling in love with the woman who would become your mother had not inspired in me such troubled questioning, because she was brilliant in science, in music, in writing and speech; she was poised and confident; she was balanced on her own center. She had found a husband with plenty of flaws, but one who would never lay a hand on her except in love, never betray or desert her. To my bedazzled eyes, this Ruth McClure seemed to have emerged into womanhood unscathed. But you were just beginning. How would you fare? Loving you, wishing you a full and free and joyous life, I set about pondering the lives of women as I never had in all the years before your birth.

On hearing that we'd had a baby, many of our friends and acquaintances, women as well as men, asked first of all: "What is it?" I was sorely tempted to answer, "Human," yet I knew what they meant, of course. So I played along, saying, "She's a girl, a hungry, fidgety, wonderful girl." Only then did they ask your name, your weight, the color of your hair and eyes, and how the delivery had gone.

Among the books we read while preparing nervously for your arrival were several on gender bias in childrearing. The pink and blue treatment begins early, we learned. Studies of delivery rooms show that nurses tend to handle boys more roughly and speak to them more loudly. Mothers of newborns often carry on these distinctions, holding girls closely and gently, holding boys loosely and distantly, murmuring to the girls and talking firmly to the boys. So from the outset, the paths begin to fork, and for a child nudged in one direction or the other, there may be no going back. In videotaped experiments, mothers presented with toddlers whom they do not know tend to be more verbal and soothing with those dressed as girls, gruffer and more physical with those dressed as boys; they keep the girls close by, within easy reach, while they encourage the boys to move out and explore the room. Supplied with an array of toys, these mothers will usually offer trucks and balls and hammers to the infants whom they take to be boys, dolls and mirrors and dress-up clothes to the ones whom they take to be girls. I suspect that fathers might have acted in similar ways; but the experiments appear never to have included fathers, perhaps because the men were busy driving trucks and swinging hammers and roving about.

Reading all of that before your birth, and not yet realizing how stubborn human character and culture are, your mother and I vowed to resist these warping influences. We would rear you purely as a child, neither girl nor boy, so that you might grow like a tree in full sunlight, taking on your own natural shape. You arrived early in 1973, after all, a time when many of us who were under thirty considered nature to be all-wise and culture to be a snarl of rusty chains, easily broken. We would seek out playmates for you whose parents were also striving to break the old gender shackles. We would allow into our house only those books, magazines, television programs, and visitors that honored your right to become whatever your heart and mind led you to be. We would put before you the whole rainbow of human possibilities, and let you choose.

Yet there you were, two days old, riding home from the hospital swaddled in a pink blanket. It was a gift from someone so close to us that we could not say no, the first of many such gifts. Clearly, whatever Mom and I might decide about rearing you, the world would have its say, right from the beginning, and the world's say would grow louder each year.

By the time I carried you into the house, presents had already begun to accumulate there in drifts, most of them cuddly, frilly, and pastel. Enough dolls to start a nursery, a teddy bear that mooed when it rolled over, a robin's-egg-blue satin pillow with music box inside that played a Brahms lullaby, morally uplifting storybooks, pale baby duds for every occasion, and soft mobiles to dangle over your crib. I didn't rush out and buy you a GI Joe and miniature chain saw and baseball glove to even things up. But I did make sure you had a toolbox fitted with toy hammer and screwdriver and wrench, and a board rigged out with plastic hinges and bells and gears, and a little bench for pounding. Thus, I began smuggling into your life my own hopes for who you might turn out to be.

Try as we might, Mom and I could not shield you from everything the world expected of girls, least of all from the expectations buried deep in ourselves. We could not undo our own upbringing, could not erase the hundreds of films and thousands of books and millions of images we'd taken in. Each of us had built up a composite notion of maleness and femaleness from all the boys and girls, men and women we had met, beginning with our own parents. Even though we wrestled with those notions, trying to break their hold, they still left their marks on us, visible and invisible. When we cuddled you, spoke to you, played and romped and dreamed with you, who could say what unconscious impulses reached you through our hands and lips?

You certainly kept our hands and lips and every other bit of us occupied in those early months. For the first year or so, you rarely slept more than two or three hours at a stretch, and never through the whole night. Although I must have been tired, the weariness has washed out of memory, and now I remember only the bliss of watching you, tracing the weather of your face; I remember feeding you the one nightly bottle that gave Mom relief from nursing; I remember bathing you in the sink, with a towel underneath to shield you from the chilly porcelain; I remember rocking you, or flying you around the room at arm's length, or spinning a leaf in front of your face so it tickled your nose, or showing you snow. I remember carrying you for hours each night as I paced around the apartment, and soothing you with songs. As soon as you found your voice, you began to sing along, in a skittery language known only to babies and sleepless parents. When I exhausted the repertoire that I could remember from my own father's singing, I worked my way through anthologies of folk songs, from immigrant ballads through whaling chanteys and spirituals and lullabies and love ditties and blues, skipping only those selections that featured bloodshed, drugs, or booze.

You've heard most of these memories before, even read some of them in my books, for I never tire of talking about you. When I sit down to make this small present of words for your wedding, I can't help recalling the child you were behind the woman you've become. There wouldn't be paper enough to hold all the memories of your growing up, so I recount only a few from the early years, when your character took shape.

In your very first spring, one blustery March day I was carrying you, bundled in a blanket, along the sidewalk from house to car. Before I reached the street, you stiffened in my arms, twisted your face about, and gazed with a startled look into the empty air. I stopped, looked around, but could not figure out what had provoked you. "What's up, Kiddo?" I asked. You weren't saying. I snuggled the blanket around you and took another step. Again you jerked, swiveled your head, stared. Only then did I feel what you were feeling, the breath of March. My eyes flared wide, and my face turned into the amazing wind.

Later that same spring, I was pushing you in the stroller one afternoon when you noticed a peach-pit moon near the horizon. You reached for it, fingers splayed, and started fussing when you discovered that your arm wasn't long enough. "That's the moon," I told you, "and it's far, far away." Months later, when you were just beginning to put sentences together, once again we came upon a ghostly moon during a walk, and this time you announced, "There's the moon. Want it, Daddy." Even if your arm wasn't long enough to reach it, you figured, then surely mine would be. I had to disappoint you, of course, and also to disappoint myself, because your hunger for the moon revived my own.

Again and again, your frank wonder stripped away the glaze of familiarity from the world. Look at that fiery ball in the sky! Smell that dirt! Taste that good water going down! Feel those wavy lines in wood! When it stormed, you and I would sit on the porch in a rocker, the rumble of thunder and sizzle of rain in our ears, mist on our faces, as still as we could be. When the leaves fell, we raked up heaps in the backyard and you plowed through them, grabbing and flinging, nibbling, yelping. What a universe! What a life! Was there no end to the surprises? You squatted tirelessly to study bees nuzzling the throats of flowers. You gawked at butterflies as they tilted overhead, spinning around until you grew dizzy. You rushed from firefly to firefly as they simmered in the grass. Anything living would captivate you—a dog, a cat, a spider, a roly-poly on the windowsill, a blue jay scrawking in the maple tree, a fern breaking ground, another child toddling along, a grown-up's idly jostling foot. How exactly right that a girl who stopped in her tracks whenever she spied a bird, who fed bread to ducks and swans, who picked up every feather she found, who tilted her face skyward in spring and fall when the geese went honking by—that such a girl should grow up to become a biologist and study birds.

As birds seem to embody your love of air, so whales seem to embody your love of water. That affection, too, began early on. You first met the ocean at Little Boar's Head beach in New Hampshire, when you were eighteen months old, squealing with surprise as the waves licked your bare feet. On our return trips to New England, up and down the coast from Cape Cod to Maine, you dipped in the chilly Atlantic or rode in boats on its choppy waters. You would stare at the surf with the same focused eagerness that you once showed when nursing, and with the same reluctance to break away. You were five when you met the Pacific, at Haceta Beach near Florence, Oregon. You clambered through a maze of driftwood logs, lurked around tide pools, stood watching waves break on rock. From a bluff on that same coast you saw your first whales, California grays migrating north, and ever after you took these great creatures to be the soul of the sea. For years, whenever anyone asked what you hoped to do when you grew up, you would answer, "Study whales."

The whales eventually swam away from the center of your imagination; but the ocean remained. Clearly, though you were born and bred a Midwestern girl, and though you've come back here to the landlocked heart of the continent to get married, some deep part of you hungers for the sea. Or perhaps what you hunger for is not so much the vastness of ocean as the force of moving water. From your earliest days, you've been drawn to the roar of rain, the flow of rivers, the tumble of falls, the sluice of snowmelt in the street. You may have caught some of that passion from me, but not all of it. During the year we spent in Exeter, when you turned two, our favorite destination for walks was the bridge over the Squamscott River where the old mill stood. You would gaze down from one side of the bridge at the tumbling water for a long while, then take my hand and cross the street to gaze down from the other side. No matter what your mood when we set out, after a few minutes at the river, you would grow calm and clear and gathered, and so would I.

In contrast to that serenity, your other dominant mood has always been a fierce whirl of energy, finely controlled. You began gymnastics and dancing the same year that you first spied whales. In our rented house, you would race full tilt down the hallway, plant your hands on the arm of the couch, and go vaulting over onto the cushions. On the springy grass of the backyard, you turned endless cartwheels and flips, asking me to spot you on the tricky ones. At the ballet studio you began the long training that would one day send you gliding down the aisle with a dancer's grace. There was nothing delicate or fragile about you when you leapt and turned, but rather a dazzling strength, akin to the strength of wind blowing and water flowing and wild creatures moving freely. What are birds, after all, but the most accomplished dancers, who can maneuver in thin air?

Whether in motion or still, you've always been a rapt observer. From the beginning, we took you with us when we visited friends, and you would sit in the midst of the grown-ups with saucer eyes and avid ears. At bedtime, no matter whose house we happened to be in, we could lay you down on a blanket on the floor of a nearby room, and you would go to sleep without a peep. That was the price you paid for getting to tag along and overhear adult conversation. Although you had lots to say when you were alone with Mom or me, in company you preferred to listen and watch.

That is the essence of what you do now, as a scientist, listening and watching. Only now, instead of a roomful of grown-ups, what fascinates you is an aviary full of birds, or a field thick with grasses and insects, or a river churning with otters, or a notebook full of data. You have a head for discovering patterns, and a heart for loving them.

So do I, darling Eva, although the patterns I care about are made mostly of language and memory. To a surprising degree, marriage is made of the same ingredients. You begin, if you're lucky, with a rush of romance, but you continue at the slower pace of shared history, a history that stays with you in stories, habits, recipes, photographs, clothes, art on the walls, rumpled sofas, potted plants, and, just maybe, in children. The two of you talk. You touch. You reminisce. You plan. You cook and clean and cope. Together you weave a fabric that neither of you could have made alone. The strength of that fabric depends on circumstances beyond your control, of course, but also on the care and patience and commitment you bring to the effort.

I started out this rambling letter by recalling your birth, because a wedding is a birth of another sort. In becoming husband and wife, a man and woman do not cease to be individuals, yet they become in addition someone new, a compound self. Two shall become one, as Jesus said. Maybe in this paradox there is something of what twins experience, each one distinct and yet each one dwelling in constant awareness of the other. Living with a mate is harder than living alone, but also richer. No learning in my life has been more difficult, humbling, or surprising than the daily lessons of marriage. As you begin your own marriage, I want you to know that I still rejoice in the wife of my youth. After thirty years, I am still infatuated with her love. I don't count this fidelity as a virtue of mine or hers, but as a great and enduring gift.

Since I held you on your first day of life, dearest Eva, I have been fretting about the cruel and belittling images of women that circulate out there in the big, bad world. I would erase them all if I had the power. And while I was making the world safer for you, I would work a few changes on men, as well. The prospect of your wedding has made me worry afresh about my half of the species, with our penchant for selfishness and surliness, our insecurities, our aimless hungers, and our yen for power. I keep reminding myself that you are not marrying men in general but only one man, and by all appearances a good one. My wish for your marriage is that you and Matthew may fashion your own history of shared work, talk, music, nourishing meals, memorable journeys, fine friends, mutual aid and respect and joy. Being married is a life's work, as demanding and rewarding as anything you will ever do.

Building Back through Time

Bill Mayher

AT LAST it is winter. My daughter, Jenny, is visiting us on the Maine coast and one way we plan to celebrate her homecoming is to spend a day outside. We have always enjoyed woods work; the sweet pungency of fresh-cut spruce and fir, the chance to share the resonant quiet—when the chain saw quits its yacking—of frozen woodlands. As indoor muscles stretch and grow limber to the rhythm of outdoor work, we will relish those first prickles of sweat breaking out against the solstice cold. There is a comfortable cadence to the work, from felling and limbing out, to the steady grunt and trudge of hauling four-foot lengths to the roadside stack. By noontime we will touch off brush piles and watch towers of sparks build against an evergreen backdrop while we eat frosty sandwiches and swig water from a jug. Finally at day's end, we have a chance to sit our aching muscles down and be hypnotized by the glow of pulsing embers through the quick December dark. Jenny was nine when we began clearing these woods to build our house. Now she is twenty-five, a woman of the West, at home with ranch work and mountain wilderness. I look forward to her help, but even more to seeing her easy competence in the out-of-doors.

When we leave for the woods, we know the deep snow from several previous storms might give trouble, but we shoulder our bright luggage of chain saws, fuel cans, and pulp hooks, and with our pockets stuffed with sandwiches, head out anyway. At groves and crossings, red squirrels announce our arrival and then cheer, with greater enthusiasm, as we pass below down the woods road. Chickadees and nuthatches flit and twitter. Crows, with their own suspicions, raise a ruckus from the high branches of impenetrable spruces.

All along our way the snow stays consistently deep, and by the time we reach the trees beyond the clearing where we are set to work, we know it's no good. Even in these dense woods, the snow level is above the knee and neither of us looks forward to a morning spent lunging about on rough terrain with a chain saw going lickety-split. So we retrace our steps, put the cutting gear away, and then stand outside the barn, momentarily stranded, like a pair who has just missed a bus, wondering what to do next.

There are paths to clear, however, so we get out shovels and open ways to the compost bins and various outbuildings. It is then we notice that with each shovelfull, the snow comes away in crisp units. Eskimos, given their rich arctic vocabulary, probably have a dozen words for such snow. Suffice it to say that what we are dealing with is two storms' worth; a couple of feet that has settled, been warmed by an eccentric day of thaw, and then reborn in the previous night's cold into dry, sparkling crystals.

This is tender stuff, but if we lift blocks carefully with the flat of our shovels, we quickly see they will form a wall. Instantly this realization brings to life the latent little snow engineer that dwells within so many of us. After childhood winters spent tunneling through snowbanks and rolling sticky balls into complex fortresses, we have at last the chance to construct an igloo, that most elegant and elusive of all snow structures.

We find a section of level, untrampled snow near the barn, and working back-to-back, begin to cut blocks and arrange them in a circle. Later we will wish we had tamped down the foundation layer beneath these first blocks, but still unsure how high we can stack them before tumbledown, we plunge ahead.

But stack this snow surely does, and soon we divide our labor. Jenny stays inside the rising circle to settle blocks in position and chink from the inside. I cut new ones from the outside and serve them up, ever higher, from my shovel. By luck, a spiral develops as we work upward, making the structure more stable. This stability allows Jenny to form the dome by laying each successive course slightly inboard. If we squeeze or push too hard, blocks explode in a sparkling shower, but mostly they hold their integrity until first Jenny's grin, and then her purple hat, disappear behind the ascending wall. In this partnership of heft, balance, and trowelling out, the rest of the world vanishes. Nothing else counts. Frozen gloves and soaked knees go unnoticed. All that matters is the feel of snow and the magic and improbable closing of the dome.

At last, only one engineering problem remains: to cut a door in from the outside so Jenny can get out. But as I slice through the wall—with a sudden and dramatic BA-WHUMP!—the edifice drops a full ten inches. We expect the hilarious catastrophe of total collapse. But instead of chaos, that downward stroke, like the final thrust of a conductor's baton ending a symphony, settles the igloo with startling symmetry. If anything, the compression makes it stronger. I gingerly trim more snow from the doorway, and Jenny slithers, seallike, back into the sunshine.

An Eskimo could have built it better and certainly faster and someday it would be interesting to see an igloo made by expert hands. But we would never trade what we have done that morning. We have always tried to live by the elusive notion that it's the lucky man who plays at work, the lucky child who works at play. Now, fully immersed in shining snow, the thin membrane dividing work and play dissolves altogether. We inhale the intoxicating air of two generations of childhood fused into one, and when at last, we crawl in through the igloo's tiny door to sit together under the enchanted dome of ice-blue light arching above us, we feel, in that moment, whole decades strip away.

Border

William Petersen

FROM MEXICALI we took the train. In the murky morning light the station was dim and dusty. Nearly everyone wore dun- or khaki-colored clothing. We waited in a long line with people carrying bundles and cheap suitcases. It looked like an evacuation. It had been my daughter Christina's idea to take this trip into Mexico, her reward for finishing the year at Berkeley. Her first year of languages, her second year of leukemia.

Christina and I were the only gringos on board. The train was grungy, the high-backed seats stained with years of use. But, as Christina put it, you could imagine that you were traveling through the Old West, and really believe it. Christina moved all over the train trying out bits of Spanish. Her energy could be hard to fathom, and cruelly deceptive. I was depressed and jet-lagged but I would get up from time to time, feeling useless in my stupor, and track her down to see if everything was okay. I'd find her in the club car sipping a beer, taking air between the cars, asking the conductor about upcoming stops. Christina's Spanish was not even up to mine. I don't think it dawned on her at first to speak in anything other than the present tense, she just plunged ahead. The Mexicans responded generously to her enthusiasm.

A woman with two young sons was seated across the aisle from us. The boys were taken with Christina. After watching us carefully they finally asked her in Spanish where we were going.

We don't know where we are going, Christina said. We are just going. *No somos turistas*, she told them in a low voice and with mock solemnity, *Somos desperados.*

Where do you come from desperados? the woman asked.

San Francisco, Christina said, though actually she'd been living in Berkeley and I'd just flown from New York to meet her at her mother's in L.A.

Oh, San Francisco! We are going there someday, the woman said. Such a pretty city. Such a handsome couple, she said.

My father, Christina said, tilting her chin. She was happy to be a part of something handsome, I think, and so was I.

I couldn't help asking her then about Ted. Originally, the three of us had talked about taking this trip. Christina went to Berkeley more or less to be with Ted. To go to school yes, but to be with Ted. They had been high school sweethearts and were a lot alike, I'd always thought. Pale, blond, smart. He was a couple years older and she started late because of her illness. He got a chance to go to grad school at Harvard and couldn't pass it up, Christina said.

He seemed like such a nice guy, I said.

Nice guys are bastards too, she said.

I took Christina's picture with the woman and her sons and we exchanged addresses. They wanted to correspond. It was pleasant to think this but no one would actually write, of course.

The woman told us about Piedras Blancas, a place where *mexicanos* take their vacations, she said. A paradise Americans hadn't discovered yet. Just what Christina and I were looking for. They wanted San Francisco. We wanted the sea and the jungle. But what we had at hand was the desert. Sand seeped through the windows and had even invaded my camera, I discovered when I opened the back to change film.

Christina slept like a baby; I did not sleep at all. I looked out the window as we passed mile after mile of desert, sadness coming on me as night overtook the train. Cactus and the occasional shantytown were covered with blown sand, sand so pervasive and so white in the moonlight that it could have passed for snow.

I have been a photographer all my life. I learned in the Army. I can still call up a slight chill when I think about the first time I put exposed paper into a tray of developer and shook the image alive. I served in the Korean War, doing aerial reconnaissance.

I married Christina's mother. I had ambitions and there were other problems. I was a philanderer. Somehow the ambition and the philandering went together. Eleanor and I divorced and soon after I went to New York, a move I'd had in mind for years. I became known for my portraits and quickly began to make a very decent living. I have taken pictures of thousands of faces. I have never asked anyone to smile.

The next morning we took the bus from Tepic. The road wound down through the hills to the coast. It began to rain gently. A relief from the desert, though only temporary. We crossed a river and the vegetation changed dramatically. Gentle, green, lush. Oh, this is nice, Christina kept saying, I'm glad we're doing this. Trees with extravagant orange blossoms stood in the turns of the road. Shirtless men walked along the shoulder, unsurprised and unhastened by the rain.

When we arrived at Piedras Blancas we walked directly out to the beach which curved southward for miles. Burros and horses grazed, unfenced on the strand among tall thin coconut palms. Oh, this is nice, Christina said.

As we scouted the town a young man approached us, smiling. He was thin with the barest mustache. Have you found a place to stay? he asked. His Spanish was hard for us to understand. He had an odd lisp and Christina tried to tell him so. He laughed and shrugged. I'm from Oaxaca, he said.

Where do you come from? he asked. And to her response, said, Oh, I am going to go there someday.

He sent us toward a hotel where he thought we would be comfortable. Tell them Felipe, he said. We liked it. Just what we were looking for. A central courtyard with ceramic tiles, a hammock, lush plants. The suites were inexpensive and had showers.

We decided to hike down the beach, toward what Christina called "serious jungle," but the heat and the humidity defeated us within a mile, so we retreated to the square and hung out for a while.

It's too hot to eat, Christina said.

You're having something, I said, guiding her by the elbow along the row of vendors. One man sold roasted ears of corn from a zinc washtub.

We had two ears each with lime and salsa, washed down with beer. If it was novel she was willing to try it for the experience.

A pair of tourists came onto the square, laughing. I surmised even from their laughter that the man was an American and the woman European. Perhaps I was keying in on other cues, I don't know. I had the feeling the woman knew I was watching her, though if she saw me it was from the corner of her eye. They crossed the square and disappeared onto the beach.

I asked Christina if she wanted a *liquado*—a shake with fruit, something she would agree to have often enough—and then walked over to the vendor on the strand. Scanning with the telephoto on my camera, I found them some distance away down the beach. In the viewfinder the woman turned to look directly toward me. I snapped her picture. Then I felt ashamed. The woman looked so much like Christina, the same thrust in her chin, the same even gaze.

Sometimes I get tired from so much looking. I have lived for my work. I have lived for pleasure. I have lived selfishly.

That night when Christina and I turned in she came into my room and joined me on the bed. It was sad to see her so pale. It was sad to see her so beautiful.

We read separately for a while, her legs crossed over mine.

It often surprised me how easily she made physical contact with me, as if there had never been gaps in our lives. I was always grateful for such moments. I remembered when she was a little girl visiting and we were both tired, lying on the floor in the afternoon, she would climb on to my back like I was a rock and doze off.

Christina asked me to read to her. You have such a good voice and you pick just the right things, she said, knowing how to get to me.

After the first story she slipped under the covers and turned away.

If you are going to sleep, I am not going to read any more, I said.

Don't stop, I have my good ear up, she said. I'm listening.

It was an old game. I would read to her for a few minutes and then see if she was still following by making up nonsense or sticking her name into the narrative. At certain points she might surface from the brink of sleep and struggle for meaning but she would never make it all the way through.

Dad, she said, I'm not doing it any more. I'm not taking the treatments. Nothing works. I'm just going to do what feels good.

I know, honey, I said.

I'd heard from her mother that she'd been thinking in this direction. We'd talked before about all of this when I flew her East to meet me and see a specialist at the base in Maryland.

I read to her and we left the door open and listened to the rain. This is lovely, she said.

On the square the next day we ran into Felipe, who helped us barter as we bought things from the vendors. We both bought hats. For me, Christina selected a huge, high-domed straw hat. For my ego, she said. For her, a pointy, magenta thing. For her humor, I said. She looked dopey and beautiful all at once.

Christina and Felipe taught each other as many swear words as they could think of.

Pinche cabrón, maricón, puta, he began.

Bastard, asshole, motherfucker, she said.

Christina took a T-shirt advertising *Rolling Stone* from her bag and Felipe, thrilled, changed into it on the spot.

That evening Christina and I investigated the town. We went into a cinema featuring a Fernandel movie. I was surprised to see that he was still making movies. The audience seemed to be enjoying themselves well enough. It was too corny for us but we watched it for a bit, seeing if we could stay with the Spanish.

Who does he remind you of? she asked.

Felipe?

She nodded.

Next door to the cinema was a club where we witnessed two plump women in one-piece bathing suits with tassel fringes strutting up and down a ramp to what sounded like mariachi music. They too seemed to be for local consumption, their movements no more suggestive than you would see at the average beauty contest.

One of the dancers lingered playfully at our table. She likes you, Christina said happily. But my response was not enthusiastic enough. The dancer said something to Christina about me—that I was a dreamer, a sleeper. Something. A pill of some sort. That was clear. Our Spanish was not adequate to the insult. Or was it merely a taunt? But when she stopped coming to our table I missed the pull of her attention. And then of course there was the question of whether a woman was welcome as a patron in such a place, even if she was a gringo's daughter who didn't know better.

We found an American bar that Felipe had told us about. The owner had been a hunter, Felipe told us, and who knows what else, or how he had ended up there. Trophy heads were mounted behind the bar, stuffed animals and birds posed on the shelves. Along the walls were eight-by-ten photographs, frontal shots of hunters, porters, and felled beasts. Christina drew my attention to the captions. Many were unintentionally funny, some sad. A lion, said to be "about to spring," looked more like he was about to doze off. There was a picture of an elephant heart, the caption marveling at its weight.

We sat at a table across from the jukebox stocked with old rock-and-roll and crooner ballads. I ordered turtle soup with my meal and I got Christina to try a little of it. She was a vegetarian. Sometimes I think that is what got her into this trouble. She is too frail for these experiments. But it's sad to think of eating a turtle, she said. And who could disagree? Once I saw a live turtle torn open for its flesh in a Chinese market on Stockton Street. Also I remembered reading somewhere that a turtle's heart can go on beating for hours, slow but steady. I didn't mention this.

We started in on the tequila, which Christina insisted on trying, and listened to desperado songs. Felipe came along, still wearing his T-shirt. He danced with Christina and they went out to the deck that overlooked the river.

I looked up to see a woman making selections at the jukebox. When she turned I realized it was the German woman I had photographed on the beach.

The picture maker, she said to me.

I don't feel so hot, Christina said, when we got back to the hotel.

I think we should get over to Guadalajara and catch an airplane back, I said.

I'm okay, she said. I shouldn't have drunk so much. I don't want to go back. This could be our last chance to do something like this together.

All right. Another day or two, then. We'll see in the morning.

I'm going to take a shower, maybe puke. Felipe wanted to seriously drink. I liked it at first—before he got completely wasted. He started yelping like a coyote and calling me blondie and acting really scary.

She laughed. It's funny now, but it was disgusting then, she said.

She went into the bathroom and screamed. I found her a standing on a chair staring at a large cockroach poised near the shower drain. I captured it with toilet paper and flushed it.

La cucaracha, la cucaracha, she sang. *Felipe es . . . una cucaracha. Ted también. ¿Quién es más macho? ¿Una cucaracha o Ted?*

Una cucaracha, I said.

She giggled.

She used me to steady herself. She was alarmingly frail. She looked adolescent in her plain cotton nightgown. She got into bed.

Dad? Am I pretty?

Yeah, honey. You're gorgeous. You know that.

Will you read to me?

You bet. But by the time I fetched the book and found something, she'd fallen asleep.

I lay on top of the covers and thought about women. How men and women are different and how they are the same. I thought about the Mexican dancer giving me a hard time, the German woman at the juke-box, Christina standing on the chair, Christina's mother Eleanor, my own dead mother, a picture of her mother who died in Denmark before I was born, pictures of my mother when she was a little girl and pictures of Christina who—to Eleanor's chagrin—bore a striking resemblance to my mother. And how that small sweet fact seemed swallowed in oblivion.

Sleepless, with dawn near, and still a little drunk, I freshened up and went out with my Leica. As the light came up I walked around the town snapping pictures of the square, of the church, of a monument of St.

Francis blessing the fishermen. I made my way up a street that zig-zagged up the hill.

Some of the better homes faced this street, surrounded with adobe walls with prongs, nails, and broken glass imbedded in their tops to prevent trespassing. I took several close shots, with the wide-angle lens, the encrustments sharp in the foreground, the town and bay below in softer focus.

I knew that I presented a spectacle, startling early risers as they came out of their gates, a tall gringo sporting a camera and wearing a high-domed straw hat. But I enjoyed being perceived as ridiculous.

At the top of the hill I took panoramas of the city and the sea. Christina would like these to show back at home.

I decided not to go back down the way I had come. I'd taken longer than I'd meant, and was becoming uneasy that Christina might have wakened. Cutting across a field and suddenly finding myself in the midst of a shantytown, I felt clumsy, ashamed, humbled. Everything before me was meager, but scrupulously defined. There were little garden plots with squash, corn, and beans; shacks of cardboard and plywood; a small latrine. But I could not tell which path led where. Kneeling in front of her hut, a woman with full, bare breasts suckled a baby.

I turned down another path. There were crosses everywhere.

When I returned, Christina was still in her bed, lying on her back, her arms folded behind her head.

I dreamed in Spanish, she said. Once you dream in a language it's all the way in.

It was cooler that evening. We decided to take another try at hiking down the beach. The mosquitoes were intense because of the recent rains. Though Christina escaped them unscathed, my back was riddled with bites.

My back is hamburger, I said. Why do they want me?

Because your blood is sweet, Christina said.

Christina went in for a swim, negotiating the waves easily. I remembered going with her on Saturdays to Larsen Pool where she had learned to swim as a child, and my feeling quite nervous the first time she swam the length of the pool crossing over the deep end. She had this odd way of rolling over on her left as she stroked. She corrected that in time.

Christina stood up out of the water, her hair wet, her skin satined. Beautiful, smiling. Soon she is going to die, I thought.

It's funny you can't swim, Dad, she said. Think you'll live forever?

We continued walking down along the shifting hem of the ocean. I thought of nothing, became aware of the sound of our feet scudding the wet sand, of waves lapping. I was thinking: there is no way out of this one. We are not going to get out of this one.

Is it always going to be like this? Christina complained.

Like what?

Like someone is always walking along beside us?

I don't know, honey. Someone is tagging along, I said.

She walked ahead of me and when she turned back to look, I took her picture.

She began to cry. I took her picture.

She went to her knees. I took her picture.

I knelt and held her. Jesus, I thought. I'm on my knees.

I'm tired, she said. We lay down on the towel and I held her until she went to sleep.

The tide was working forward. I waded out slowly. The bottom was soft and gently sloped. The ocean swelled around me, alive. Thunder crackled in the mountains. *Tormenta tropical,* I thought. Tropical storm. It was the right phrase, I think, but I couldn't remember ever having heard it. I didn't know where it came from. It just came. *Once you dream in a language it's all the way in.*

It's true that even though I have lived near the water all my life I can't swim. I waded farther and farther into the ocean. The water was warm, warm as blood. I looked at the beach curving and stretching away southward. At Christina crumpled on the sand. *Tormenta tropical,* I kept thinking. Everything will pass. But no, some things are unacceptable. There are some things you cannot accept. The water rolled under my neck forcing me at times to stand on my toes. I do not change easily. I am a man without faith who always looks for signs.

6

Coda

Ordinary Blessings

A LETTER TO MY DAUGHTER
ON THE EVE OF HER BIRTH

....

George H. Smith

Dear Julia Danielle,

A quite commonplace and extraordinary thing is happening: I'm going to be a father! I've known this for a little over four months now, though the news has yet to sink in. I only returned home yesterday, having spent the summer in Iowa City, separated from your mother and the day-by-day developments. Three weeks ago she called to tell me we were going to have a daughter. I received a picture in the mail, though I could scarcely distinguish your head from your tail, had forgotten, in fact, that human embryos repeat the stages of evolution, resembling numerous creatures of the past and present before they resolve into themselves.

You and I are on the threshold of something that can't be prepared for, that can only be truly known by being experienced. Is it merely coincidence that the whole world seems now poised on its own threshold, from which there will be no turning back regardless of the directions taken, the choices made?

I once heard that it is customary for Vietnamese parents to speak to their unborn children, and though I am of European descent, I would like to perpetuate that custom here, as much for my sake as for yours. There is a tendency for fathers to feel unimportant, even in the way during this period, but I think that this is more than a time of mere waiting, and that there are things worth considering now, things worth saying that might easily be forgotten later.

As I write this, you are nine inches long, a lithe shadow superimposed on others in a bell-shaped sonogram, but also a living presence in your mother's womb. Already, you demand attention, deference, special consideration. Your mother, for example, can no longer sleep on her stomach (her usual preference) or on her back. You will protest, kicking fiercely if we make love in the wrong position. Already, you occupy the majority of my thoughts. You invade my dreams, dominate my prayers, moving other matters aside as if they were of no import at all and never had been. I am reminded that you are fashioned, in part, of my flesh, of genes and chromosomes, molecular helixes, impressed and programmed aspects of myself too small to comprehend, and I have my hands full here wrestling with the implications.

Everything frightens me, the familiar as well as the strange. Reading about childbirth and development, ostensibly for assurance, I encounter the names (often unpronounceable) of scores of prenatal and infant maladies, complications that can occur at any time or place without warning. In the introductions to these books, the authors assure me that I am not alone, that there is no reason to panic, though it is difficult to take comfort in this. I am reminded of the emotional and physical frailty of human beings, and see that being childless these forty-eight years was a luxury of ignorance, even as it was a deprivation. I have many questions for which the "experts" have no answers, though it is unclear to me why this should be surprising.

The truth is, there is much selfishness at the heart of my fear. Anticipating your arrival, I am forced to concede my own mortality, to view it head-on, unflinchingly, as an indelible part of a process both larger than myself and beyond my control. Parents, by definition, are obliged to hand down, pass along, inevitably stand aside. When you enter the world, I will cease to be the master of the house your mother lets me pretend to be, the be-all and end-all I have too long considered myself. To this reordering of things I hear the protests of my own inner child. His is the voice of a boy growing up mostly alone, smug in a world of his own creation in which he is king, author, prisoner, president. His creation is his child; he could never countenance or understand the need of having another.

I must do my part to make room for you in our home, in our lives. I must make you feel welcome. I'm afraid if I fail to do so, you won't come. But I wonder if I'm at all qualified for this. It seems that a man should first come to his own true estimation of the worth of being. I wonder even now, at the end of the millennium, in the midst of all that we are in the midst of—my well-blessed American life a leaky boat in a sea of lies and contradictions—if I can honestly affirm the worth of existence. At least there was a time when I was (in my own estimation) unfailingly optimistic, but that's less than history now. I look upon it as an artifact, a scrap of someone else's memory.

The baby books don't discuss these feelings, yet I can't help believing that others share them. Which are the appropriate attitudes? Where might one find consolation?

I am home now, back in the West. Exhausted from the drive across country, I re-enter my house, and my house re-enters me. My house is more prepared for your coming than I, filled as it is with birthing manuals, instructional videos, miscellaneous equipage. Clint Eastwood's wife has sent us a box of maternity clothes, as has your Aunt Karen. We have acquired a crib, a car seat, and a backpack. Few of these items were here when I left in early June. Seeing them now, I am disoriented, taken off guard as the reality of your coming approaches me from an entirely new angle.

I sit alone in the room we have designated as yours. By chance, most of the objects in this room, the paintings, bedspread, and rugs are blue, a circumstance that will have to be remedied, inasmuch as I am unwilling to buck tradition in a realm in which I have so little comprehension, let alone authority. On the shelves of the bookcase here, and on the cedar chest beside it, your mother has arranged some of the things that will greet you when you arrive in this world. Already, we have begun to collect baby clothes, pink and yellow jumpers, socks and booties. Family and friends have begun to take an interest in you. Gifts, those universal gestures of encouragement, commiseration, support, have begun to stack up: a rattle, a teether, an orthodontic pacifier, something called a "bubblegum buddy," picture books, refrigerator magnets bearing the faces of cartoon characters, crayons and a coloring cloth (ages three and up, which reinforces the permanence of this change in our lives), pink rabbits, orange Pooh bears, a milk bottle with metric and standard demarcations. There are humorous reminders of the narcissistic pathology of our times: a pastel T-top with the graffitied logo of its world famous designer, a pop-star lunch pail, a miniature sports bottle.

What is important, of course, is the atmosphere all this creates. Here, in this room, bright, soothing colors predominate; things are soft that they might be hugged, stroked, cuddled. Not since my own childhood have I been immersed in such an environment, surrounded with objects whose primary function is to delight and amuse, to soothe and secure. In rooms like these, love of life is nurtured, encouraged to thrive to the extent that anything so fundamentally natural might need coaxing. There is a delicious superfluousness to it all, a quite intentional silliness, and I am reminded how utilitarian my adult world is—more so than I'd care to admit—and how such utilitarianism dims our vision and creativity after a time, stifles our enjoyment and appreciation of ordinary blessings.

Soon, after a long, sterile hiatus as a grown-up, I will have toys in my house again, mine to enjoy if only vicariously. Toys link us, ultimately, to stories. Like blank medallions ready to be stamped, they are fodder for the mind at play, tangible objects upon which the imagination can project itself, refine, deepen, expand its interpretations of the Real.

I am forty-eight, thirteen years older than your mother. With the exception of a half-brother I hardly knew, I was an only child. (I used to joke that I was an endangered species, though I don't find that so funny anymore.) My parents had me late in life, though eleven years earlier than I propose to have you. Your mother, by contrast, has two brothers and a sister, four nephews, numerous aunts, uncles, cousins. The full menagerie. Family is important to each and every one of them. Nothing gets in the way, and I admire them for this, though sometimes when they visit the noise and commotion overwhelm me and I have to take a walk, or go to a bar or a coffee house to regain my composure. I feel guilty whenever this happens. What in the world is the matter with me?

What must they say to one another on these occasions when I am out of earshot, or later, when they go back home?

Friends and acquaintances tell me I will make a good father, though I wish they wouldn't, since I feel the pressure to measure up more than any ability to do so. I think of my own father, possessed of rare empathy and understanding, who set a standard I could never hope to meet. His father died in the same hospital where I was born, at roughly the same time, obliging him to run back and forth from one floor to another, from a state of grief to one of ecstasy. I have often wondered how he managed that, what conclusions such an odd juxtaposition of life events might have led him to. Perhaps this is where he learned to endure my delinquent exploits, the ongoing war between my mother and me, with such quiet strength and resolute acceptance. Utterly unflappable, without bluster, flourish, or self-aggrandizement, he weathered my stormy childhood with affection and (in times when a saint couldn't have mustered it) a rough pride. It is no wonder I thought of sitting out a whole generation of parenthood for fear of coming up short, more than content to rest on his laurels.

There is little I know for certain—only that you will be wholly dependent on me for love, compassion, and guidance, that my best resource in this will be a dim memory of having once been wholly dependent myself.

There are many questions in the new world that that didn't exist in the old. Where and how, for example, will you play? I'm told children don't simply go out on their own anymore. Spontaneity bows to the dictates of security. My friends make "appointments" for their children to get together. More often than not, play is supervised. As a product of the old world, I can't imagine growing up that way. Like adults, children need freedom from scrutiny, the opportunity to be alone.

But in the new world aloneness itself is suspect, actively disapproved. Can fear of crime be the sole reason for this? A child found wandering alone in the woods is, more often than not, presumed to be in trouble or suffering some crisis. One could imagine her being sent, forthwith, to the school psychologist for an evaluation. Would I be neglectful if I encouraged you to strike out on your own? Could I forgive myself if you were harmed as a result?

What could I hope to know of bringing up a girl? Ever conscious of your impending arrival, I now look at young women differently, imagining how I would measure up as a father to them, what they would expect of me, or praise or condemn. In a lifetime of wooing and pursuit, passion and compromise, I never fully understood what women wanted, or how they suffered for what they lacked or were told they did. I have known quite a few: those who looked to men to tell them what to want, how to feel; those who lived in solitude, hopeful or despairing; those who couldn't bear, even for a minute, to be alone. Yet I am as ignorant of them now as ever, more so for the obfuscation of fantasy, memory, and desire which has accumulated over the years.

But I doubt my ignorance to be unique, and in any case it can't be helped. We must make the best of it, which I don't mean as a platitude, but as a guiding principle, one of the few we can hope to hold onto.

I have made a few resolutions. For example, out of naïveté, pride, or misguided moral compunction, I have vowed to always tell you the truth. Preposterous, perhaps. Who knows if I will be able to keep this promise, which could easily prove to be my first and most serious blunder as a parent? Needless to say, having so vowed, I fear each of your questions.

In all but matters of strictest discipline, I vow to treat you like an equal. I will limit "baby talk." I will make eye contact. I will anchor what I say in sincerity, or rethink saying it at all. When I don't know the answers to your questions, I won't try to bluff, but will confess my ignorance. To the extent possible, I will give you reasons for the things I ask you to do or not do.

It is certainly not an ideal world to bring a child into. Your mother and I often consider this, though we have no way to reconcile what we know with what we believe in our hearts to be our responsibility. It is not a world that bends to our wishes, or heeds our concerns, nor is it an especially safe, or kind, or nurturing one. Whenever one of us brings this up, we grow silent. One or both of us look away as if straining to think of some reassuring thing to say on the subject.

But what can anyone say?

We live in a time of transition, of chaos. It is the kind of chaos that is produced by an exhausted culture, one of hucksters wielding slogans, politicians mouthing sound bites and empty promises, one that lauds selfishness and self-focus at the ironic expense of individuality. Original thought is suspect, mutual respect nearly unheard of. Dialogue between the young and old has been marginalized to a whisper. The noble warrior, stripped of true nobility, makes his or her final stand on the back pages of comic books. The old myths have been declawed, relegated to the realm of the quaint and obscure, regarded as mere fairy tales. Nor are there new ones waiting to take their places. We suspect every invitation to human contact, while at the same time honoring nothing larger than ourselves. In the absence of core values, we play it safe, making much of little. Ignorance and heartlessness, the waste products of a techno-marketing mentality, spawn mass apathy, disenfranchisement, psychosis: the etiology of both motiveless crime and lackluster aesthetics. We hear much of this, and yet on the eve of having a child, the problem takes on new significance. It plagues me with a nagging insistence.

What will become of your potential to realize yourself?

In chaos lies opportunity, the chance to reorder and make things right. According to the *I-Ching,* "Before there can be great brilliance, there must be chaos. Before a brilliant person begins something great, he must look foolish to the crowd."

We are all fools now, it seems, on the eve of the twenty-first century. Hounded to our graves by inane advertisements, bombarded with disconnected bits of information, we turn to our very tormentors for solutions, using consumerism, the end product of a cheapened science and technology, as a shield against our own stubbornly resilient humanity, dancing awkwardly to the same discordant music, wondering when and how things might resolve themselves into a cohesive whole.

Out of fear and frustration, we laugh ourselves silly.

Regrettably, our laughter, more often than not, sounds canned, like that of cheap sitcoms. All we can muster is a bullying, ghoulish flippancy at the expense of others, mocking people and ideas we would do better to revere. In an atmosphere of near panic, hatred and derision are easy crutches to reach for. So much is belittled and so little embraced, it is no wonder we have begun to break out of the molds that sustain us, accelerating beyond the gravitational pull of our own history.

I worry for you. That much must be apparent. I worry about the usual calamities, the things that can go wrong in childbirth and everything after. But I also worry for your soul on earth, the person you become, what you choose or don't choose to hold sacred in your life.

We are moving in new directions, modes of evolution that seem to necessitate, by virtue of an ignoble and self-sustaining momentum, the wholesale erasure of everything that has come before. The physical manifestations of this are visible everywhere. Old-growth forests are being relentlessly logged for short-term profits. Old buildings are being knocked down, small businesses bought out, or driven out of neighborhoods by look-alike franchises. The products of individual effort are quickly seized upon, institutionalized, subsumed under grandiose national or multinational corporate headings. Nostalgia—the whimsical, and largely commercial reverence for certain eras, styles, modes of speech—passes for history itself. Einstein, Beethoven, even Christ are usurped, their images depicted on T-shirts, buttons, coffee mugs until our awe is replaced with incurious pity, wry amusement. In this fashion, genius is brought to its knees, devalued by the common-denominator mentality that has become our principal national export.

Quality of thought and deed, nobility of purpose are downplayed in the headlong rush to achieve and acquire according to the dictates of the market-based culture. While loneliness flourishes, privacy is scarce. Shopping malls have become social meccas, gathering places for the young. A wretched sameness, perverse and seemingly inexhaustible, is spreading over the planet, hounding the beautiful and mysterious to extinction. Cities are renovated, neighborhoods gentrified until they meld into clones of some unspecified prototype. Small towns begin to resemble suburbs. People, too, seem to be changing, their psyches reflective of this "new" look. You hear it in the standardization of voice. In movies, and on television, even on the streets, there is a push in the direction of accentless speech. Communicators seem increasingly to be aiming for a smoothness of rhythm and syntax that will appeal to the masses, even if at the expense of depth and diversity. In the words of Barry Hannah, "Everyone wants to sound like a newscaster from Indiana."

Information abounds, too much about too little. Advertisers and

public relations consultants dictate interior as well as exterior land-
scapes. We revel in scandal, repetitions of the trivial. Fame and notori-
ety have become goals in and of themselves. In the absence of pervasive
myths, a comprehensive moral code, incidents are mistaken for stories,
superficial traits for character itself, appearances for realities. Our news
services elevate tragedy, scandal, insignificant exploits of small-
minded people to the status of legend. It is a fragmented, exploitative
mind-set ever in danger of consuming itself, falling into a moral vac-
uum of its own making. There is no heart in it, even (or especially) in
matters of the heart. The result of this, not surprisingly, is widespread
alienation: of the races, of men from women, of citizens from government, children from their parents. Even within the individual one de-
tects a growing rift between the heart and mind, so that more and more
is surface.

Environmentalists fight to save trees, whales, three-toed frogs, but
who will fight this tidal wave disenfranchising the essence of what's
both human and natural?

I wonder if any of this will interest you. Or if I will ruin the experience of your youth with my braying and ranting, becoming the very cli-
ché of a grumpy and irrelevant adult I so decried as a teenager? How can
I express these feelings without undermining your own optimism, depriving you of the joy of innocent discovery?

Paranoia strikes deep. Much is suspect now, and little is clear. We are
told what to think by institutions that are clueless themselves. Eventually, the language becomes infected. Men no longer "flirt" with women,
for example. They now "hit on" them, a pejorative term suggesting that
an approach occasioned by romantic interest is, a priori, both unwanted and violent. The predictable effect is (again) alienation, polarization, disaffection.

In the old world, men were taught to care for women, to protect them
(though the later term has acquired a clearly pejorative connotation).
In the early stages of courtship, a man's willingness to assume such a
role was expressed in oafishly simple gestures: holding open doors,
lighting cigarettes, pulling back chairs. Care was symbolized in the repetition of these and other mindless rituals. Courtship itself has ceased
to exist, of course. The word is antiquated, laughable. There are no as-

sumptions in the new world, unless of hidden agendas, ulterior motives. Care is neither promised nor delivered in the mad rush for the identification of the self along pop-culture-inspired, media-dictated lines.

Not so many years ago, young people (I was one) joined in a nationwide rebellion against conformity. Though in many ways ill conceived, this rebellion seemed to be a last-ditch attempt to ensure the survival of humanistic sensibilities in the modern world. People espoused universal love and the celebration of life. They wore bright clothes and danced and marched in the streets. Who knows what went wrong? Perhaps the movement to end the Vietnam War siphoned off people's energy. Too much grim reality, offered up nightly on television, may have dampened spirits beyond redemption. A fixation on drugs and self-indulgence opened us up to ridicule, fragmentation of thought and purpose.

Today, the beatific smiles of Woodstock, scorned as simple minded, or drug induced (which, admittedly, they often were), have been replaced with scowls, threatening gestures, and cocky sneers. Body piercing, tattoos, and shaved heads mimic the mutilations of war and the atrocities of concentration camps. Drugs once touted as "expanding consciousness" have been replaced by ones that obliterate it, supplying short-lived illusions of well-being, power, and omnipotence. Ten year olds (even those who don't carry guns) dress like urban guerrillas, in baggy clothing inspired by the martial arts. Gang clothing and school uniforms occupy opposite, nearly connected ends of the same spectrum, each demanding rigid conformity at the expense of self-expression.

Almost daily, new laws are passed, new causes of action and phrases describing and proscribing human behavior. In the twenty years I have practiced criminal law, the California penal code has at least doubled in thickness. Has human behavior changed so dramatically? What are these new laws our legislators feel obligated to enact for our protection and the preservation of our way of life?

Abstracted social issues are dissected in tabloids and on talk shows. Lurid headlines reflect the culture's hunger for the titillating and self-explanatory. Lawyers increasingly yield to the temptation to try their cases in the media, where the focus abruptly shifts from litigation to exploitation. The determination of guilt or innocence, responsibility and compensation, take a back seat to accusation and counteraccusation, which become media events, complete and consequential in and of themselves.

Your mother and I have both lived in California the majority of our lives, but I wonder how long we will wish to remain here. Here in the West—in what must be one of the glaring ironies of our time—stillness and solitude are at a premium. Those of us who live out here—there are millions more each year—can't escape each other anymore; there is no mountaintop so removed that a dozen others might not already have climbed it on any given day, or arrived—complete with picnic and lawn furniture—by helicopter. The region is rapidly becoming the harbinger of rage and frustration, hair-trigger tempers. I witness this daily in the courts, but also in the jostling of crowds on the street, in the way people drive, ever increasing incidents of road rage. The newspapers are filled with accounts of drive-by shootings, home invasions.

There is a new breed of human being wandering around out there, chillingly lacking in remorse or comprehension of the distinction between right and wrong. Not long ago, I watched a young man laughing as a police officer put him through field sobriety tests. He had just run down a young girl on a bicycle, and she was still lying there, a few feet away under a blanket. I interviewed a codefendant in a juvenile case a few years ago, a fourteen year old charged in the shooting death of a marijuana farmer. As long as I live, I will never forget our meeting. As we sat together in a concrete holding cell at Juvenile Hall, he described to me with complete detachment the fashion in which he had gunned down his victim. He knew how much time he would do, and that he would in all likelihood eventually be returned to the custody of his parents. There was no emotion in his voice or facial expression as he detailed the circumstances of the killing. "It just happened, you know," he said. "He was there, and I was there, and one thing led to another."

How long should we hold out? Indeed, where can we go? Thousands of years ago, Lao Tsu counseled, "There is no safe place on the earth." I have long believed in the deliverance of creativity, its potential to reclaim the afflicted heart.

But even this refuge is threatened. Political forces labeling themselves "conservative" are cutting funding for the arts, even as they antagonize the poor by crippling welfare and education. For peace of mind and transcendence you and the other children of the new world will have to look into your own hearts, and those of us who care will have to equip you to do so. This, without depriving you of your vested right to make your own way, to find your own solutions. I am afraid of the choices you will make, simultaneously of my ability and my inability to influence them.

What strategies would you adopt if you were in my place?

It is common knowledge that children rebel against their parents, and that this rebellion often includes a wholesale rejection of parental standards and ideals. I wonder how I would weather that? I have considered reverse psychology. Great books will be censored in our house, stored in rooms you will be forbidden to enter. Literature will be taboo: Chekhov, Tolstoy, Shakespeare. Even the Americans, Flannery O'Connor, Tennessee Williams, Virginia Woolf, will be kept under lock and key. Likewise, all classical music, blues, and jazz, any and all rock-and-roll songs with insightful lyrics.

Backpacking, foreign travel, tolerance and appreciation of the language and customs of others will be discouraged.

But no. Something tells me even this wouldn't work.

What I owe you is the past, the foundation on which the new world is built, a past which is at once fleeting, undervalued, and misunderstood. My parents are both eighty-five. My mother, dying of Alzheimer's, couldn't tell you what year this is. "I don't keep track of that sort of thing," she would say. "You'll have to ask your father."

Even so, I know she has visions of the past: faces and names, disjointed stories, accounts of love and pain that visit her in dreams forgotten on waking. There are boxes of photographs somewhere, sepia and black-and-white, crazed and stained, with curled edges: pictures of men with beards and handlebar mustaches, women in high-buttoned dresses.

Who were these people? How did they see themselves?

I must ask your grandparents while I still can. I must write down their answers. Memory isn't to be trusted, though for generations the stories of families all over the world relied on little else, passed down by word of mouth.

Here is what I know so far:

We were peasants, shepherds and dirt farmers who emigrated from the high Alps of Italy, France, and Switzerland. At the age of sixteen, your grandmother's father and uncle got on a steamer in Marseilles and came to America, never to return. Young people did such things in those days. The four sides of my family lived within thirty kilometers of each other in those three different countries, but never met until they reached the new world. Some (quite a few of us, apparently) were criminals. Your great-great-grandfather on my father's side ran a gambling boat on the Sacramento River delta. He was stabbed in the heart one night, presumably over a disputed debt. Somewhere back on your French grandmother's side there lurks a Royalist highwayman. My cousin Edward, a Jesuit missionary in Manchuria, was excommunicated for falling in love with the daughter of a Parisian lawyer.

Our lives, yours and mine, stand on the remnants of these. To what extent might they contribute to our sense of identity? I wonder if there are trends, mistakes we keep making as a family. There is something in my personality that prefers squalor, bare-bulb hotel rooms, greasy spoon cafes. I have always been uncomfortable around people with money, a feeling that persists even now that I have a little of my own. Does the past shed any light on this? Are we haunted by themes and causes that arose in the time before memory?

Mostly, I want you to know that I envy you.

Does that seem incongruous, given my complaints and trepidations? In chaos there is, indeed, opportunity. Perhaps in the bright lights of the new millennium, evil will have nowhere to hide. Your generation might discover its common humanity. I can't imagine a more worthwhile journey than one that would take you to such a place.

I haven't given up, and neither should you. I want you to hear and accept this, even if you have to take it on faith for the first few decades. At the risk of appearing sentimental, I will say that the world is a marvelous place, and completely worthy of whatever enthusiasm you can muster. Life can indeed be the adventure that dyed-in-the-wool optimists claim it is (though I am no friend of dyed-in-the-wools otherwise).

You should know that there have been times in my life so astoundingly beautiful, transcendent, even magical (regrettably, a disfavored word in the new world), that they were worth all the rest: the pain of losing loved ones; of seeing dreams shattered; of faltering, shamefaced and impotent, in moments of truth. The greatest secret is that greatness can be coaxed to appear with the right attitudes: respecting mortality, for example, having and holding a loving heart, for another.

In closing, please forgive me (it is best to ask in advance, don't you think?) for my failures, of which I am sure there will be many. I, in turn, naturally forgive you yours, though it is no bargain for me to offer to do so. Of the two of us, if I haven't already made it clear, I have the most faith in you, coming as you do from a place the rest of us have too long forgotten.

There is something else. It is not easy to talk about, nor does it need to be said, and yet I have a desire to try. I have never considered myself a religious person. I am still profoundly suspicious of those who proselytize, and still believe that organized religion and religious fervor have done this world more harm than good. When people tell you that they believe "in" something (as opposed to simply believing it), they usually mean that they have adopted others' explanations. There is a passivity in such attitudes that is deeply disturbing. Having "decided" what is true, these people have, in short, stopped thinking.

A shame. And yet, I must confess that I, too, have become a believer of sorts, though it seems oddly like heresy for me to confess it. I believe, for example, in intimations of immortality: moments when a sense of what Wallace Stevens called "the sleight of hand man" creep into your perception of the otherwise ordinary. It might come to you as a glimpse out the window of a speeding train, or an image in a dream that persists for days, as if begging you to comprehend it. It might devolve from an intense appreciation of something in the everyday world, something you seize on at a time when others seem oblivious. It helps to spend time alone, regardless of what others may think. Ultimately, you will have to teach yourself the things that matter most. The rest of your education, important as it is, will deaden your senses to a degree, as will the attentions of friends, lovers, and family. You must develop a vigilance. Years pass with few encouraging signs. It is much like groping in the dark. I can't tell you what you are looking for, or even what it will look like if and when you find it.

Try to avoid being manipulated. Seek out and nurture kindhearted people. (Time is too precious to waste on the rest.) You would do well to question every fact, each and every opinion, even the ones you encounter here. Ideally, you will develop the ability to forgive yourself when others, even your parents, are unable to. I pray that you will find love, and offer you this small token of mine. Above all, I wish you the strength, courage, and exuberance to praise this world, which deserves no less.

Rejoice, then.

Have a good life.

Love,
Your father

CONTRIBUTORS

RICK BASS is the author of eleven books of fiction and nonfiction, including *Winter*, *The Lost Grizzlies*, *In the Loyal Mountains*, *The Book of Yaak*, and, most recently, *Where the Sea Used to Be*.

ALAN CHEUSE is the author of many works of fiction and nonfiction, including *The Light Possessed* and *The Grandmothers' Club*. Book commentator since 1982 for National Public Radio's *All Things Considered*, he lives in Washington, D.C., and teaches writing at at George Mason University. A new collection of his short fiction is forthcoming.

NICHOLAS DELBANCO has published seventeen books of fiction and nonfiction, most recently the novel *Old Scores*. He directs the Hopwood Awards Program at the University of Michigan, where until recently he also directed the MFA in Writing Program. He is a founding director of the Bennington Writing Workshops.

GERALD EARLY is director of African-American Studies at Washington University, and the author of three books, including *Daughters: On Family and Fatherhood*. A recipient of the Whiting Writers Award, his work has appeared in *The Atlantic Monthly*, *The Hungry Mind Review*, *The New Republic*, *Harper's*, and *Emerge*. He is currently at work on a book about Fisk College. He lives in St. Louis.

DEWITT HENRY was the founding editor of *Ploughshares* literary magazine and has edited two fiction anthologies, *The Ploughshares Reader: Fiction for the Eighties*, and *Other Sides of Silence: New Fiction from Ploughshares*. His personal essays have appeared in *The Pushcart Prize*, *Boulevard*, *The Iowa Review*, *American Voice*, *The Nebraska Review*, and *The Colorado Review*, among others. He teaches at Emerson College.

HOWARD JUNKER is the founding editor of *Zyzzyva*, a journal of West Coast writers and artists; he has edited three anthologies of material from its pages, most recently *Strange Attraction*. Madison Junker is at this writing a fifth grader who runs cross country and plays power forward for her school basketball team. A drawing of hers appeared in *zyzzyva 37*.

RODGER KAMENETZ is a poet and essayist. His books include *Stalking Elijah: Adventures with Today's Jewish Mystical Masters; The Jew in the Lotus*, now being made into a film; and *Terra Infirma*. His most recent books of poetry are *Stuck* and *The Missing Jew: New and Selected Poems*. Kamenetz lives in New Orleans and teaches poetry and nonfiction writing in the graduate program at Louisiana State University, Baton Rouge.

PHILLIP LOPATE is the author of a triology of personal essay collections (*Bachelorhood, Against Joie de Vivre,* and *Portrait of My Body*), and editor of *The Art of the Personal Essay* and *The Anchor Essay Annual*. He holds the Adams Chair in Humanities at Hofstra University.

After teaching history and doing college counseling at the secondary school level, BILL MAYHER now works as a free-lance writer on the Maine coast. His work has appeared in *Wooden Boat, Sail, Maine Boats and Harbors, Yankee,* and elsewhere. His book *The College Admissions Mystique* was published by Farrar, Straus, and Giroux in 1998.

JAMES A. MCPHERSON's nonfiction book *Crabcakes* appeared this year. He has published two collections of stories, *Hue and Cry* and *Elbow Room,* for which he won the Pulitzer Prize. He has also edited *Railroad: Trains and Train People in American Culture* (with Miller Williams), and contributed articles and stories to numerous anthologies and magazines. He teaches in the Writer's Workshop at the University of Iowa.

MARK PENDERGRAST is an investigative journalist, whose 1993 book, *For God, Country and Coca-Cola* was named a Notable Book of the Year by the *New York Times*. With *Victims of Memory,* the author explores the hunt for "repressed memories" of sexual abuse. Pendergrast, who lives in Vermont, hopes that his book will facilitate healing and reconciliation, particularly with his own daughters.

WILLIAM PETERSEN has worked as a photographer, film and video maker, musician, and chef. He currently supports himself as a fishmonger in San Francisco where he continues to work on a collection of short stories and a novel. His work has appeared in *The North American Review* and *The New England Review*. This past summer he received a Hellgate Writers Scholarship.

SCOTT RUSSELL SANDERS is the author of more than a dozen books, including, most recently, *Writing from the Center,* which won the 1996 Great Lakes Book Award. For his work in nonfiction he won a Lannan Literary Award in 1995. He teaches at Indiana University, in Bloomington, where he lives with his wife, and where his daughter Eva is currently a graduate student in biology.

ADAM SCHWARTZ's fiction has appeared in *The New Yorker*. He teaches at Wellesley College.

SAMUEL SHEM is the pen name of Stephen Bergman, a psychiatrist at Harvard Medical School. As Samuel Shem he has published many novels and plays, including *The House of God* and *Mount Misery*, and with his wife Janet Surrey the play *Bill W. and Dr. Bob*, about the founding of Alcoholics Anonymous. Drs. Bergman and Surrey are codirectors of the Gender Relations Research Project at the Stone Center, Wellesley College, and are publishing a book on their work, *We Have to Talk: Getting from Me to We*.

GEORGE H. SMITH is a writer and criminal defense attorney in Santa Cruz, California. He and his wife, Jan, welcomed Julia Danielle (their first) on December 13, 1997. "Ordinary Blessings" is his first published essay. He is currently at work on a novel.

GARY SOTO is the author of several prose reminiscences, including *Living Up the Street* and *A Summer Life*, as well as collections of poetry, most recently *Junior College*. In addition he has written filmscripts, plays, fiction, and children's literature. He divides his time between Berkeley and Fresno, California.

M. G. (MICHAEL GREGORY) STEPHENS' nonfiction includes *Green Dreams: Essay under the Influence of the Irish*, winner of the Associated Writing Programs Award in Creative Nonfiction, and *Lost in Seoul*, a memoir about living in contemporary Korea. Among his works of fiction are the novels *Season at Coole* and *The Brooklyn Book of the Dead*. His play *Our Father* was recently published by Spuyten Duyvil Press in New York City. He is writer-in-residence at Emerson College.

FRED VIEBAHN has published seven books in his native German; written for radio, television and theatre; and worked as a journalist and editor. Among his honors are the German Book-of-the-Month award for his first novel, *Die schwarzen Tauben* (The Black Doves) in 1969, the literary prize of the City of Cologne, and a residency at Jerusalem's Mishkenot Sha'ananim. He met his wife, the poet Rita Dove, in 1976 when he was a Fulbright Fellow in the University of Iowa's International Writing Program. *The Stain*, the revised American version of his 1979 novel *Die Fesseln der Freiheit*, was published by Story Line Press in 1988. Mr. Viebahn lives in Charlottesville, Virginia.

CREDITS

"The Driving Lesson" by Gerald Early first appeared in *Emerge;* reprinted by permission of the author.

"The Mistake Game" by Rodger Kamenetz first appeared in *Ploughshares;* reprinted by permission of the author.

"Delivering Lily" by Phillip Lopate first appeared in *Creative Nonfiction;* reprinted by permission of the author.

"Building Back through Time" by Bill Mayher appeared in slightly edited form in *The Christian Science Monitor* on February 9, 1996, as "The Elegant and Elusive Igloo Takes Shape."

Excerpts from *Victims of Memory: Sex Abuse Accusations and Shattered Lives* by Mark Pendergrast appear courtesy of Upper Access Books, P.O. Box 457, Hinesburg, VT 05461.

ACKNOWLEDGMENTS

Thanks to my wife, Connie, to Don Lee at *Ploughshares,* to John Skoyles, to Judith Friedericy, and to Victoria Morrow for suggestions; to our editor Helene Atwan; and to my graduate assistants at Emerson College, Mike Kula and Tara Godel, for research and proofreading.

—DeWitt Henry

Thanks to Mrs. Julia Smith, Gerald Freund, and Jack Leggett.

—James Alan McPherson